DRAMA IN THE TIME OF COVID

50 Plays of Love, Loss and Hope

Editors

Robert Paul Moreira & Philip Zwerling

Assistant Editors

Denisse Zecca

Arnold Gonzalez

Aziz Quenun

FlowerSong Press

ISBN: 978-1-963245-00-4

Published by FlowerSong Press
in the United States of America.
www.flowersongpress.com

Cover Art: Carlos Fidel Espinoza
Cover Design by: Carlos Fidel Espinoza
Set in Adobe Garamond Pro

Contents

Introduction

Humans birthed theater when the earliest cave dwellers picked up spears and reenacted the day's hunt around the evening fire. Thus, the playwright was born. Since then, from Aeschylus to Ibsen to Albee, across the centuries from Greek theatrons to the La Jolla Playhouse, theater has displayed human existence in all its blood, sweat and tears, and audiences have loved it.

Then in 2019, COVID killed the Theater…presumably. The coronavirus pandemic closed performance venues from New York's Broadway to London's West End to Avenida Corrientes in Buenos Aires and every world capitol in between. Actors and directors collected unemployment and lived hand to mouth, locked out of even their old wait staff jobs as restaurants shuttered. Playwrights holed up in their apartments to wait the pandemic out, or even worse, returned to living in their parents' basements.

But even COVID could not kill Theater. Playwrights, actors, and directors all found ways to keep theater alive. They took to Zoom and YouTube and outdoor venues or friends' living rooms to stage their work. This collection celebrates their survival in all its colorful dramatic diversity. From Joe Gulla's heartfelt *Members Only* to Phil Darg's musical comedy *Quarantined!*, these plays run the gamut from somber to comedic to downright bizarre, each probing the human pandemic experience all across the world.

COVID did not kill Theater, because COVID never killed the Human Spirit. In the midst of disease and death and masks and vaccine mandates, playwrights remained at work making theater, and we thank them for doing so.

So, read a play. Write a play. See a play. Act. Direct. Tech. Why? Because Theater lives.

Robert Paul Moreira and Philip Zwerling

Spring 2024

THE LAST SUPPER
by Lindsay Adams

CHARACTERS

MAN	20s-30s. Any Race
WOMAN	20s-30s. Any Race

SETTING

A Zoom Call. Now.

(At Rise, the Man and the Woman are on a Zoom video chat together. Each has a plate in front of them.)

MAN: So, this is it.
WOMAN: I guess it is.
MAN: The last supper. See?

(He changes his video background to The Last Supper by Leonardo da Vinci. He switches the background back to his kitchen momentarily.)

WOMAN: Geez, that took it to a dark place. Who's Judas in this scenario?
MAN: Well dibs on Jesus.
WOMAN: So, I get to be Judas then.
MAN: Maybe nobody's Judas. Maybe you're Peter. Or Paul. One of the P's.
WOMAN: Somebody's always the Judas…So…what do you have?
MAN: I have cooked tofu that has been breaded with stale potato chips. Topped off with a soy sauce reduction. I even plated it.
WOMAN: Very nice.
MAN: I do what I can.

WOMAN: And that's everything you have? All the food left in your apartment?

MAN: Yeah. What about you?

WOMAN: I just made a sandwich.

MAN: Of?

WOMAN: Bean Sprouts, Apples and Tabasco.

MAN: What?

WOMAN: Sweet and spicy you know. I have one extra piece of bread, so I'll have that for dessert.

MAN: But how is that a sandwich. The bread has to be so soggy.

WOMAN: A little bit. We should eat soon.

(She touches her face. Maybe she scratches. Or maybe just one of those involuntary touches.)

MAN: Hey. Wash your hands, don't touch your face.

WOMAN: Sorry, I feel like I've gotten even worse about that since… somehow. Like by thinking about it I touch it more. If you were here, I could just touch yours.

MAN: Bon Appetit?

WOMAN: Yeah, sure.

(They eat.)

MAN: How…is it?

WOMAN: It's not half-bad. You know. The Tabasco really takes over.

MAN: Makes sense.

WOMAN: Yours?

MAN: Turned out alright.

WOMAN: Nice.

(She finishes. She waits as he keeps eating. She seems unsettled. He is

contentedly still eating.)

WOMAN: Is this fine?

MAN: Is what fine?

WOMAN: This.

MAN: Yeah, it's fine.

WOMAN: Okay good…Like you don't seem fazed at all. You just seem fine, with being stuck at home.

MAN: Well, I like time to myself. And I can get more done around the apartment.

WOMAN: Sure, yeah.

MAN: I'm fine.

WOMAN: Okay…good…I just…miss you a lot…Like not even just touching me. I mean yeah also that. But just like you being around. Smelling the stuff you put in your beard to make it soft, when you're reading or thinking about something. You do that absentminded thing where you stroke your beard, even though you hate it when I stroke it.

MAN: I don't hate it.

WOMAN: Sure, okay, you just wince every time. But anyway, it makes it smell more when you touch it, the stuff.

MAN: Beard balm.

WOMAN: What?

MAN: That's what I use. To make it soft.

WOMAN: Okay, yeah. That. I just…I don't know what I'm saying exactly now…I lost my train of thought.

MAN: It feels like you're petting a dog sometimes.

WOMAN: What?

MAN: I just wish you would be more…still. Just, you're always moving.

WOMAN: Okay.

MAN: I just…that's what I don't really like.

WOMAN: So basically, um, you don't like how I touch you.

MAN: ...

WOMAN: Let's just have a nice dinner. Eat. Finish...eating.

MAN: Are you okay?

WOMAN: It's fine, I'm alright.

MAN: Clearly, it's not alright, because you're about to cry.

WOMAN: Sometimes I'm just sad. I get to be sad too...sometimes. I know you're dealing with everything with work. And now you're stuck in that and the economy is shit and will be shit probably for...who knows, but a while. But everything is shit, okay? Right now. And I still get to be sad. Even if you're having a bad time and you're unhappy.

MAN: I'm fine.

WOMAN: No, you're not. No, you're not and I can tell, but you won't say anything.

MAN: What am I supposed to say? Talking about things doesn't help me.

WOMAN: Well, it helps me, and it lets me know what's happening. I literally don't know where you're at.

MAN: I'm in my apartment. You know, the only place any of us get to be right now.

WOMAN: You know that's not what...I mean like emotionally.

MAN: ...

WOMAN: I just want to be there for you, and you won't let me.

MAN: I do, too.

WOMAN: Okay, then you'll let me get groceries for you, like I offered to.

MAN: ...

WOMAN: Is that a yes?

MAN: I...um...I don't need groceries.

WOMAN: I'm sorry, what?

MAN: I got off early today, so I already went to the store.

WOMAN: You're fucking kidding me. You said that was it. The meal was all you had left.

MAN: I really wanted this to be a good night.

WOMAN: By lying? I can't believe you did a grocery run. It is so unsafe for you.

MAN: I was fine.

WOMAN: You're at risk.

MAN: I was safe.

WOMAN: You only have hand sanitizer because I made you take mine.

MAN: I wash my hands.

WOMAN: This was the last meal. The last supper as you put it. We were making the whole not having food left into a game. It was supposed to be fun and like something like a date or…What are we doing?

MAN: We're still having dinner together.

WOMAN: You really don't care?

MAN: What do I not care about?

WOMAN: You like having dinner over a screen. It's like you wanted this all along.

MAN: I wanted a pandemic. I wanted to not be able to see people.

WOMAN: You wanted this. With us. You have been so distant with me. And with all of this, I already feel pretty fucking alone right now. I don't know what…I try really hard to be happy and upbeat and to be your cheerleader and to make things better. And not to bring anything else in to make this situation worse but I can't just keep…Please say something, you know I just keep talking when you don't RESPOND to me.

MAN: What am I supposed to say to that? Sorry, I'm the awful person who doesn't care about you enough.

WOMAN: It's not that you don't…But you don't say it or show it or—

MAN: How am I supposed to show it right now?!

WOMAN: No, but before.

MAN: I don't remember before. All my life is just Zoom meetings and putting out fires at work. And now having to have conversations about our relationship. It feels like it's been fucking eternity here.

So, I don't know what I did or what I wasn't doing.

WOMAN: You wouldn't go to things. When I invited you, or other people. And then like even when we were still seeing each other. In person. But not seeing anyone else. When the group has Zoom parties. You would always make up something. So, then I wouldn't go either because I was with you. I'm really worried about you. Like have you been talking to anyone else?

MAN: I want my keys back.

WOMAN: What?

MAN: I want them back. I want you to give them back to me.

WOMAN: We're sheltered in place. What do you think I'm going to do? Like I'm gonna go pour bleach on your clothes or something?

MAN: I want you to get them to me.

WOMAN: Is this seriously how you're breaking up with me?...Are you going to say anything after that?

MAN: I just need some space.

WOMAN: All you fucking have is space.

MAN: I've just been thinking about this a lot, about what I need, and I'm not sure that this is what I need right now. I need someone who cares about me.

WOMAN: What the fuck does that even mean. How about you care about yourself? You don't even keep yourself safe. You won't even let me get you groceries.

MAN: I need someone who isn't always critical of everything that I do.

WOMAN: That's it. You're not going to even yell or...just yell at me, something. Like any of this mattered to you. Like I mattered...

MAN: You really like playing the victim, don't you?

WOMAN: No, I don't. You make me that. You're Judas.

MAN: What?

WOMAN: You're the Judas.

MAN: Wow, okay.

WOMAN: You are. You're Judas. Way to fuck up the Last Supper, dude.

MAN: I'm not having this conversation with you.

WOMAN: Just like every other one you refuse to have.

MAN: I want my key back. I'll come over there if I have to.

WOMAN: No! You won't!

(She gets up with her phone and moves into the kitchen.)

MAN: You don't get to give me permission.

WOMAN: Well, there won't be any purpose if you do.

(She has found the extra piece of bread.)

MAN: You won't let me in? I will make a scene if I have to.

(She pulls the key off the key chain.)

MAN: Are you saying something? Are you talking to me? I can't hear you if you're talking to me.

(She places it on the bread. Making a sandwich.)

MAN: You…wouldn't.

WOMAN: Time for dessert.

(She eats the bread.)

MAN: Are you crazy?

WOMAN: You aren't getting your silver, Judas.

MAN: You're fucking insane.

WOMAN: Happy Last Supper to you, too.

MAN: You goddamn, crazy bitch.

WOMAN: You can get a new key next month!

MAN: I can't... What the fuck... You...

(He logs off the Zoom call. She spits the key out of her mouth. She starts crying.)

WOMAN: Just stay inside.

MUM'S THE WORD
by Maripat Allen

CHARACTERS

JENNY	A young woman
MICHAEL	A young man

SETTING

An apartment in an American city. The time is the near future. A deadly pandemic has been ravaging the world and become a permanent condition. Because of this non-family members are strictly forbidden by law from touching, or even getting within six feet of each other. Most people work remotely and there is very little social contact in general.

(At Rise, Jenny enters from the front door. Michael follows, six-feet behind. Both are masked. They sanitize their hands immediately upon entering. Throughout the action the two of them will take great pains to stay six feet away from each other.)

JENNY: Come on in. Welcome to my humble abode. I wouldn't normally invite a man in on the first date, but…six feet and all…

(She laughs awkwardly.)

MICHAEL: You're safe with me, even without the six feet thing. I'd never— not that I wouldn't want—it's just that I—and not just because of the virus, I—

JENNY: I know what you meant. I'll open some windows then we can take off our masks.

(She opens some windows and unmasks.)

MICHAEL: What about the sentinels? Your neighbors reporting us?

JENNY: They have nothing to report as long as we follow the new rules: open windows, social distance, and no socializing more than twenty minutes.

MICHAEL: *(Unmasking)* Okay, I'll set my timer.

(He does so, on his phone.)

JENNY: *(Indicating chair)* Have a seat.

MICHAEL: Are you sure?

JENNY: It's okay, it's leather. I'll just sanitize it after. I stocked up on wipes before the last spike. Don't tell anyone!

MICHAEL: Mum's the word! I'm glad they relaxed the restrictions at least a bit. It's amazing to be in someone else's house, sitting in another person's chair…

JENNY: Talking to someone in person…

MICHAEL: Yeah. *(Awkwardly)* So, uh, I enjoyed our walk.

JENNY: Me too. I'm glad you asked me.

MICHAEL: I've been wanting to for a long time.

JENNY: Really?

MICHAEL: It's just hard to ask out someone you only see in little square on-screen, in a Zoom meeting. Kind of weird working remotely all the time…

JENNY: Yeah. Working in your pajamas is overrated. I've got some wine. Want a glass?

MICHAEL: Sure!

(During the following exchange Jenny pours two glasses of wine and sets them on a table. She sets out a box of latex gloves, takes her glass and sits down, six feet away from Michael's chair. Michael then comes to the table, puts on gloves, takes his wine, and sits down.)

MICHAEL: Having a glass of wine with someone! That's something I haven't done since…

JENNY: I can't even remember.

MICHAEL: *(Holding up his wine glass)* Cheers.

JENNY: Cheers. So, why'd you ask me out on Wednesday?

MICHAEL: I don't know. You're just so nice. That was the day you got Alice to talk in the meeting. She's so quiet but you got her to open up.

JENNY: She's got good ideas, if people would just listen to her.

MICHAEL: Yeah, and you do that! You really listen, like you're actually interested. Anyway, I'd had this plan to ask you to stay connected after the meeting so I could talk to you alone. Wednesday, I figured, if I was ever going to meet you in person I better just go for it.

JENNY: I'm glad you did. I was hoping you would.

MICHAEL: You were?

JENNY: Yeah. I wanted to meet you in person too. *(Shyly)* I always liked your smile…

MICHAEL: *(Shyly)* And now here we are, in the flesh, in all three dimensions, head to toe. And so, what if it's at six feet distance, right?

JENNY: Right.

MICHAEL: I'm glad you were willing. I know it's a little scary…

JENNY: Yeah, between the virus and the sentinels…

MICHAEL: *(Wiping the wine glass with a sanitizing wipe)* Ugh! Are you as sick of this as I am?

JENNY: Yeah, but let's not go there.

MICHAEL: Right. *(Beat)* That was a beautiful moon tonight, wasn't it?

JENNY: Beautiful.

MICHAEL: So big and round. Like a great big…manhole cover.

(Jenny laughs.)

MICHAEL: And the light on your skin…you looked so…glowy.

JENNY: Really?

(She dims the lights and leans toward him.)

MICHAEL: Like one of those women in a Rubens' painting.

JENNY: They're fat!

MICHAEL: No, I didn't mean that! But Rubenesque is a good thing anyway, right? Curvy! Not that I was noticing. But it was nice to see more than just your shoulders and head. Not that I was looking below that. It was your eyes…and the moonlight on your skin… the skin on your face, that is…the neck up. Your head basically.

JENNY: You like my face?

MICHAEL: Yes, very much.

JENNY: You mentioned my neck. You like it?

MICHAEL: That too.

JENNY: And my shoulders?

MICHAEL: Yes, very nice shoulders.

JENNY: And…everything else?

MICHAEL: Yes! Yes! Everything! The whole shebang! *(Jumping up and moving back)* Hoo! Six feet…

JENNY: You're sweet, you know that?

MICHAEL: I am?

JENNY: You seem so sure of yourself at work, but tonight…you seem kind of shy.

MICHAEL: It's just…this distance dating thing…It's a whole new game.

JENNY: This is a game to you??

MICHAEL: No! I loved walking with you tonight! You're so easy to talk to. Even with you on the sidewalk, me in the street…

JENNY: The city was so still, so peaceful…

MICHAEL: The river was beautiful, wasn't it?

JENNY: The lights sparkling on the water…

MICHAEL: And the bridge…I wanted to sit on that bench with you and look at it together.

JENNY: Me too.

MICHAEL: You were beautiful in the moonlight. And I wanted to look at you. I wanted to sit on that bench with you and look at the river and look at you. And put my arm around you. And smell your hair.

JENNY: I'd like to feel your arm around me.

MICHAEL: What does your hair smell like?

JENNY: *(Sniffing her hair)* Eucalyptus maybe?

(He breathes in deeply but can't smell it.)

JENNY: Maybe if you close your eyes and concentrate…

(He closes his eyes and breathes in deeply again.)

MICHAEL: I can smell it! You even smell beautiful!

JENNY: Let me try to smell you. *(She closes her eyes and breathes in deeply)* All I'm getting is hand sanitizer.

(They laugh. Beat.)

JENNY: I love your laugh.

MICHAEL: You do?

JENNY: Tonight, when that cat startled us—

MICHAEL: That was one loud cat!

JENNY: I screamed and you gasped—

MICHAEL: I wanted to put my arm around you then too…

JENNY: Then you laughed and you…you just sounded so free…just laughing at yourself, and with me…I haven't heard a laugh like that in a long time.

MICHAEL: You laughed too. Your head was back, and your skin glowed in the moonlight. Your neck was arched. I wanted to kiss your neck then, but…

(Beat.)

JENNY: Frickin' virus.

MICHAEL: Frickin' virus.

(Beat.)

JENNY: So, you want a snack? I have some granola bars. They're in the packaging.

MICHAEL: That sounds safe.

(Jenny brings out some granola bars. They eat them.)

MICHAEL: These aren't bad.

JENNY: I'd make something fresh but—

MICHAEL: I know.

JENNY: So, tell me, what do you miss most?

MICHAEL: Besides the obvious?

JENNY: Yes.

MICHAEL: That's hard, there's so much. Touching things without even thinking about it.

JENNY: You can say that again!

MICHAEL: Shaking hands—hands that aren't raw from washing a hundred times a day.

JENNY: But the most.

MICHAEL: I guess I'd have to say March Madness.

JENNY: Really??

MICHAEL: Yeah. The thing about March Madness is, I followed it with my Dad and brother. Ever since I was a kid we'd go to all the MSU games. We were all alumni and loyal Spartans. *(Singing)* "On the banks of the Red Cedar." *(Laughing)* Dad would curse out those refs when he thought they made a bad call against our team! Never heard him swear otherwise...Can you imagine seventy-thousand people together in a stadium now?

JENNY: Some people watch the old tournaments together on FaceTime. Have you ever done that with your father and brother?

MICHAEL: *(Sadly)* We used to, but Dad...

JENNY: *(Seriously)* He...?

MICHAEL: Yeah.

JENNY: I'm sorry. *(Beat)* My mother had it, but she recovered. But when I couldn't visit her...

MICHAEL: That was the worst.

JENNY: Absolute worst.

(Beat.)

MICHAEL: So, what about you? What do you miss most? Besides the obvious.

JENNY: Hmmm. Seeing people in person. Remember getting together with friends, even inside?

MICHAEL: Seems crazy now...

JENNY: I used to play volleyball! In a gym!

MICHAEL: Insane!

JENNY: Even when that all that ended you could at least see people at the store, before they started delivering everything by drone.

MICHAEL: But the very most?

JENNY: Honestly? Hugs. Skin contact. *(She leans in, playfully seductive)* You want to know my wildest fantasy?

MICHAEL: Well, yeah!

JENNY: Spooning.

MICHAEL: Spooning?

JENNY: Can you imagine, the length of your entire body—

MICHAEL: Don't torture yourself.

JENNY: Pressed against the length of—

MICHAEL: Don't torture me!

JENNY: If we could only, just a little…

(Beat.)

MICHAEL: There are those people who—

JENNY: You're not saying…?

MICHAEL: We could just try it.

JENNY: But the virus! Think about your father! My mother!

MICHAEL: I know, but we can sanitize, we can mask. We can even hold our breaths during it! And I've got a N95. Do you?

JENNY: Yeah, but…if anyone found out…The sentinels are watching!

MICHAEL: I'll pretend to leave, then you draw the blinds. Then I'll sneak back in.

JENNY: They'd throw us in jail!

MICHAEL: They'll never know! *(Beat)* It will be our secret.

(Beat.)

JENNY: Mum's the word?

MICHAEL: Mum's the word.

(Michael steps out of the apartment. Jenny draws the window blinds, then furtively lets him back in. They then get the hand sanitizer and

sanitize their hands and put on N95 masks. Then they sit again, but closer, facing each other and, while looking into each other's eyes, slowly raise their arms, reach out and press their palms together. They close their eyes and breathe in deeply.)

THE INEVITABILITY OF SUNSHINE
by Cris Eli Blak

Did you hear about the rose that grew from a crack in the concrete? Proving nature's laws wrong, it learned to walk without having feet. Funny, it seems to by keeping its dreams; it learned to breathe fresh air. Long live the rose that grew from concrete when no one else even cared.

Tupac Shakur

CHARACTERS

LANGSTON 18; an intelligent young man, thin but fit, aspires to be the next great American poet, but most of all to get out of his current living conditions; works at a movie theater (one of the guys who sweeps up the popcorn you drop on the floor during the movie)

ZOEY 17-18; a pretty middle-class girl, peppy, optimistic and pretty—but there is something deeper, more personable, smart, understanding. She works the concession stand, a perfect job for someone who loves communicating with strangers

SETTING

The Bright Star Movie Theatre, a small locally owned theatre in a small Southern town. Right now. Maybe tomorrow, maybe yesterday, maybe next week, maybe right now.

(At Rise, lights up…on the lobby of the Bright Star movie theatre, completely empty and quiet, almost a ghost-like silence filling the room. The lights are dimmed, one light bulb flickering from repair neglect. A small concessions counter sits towards the back of the space, a cheap popcorn machine barely visible in the shadow of the lobby.

It's clear that this is a local theatre, one that probably does not have any more than fifty or so seats in its one screening room. Imagine somewhere intimate, like something you would find down South, where time has passed but the city has not quite caught up with it.

Enter Langston. He wears a hoodie and holey blue jeans, which barely fit him; his belt is tied as tightly as possible just to hold them up along his thin frame. Over his shoulders hangs a backpack and in his hand is a notebook—pen writing and scribbles occupy the exterior. He clears his throat and opens the notebook to a few pages in. He looks up and begins speaking his poetic words aloud, almost as if he were speaking directly to the audience.)

LANGSTON: How do you manage
in a world full of panic?
How do you stand it
when there's a pandemic,
when the academics say it's systemic
and the Internet claims that it's all gimmick.
even though the death toll rises high above the triple digits?

(Zoey enters. She wears the typical "movie theatre" uniform, black vest and all. On her shoulder hangs her purse, in her hand she clutches her iPhone. She freezes, eyes widening, not knowing exactly what she has walked in on. She holds onto her items, mouth open halfway, wanting to say something but also wanting to listen to the rest.)

LANGSTON: They say the secret to survival
is through independence,
but old friends just see that as a

temporary life sentence,
like imprisonment,
and it's impossible to find senti-
ment from the government,
especially when you're like
me.
While this virus
is on its cold hunt
I'm just a pirate
in search of a homefront,
somewhere to prop my feet up.

(Zoey's face turns to one of concern and sympathy.)

LANGSTON: Cuz I am alone,
on my own,
owning nothing but my soul,
nothing but this body with all its
scars and cracks,
this body that's now always at risk
of attack.
Sometimes I wish I could go back—

(He turns around and sees Zoey standing there. He freezes, she frenzies.)

ZOEY: I'm so sorry! I didn't know anyone else would be here this late.

LANGSTON: Did you—?

ZOEY: Hear anything? No!

LANGSTON: Oh.

ZOEY: Yes! I lied. I heard.

LANGSTON: What all did you—?

ZOEY: I'm sorry.

LANGSTON: Stop apologizing.

ZOEY: It was good, though. Have you heard? Poetry is…lit. *(Chuckles)* Get it? Cuz poetry is literature.

(Nothing.)

ZOEY: Alrighty then. Really, though. It was good. I liked it. I mean, I didn't like it, it was pretty dark. But that can be good too! Like Edgar Allan Poe on meth, or something. Then again, what isn't dark these days, right?

(She gives a faux laugh, a stupid grin crossing her face. She turns away, nervously stuffing her hands deep into her pockets. Within a second, she turns back around and extends her hand, a youthful optimism painting her stance.)

ZOEY: Let's start over. I'm Zoey.

(Langston starts to go for her hand with his, then she quickly recoils.)

ZOEY: Oh, wait!

(She reaches into her purse and pulls out a small bottle of hand sanitizer. She squeezes some out into her hand.)

ZOEY: Better safe than sorry. Do you want some?

LANGSTON: Uh, sure.

(She pours some in his hand. As they cleanse—)

ZOEY: I'm usually not here this late. Ever since they implemented the whole curfew thing, I've tried to play it safe and get home as sure as possible.

(She reextends her hand.)

ZOEY: Zoey. My name's Zoey. I work the concession stand. I started in sodas but was recently promoted to hot dogs. *(Off his laugh)* What's funny?

LANGSTON: Oh, I—nothing. *(Shakes her hand)* I'm Langston. I'm on the cleaning crew.

ZOEY: Langston the mysterious poet. You should be getting home, too. Things aren't getting any better out there and they're getting even stricter when it comes to curfew. They barely want us working at all. You know they're even talking about shutting down the theatre?

(Langston's face turns, appearing sick. He starts breathing heavier.)

LANGSTON: Are you for real?

ZOEY: That's what I heard. No one wants to sit around strangers for two hours not knowing whether or not they're infected. And, well, the movie studios don't wanna spend money to put something out that no one is gonna go see.

(Langston starts pacing around in a circle. She notices.)

ZOEY: Are you okay?

LANGSTON: Did they say when?

ZOEY: When what?

LANGSTON: When they're gonna shut down the theatre. Did they say when?

(He's getting louder, his words beginning to mumble together. Zoey looks somewhere between concerned and scared.)

ZOEY: I don't know. For all I know it's just gossip. I'm sorry if—
LANGSTON: Stop that!
ZOEY: *(Emotional)* I'm sorry.
LANGSTON: For what now?!
ZOEY: Saying sorry!

(A beat. Langston throws the notebook down and kneels, covering his face with his palms. Zoey chews on her bottom lip, unsure about how to react).

ZOEY: I think I should get going. It's getting kinda late.
LANGSTON: *(Not looking back)* Yeah. I think maybe you should, too

(Though his words may come off harsh, his tone does not. It is more remorseful, afraid, like a child looking for his parents in a dark house during a thunderstorm.)

ZOEY: It was nice meeting you.
LANGSTON: Yeah.

(Zoey nods, accepting. She turns and starts off then pauses. She turns back around and begins towards Langston.)

ZOEY: Your uniform.
LANGSTON: What?
ZOEY: You don't have on your uniform.
LANGSTON: *(Standing)* Okay?
ZOEY: Where is it?

LANGSTON: In my backpack.

ZOEY: Why?

LANGSTON: What does it matter?

ZOEY: *(Searching)* I'm just curious. I don't see why you would risk dodging curfew just to change clothes. I really don't get why you would get so upset about not being able to come to work here. I mean, not only is this place a piece of crap but you'd be able to self-isolate and stay healthy. Who would freak out about that?

LANGSTON: You have a lotta questions.

ZOEY: You have few answers.

LANGSTON: Listen, no offense but I don't even know you. You seem like a nice girl, for real, so I think it'd be best if you just went home.

ZOEY: Fine. Walk out with me.

LANGSTON: What?

ZOEY: Walk out to your car with me.

LANGSTON: *(Stutters)* I…don't have a car.

ZOEY: How do you get to work?

LANGSTON: I…walk.

ZOEY: Great. Then I'll drive you.

LANGSTON: It's too far.

ZOEY: But not too far to walk? I promise you my car is faster than your feet. If we leave now, we can both make it home before the patrol comes out.

LANGSTON: *(Sternly)* I like to walk.

ZOEY: Start walking now and you'll never get out on time.

LANGSTON: I'll take the risk.

(They stand looking at each other, arms crossed.)

ZOEY: Cut the shit, Langston.

LANGSTON: Excuse me?

(Zoey drops her purse and sits down, crossing her legs "crisscross-applesauce" style.)

LANGSTON: What are you doing?
ZOEY: If you're dodging curfew, so am I.
LANGSTON: That's dumb.
ZOEY: Guess I'm in a dumb mood tonight.

(She lifts her hands, closes her eyes, and starts acting as if she is meditating.)

ZOEY: Ommmmmmmmmm…
LANGSTON: You're kidding me.
ZOEY: *(Opening one eye)* Tell me the truth.
LANGSTON: I don't know what you're talking about.

(She shrugs and closes her open eye.)

ZOEY: Ommmmmmmmmm…
LANGSTON: Jesus Christ.
ZOEY: You can stop this anytime you want. Ommmmmmmmmm…
LANGSTON: Of all the nights…
ZOEY: *(Louder)* Ommmmmmmmmm…

(She starts waving her hands in the air overdramatically.)

ZOEY: I am one with this world.
LANGSTON: Fine!

(She opens her eyes with a satisfied smile.)

ZOEY: One point Zoey.

LANGSTON: What do you wanna know?

ZOEY: Everything.

LANGSTON: Three questions. That's it. Then you go home.

ZOEY: Not fair.

LANGSTON: Life's not fair.

ZOEY: You're no fun. But fine. Three questions. *(Stands)* Question one: Why are you here so late? Really.

LANGSTON: Honestly?

ZOEY: Honestly.

(Langston turns his back on her and starts biting on his thumb nail. He doesn't know whether he should open up or not, tell the truth or come up with a lie. You can almost see the dueling thoughts racing through his mind.)

ZOEY: Langston?

LANGSTON: *(Quickly)* I sleep here.

ZOEY: Oh.

(He still doesn't look her way.)

LANGSTON: Happy?

ZOEY: What? No. I'm sorry…I mean, I don't know what to say. I didn't expect that. I didn't mean to make you—I don't know.

LANGSTON: Damage is done. You have two questions left.

ZOEY: How long have you been staying here?

LANGSTON: On and off since I was hired last month. Before that it was wherever I could lay my head. Hotel lobbies, benches —anywhere.

(Zoey sits back down, taking it all in.)

ZOEY: What about your family?

(He sits down beside her but the two do not make eye contact.)

LANGSTON: I am my family.

ZOEY: What does that mean?

LANGSTON: You already asked three questions.

ZOEY: A deal is a deal, I guess.

(They sit in silence. Zoey wraps her hands around her knees.)

ZOEY: Do you ever just count the seconds during a quiet moment, just to see how long the world can go on without a single sound? *(Then)* I know you think I don't get it, your situation. And you're mostly right. I don't. But I also hope you know that just because you're in one place doesn't mean you have to stay there forever.

LANGSTON: It's not that easy. Where I'm from there's barely even a curfew. You know why? Cuz most people don't even have a bed to run to. We were one of the first communities hit hard. Hardly anyone had insurance, so they just sat with it or went out and spread it to the rest of the block. Soon enough patrol comes through and starts burning down whole houses, claiming that that's the only way to contain the virus. And I mean, fine, maybe you save one life doing that, but you also just put someone out on the street. You don't hear that stuff reported on the news.

ZOEY: I remember when the first person died—the first reported person. I couldn't believe it. It was like something out of a horror movie.

LANGSTON: You were afraid.

ZOEY: Weren't you?

LANGSTON: No. What do I have to lose?

(Zoey looks to him with gentle eyes.)

ZOEY: How long have you been writing poetry?
LANGSTON: Since I started needing it to stay sane.
ZOEY: It will do that for you.

(She stands up and grabs her purse, pulling out a small notebook of her own. She flips a few pages.)

ZOEY: My dad had this game
called "music box."
He would hum a tune
and I would make up the words.
His whistle was the soundtrack of my world,
my whispered lullabies were my favorite tracks.

(Langston looks at her as she lowers the notebook to match his eyes. There is a softness to his stare now, something new beaming. They are connecting.)

ZOEY: When he went away,
off into the sky to claim his corner,
a cloud of his own,
I would wait by the window,
eyes to that sky
and I would hum the hymnals of his heart,
hoping that he would hear and come back down
to give me his words.
But he never came back.

I remembered he once took me to a garden,
guarded by green beauty.

He picked me a rose,
his red remembrance to his little girl.

(She puts the notebook down and reaches in her purse again, this time pulling out a small rose.)

ZOEY: And even though I don't see them as often anymore, when I do see a rose I make sure to pick it. You see, when I was little my dad sat me down and told me that a rose is special because it's the result of nothing but the world. And no matter what happens to use, to society, to the neighborhoods we live in—roses are still gonna grow. They don't need our permission. They don't listen when a daisy tells them they can't. They still grow. And thrive and bring happiness and love, even in times like these. You can trust that the sun will wake up every morning, even if our loved ones don't.

(She hands the rose to Langston.)

ZOEY: We're all roses. We can grow past this.

(He examines the rose, maintaining his newfound softness, nearly breaking a smile, nearly shedding a tear. We hear a phone notification ring. It snaps Langston back into reality. He reaches into his pocket and pulls out his cell phone. His face sinks.)

ZOEY: What is it?

(He looks at the phone, its screen illuminating onto his face. We hear yelling, glass breaking, screaming, wailing.)

LANGSTON: It's a neighborhood in Fresno. It was supposed to be a pro test to make vaccines cheaper, I guess, but it took a turn.

(We continue to hear the commotion. Zoey moves closer to him, bending over to see for herself.)

ZOEY: It's so many people. They look so scared. They're hysterical. I've never seen so many people so panicked.

LANGSTON: It's like they know their time is running out.

(Zoey looks away from the phone and at Langston's face. She can tell the attitude that she brought out of him is fading away. She lowers the phone from his face, picks up the rose and hands it to Langston.)

ZOEY: Or they're just waiting to grow.

(And with that the lights completely go out. It is pitch black.)

LANGSTON: Guess it's curfew.

(Suddenly, a single light shines down on Zoey. She is the only thing illuminated in the sea of darkness. She reaches out her hand. When she does another light appears, this time down on Langston. He looks around, then looks to her as she stands. Langston grabs his backpack and puts it on, then takes her hand. Zoey grabs her purse and smiles at him.)

ZOEY: I was pretty bummed out when they canceled school and stuff. I wanted to go to prom so bad. But I guess that's not happening, huh?

LANGSTON: I'm sorry.

ZOEY: Look who's apologizing now.

LANGSTON: *(Laughs)* Okay.

ZOEY: I'm rubbing off on you.

LANGSTON: I dunno about all that.

ZOEY: Dance with me?

LANGSTON: Now? Here?

ZOEY: Why not?

(He grabs for his phone, clearly a bit nervous and anxious.)

LANGSTON: What song do you want to dance to?

ZOEY: Put the phone away, mysterious poet.

(He places the phone back into the pocket of his jeans.)

LANGSTON: You wanna dance to nothing?

ZOEY: Do you prefer music?

LANGSTON: It makes it a little less weird, don't you think?

(She chuckles and reaches out her other hand. He takes it.)

ZOEY: Fine. We can have music. I'll hum, and you make up the words.

(They start dancing. Their two lights become one. We hear the faint sounds of an ambulance siren racing past, but they still dance. We hear an incoming breaking news report, but they still dance, looking each other in the eyes, now not breaking contact at all, not even for a second. The sounds fade behind them, and then their lights fade and all we hear is music.)

SIRENS IN LIMBO
by Mark Borkowski

CHARACTERS

MINNIE
KAT
VIVI

SETTING

April 8th, 2020 (worst day of the pandemic in New York City).
Late afternoon.

(At Rise, a loud siren is heard from outside. On the far side of the living room, Minnie is talking rather intimately on her cell phone. Kat is across the room, sipping a can of beer…)

MINNIE: *(On cell)* "And all at once, and over all
The pitying rain began to fall
I lay and heard each pattering hoof
Upon my lowly, thatched roof
And seemed to love the sound far more
Than ever I had done before.
For rain it hath a friendly sound
To one who's six feet underground;
And scarce the friendly voice or face:
A grave is such a quiet place."

KAT: That's just what we need, more death.

MINNIE: *(To Kat)* Do you mind? *(To cell)* Yes, she wrote in 1912, it's called "Renascence." I'll text you a link, you can read the whole poem…I'll let you know if I can make it…

KAT: Make what?

MINNIE: And again, I'm so so sorry...*(Hangs up. To Kat)* It's Evelyn's favorite poem. Was.

KAT: She just died, right?

MINNIE: Yesterday.

KAT: Why the fuck are you telling her grieving brother a morbid death poem?

MINNIE: It's not about death, it's about life—it's a declaration of life.

KAT: Sounds like morbid death crap to me.

(A loud scream offstage from the kitchen—)

MINNIE: They're trying to find poems to read at her service.

KAT: Should read something uplifting.

MINNIE: You haven't even heard the poem.

KAT: Remind me not to invite you to my funeral.

MINNIE: Why, I may be the only one there.

(Vivi enters from the kitchen, like a hurricane, ballistic—)

VIVI: Look at me! Look!

MINNIE: What am I looking at?

VIVI: I'm fucking shaking!

MINNIE: What happened now?

VIVI: *(Points to Kat)* Her!

KAT: Back off, sister.

VIVI: Don't tell me to back off. I asked you three times, nicely, to clean that goddamn kitchen!

KAT: Nicely? You threw a fuckin' book at me!

MINNIE: What book? Not my Norton Anthology.

(Minnie hurries off into kitchen.)

VIVI: Sink's packed with filthy dishes, grease splattered all over from your fucking shell steak!

KAT: Skirt steak.

VIVI: You cook it—not only does the whole place reek of meat—I hate meat, you know I hate meat—now the grease is all over the stove, counter tops—You don't even put a lid on it!

KAT: I don't believe in lids.

VIVI: What are you waiting for, the fucking maggots?!

KAT: I said I'd take care of it.

VIVI: Who thought this was a good idea?

KAT: To use lids?

VIVI: For us to come stay with you and Mom.

KAT: Ask Minnie.

(Minnie re-enters, wiping off her book.)

MINNIE: Ask Minnie what?

KAT: Why you decided to show up with this basket case, in the middle of a fuckin' pandemic, to be with Mom.

MINNIE: Kat, she's…

KAT: What? She's what?

MINNIE: Dying.

KAT: She's been dying. I should know, I've been taking care of her almost five years. While you two are "fulfilling your fucking dreams!"

MINNIE: Look, I know you've been the rock, the anchor that's kept her—

KAT: Out of a nursing home?

MINNIE: The point is, you told us she was dying.

VIVI: That's right, you did—It's why I flew 3,000 fucking miles—you said, "Mom's dying"—

MINNIE: If you didn't want us to come, you should've just said so.

VIVI: Fuck that! It's my mother, I have a right to be here!

KAT: I didn't know we'd end up in a lockdown together!

MINNIE: The woman's laying in that room, listening to you two screaming.

KAT: She ain't listening to anything. She doesn't even know what year it is.

VIVI: I fed her lunch, she thought I was Grandma. Asked me if she could go out to play.

(Another loud siren heard from outside.)

MINNIE: 731 today.

KAT: 731 what?

MINNIE: Dead. In one day. What world are you two living in? Five blocks from here they're bringing out the dead. Yeah, Bellevue has a makeshift morgue outside. People are fucking dying and you two are yammering about skirt steak?

VIVI: Not skirt steak. The skirt steak is long consumed. Now what's left is Dresden! Dishes, grease, slop—have you seen that kitchen?

MINNIE: My book was in the trash.

KAT: It was intended for my head.

MINNIE: There's more dead in New York City than half the country.

KAT: That's out there, it's not in here. Cut your Grim Reaper shit! We keep that TV set off we can pretend like it's not even happening!

MINNIE: Not even happening? My friend died yesterday!

VIVI: Personally, I'm more concerned about rats and roaches—

MINNIE: How can you say that?!

VIVI: You guys know how I am…my issues.

MINNIE: It's not that bad, Viv.

VIVI: My issues?

MINNIE: The kitchen!

KAT: Thank you.

VIVI: Yes, it is! I'm not crazy! Now I got that icy feeling, I start itching and—and —

(Vivi is shaking, practically in tears.)

MINNIE: Sit down.

KAT: Yeah, sit—

VIVI: Don't you tell me what to do!

MINNIE: Breathe.

VIVI: It's like I got maggots crawling all over me.

MINNIE: Don't let your mind get morbid, sweetie.

KAT: You got nerve. You're the one that's reciting death poetry to a grieving brother.

VIVI: What's she talking about?

MINNIE: Evelyn.

VIVI: Who?

KAT: Her friend that died.

VIVI: Death poetry?

MINNIE: Her brother doesn't know what to do. They can't have a service for her cause of this shit virus. They're just gonna put her in the ground. He and her sister are doing a little vigil of their own. Ya know, to say goodbye to her. Her brother never paid attention to her as an artist. He called me to ask who her favorite poets are. Were. She always loved Edna.

KAT: Thought it was Virginia Wolff.

MINNIE: No.

KAT: Suicidal poets all sound the same.

MINNIE: She didn't kill herself.

KAT: Virginia Wolff?

MINNIE: No, Edna St. Vincent Millay.

VIVI: Virginia sure did. She just filled her fuckin' pockets with rocks and walked into the river. She said, "I'm fuckin' outta here!"

MINNIE: Evelyn and I did a show together eight months ago. We were on stage together. We looked into each other's eyes and had some of those moments that only actors know about.

VIVI: I need a Xanax.

KAT: I thought you were trying to stop.

VIVI: I WAS but now I'm NOT! Okay?!

KAT: You really need one?

VIVI: Living with you, I need a fucking arsenal!

KAT: I'll get 'em. Where are they?

VIVI: My purse. Thank you.

(Kat goes to her purse, digs through—)

VIVI: I should never have travelled on my bad moon.

MINNIE: Bad moon?

VIVI: Everybody's got a bad moon. Plus, motherfuckin' Mercury's in retrograde.

KAT: Got 'em.

(Kat brings over the pill bottle. Hands her one—)

KAT: One for you, two for me.

(She pops two.)

MINNIE: C'mon, Kat.

VIVI: Gimme those! I knew you doing something nice was too good to be true.

KAT: Ya know what? I could pry your fuckin' mouth open and shove this whole bottle down your throat and watch you overdose, you—

MINNIE: Kat!

KAT: "Too good to be true?" I'm here taking care of that black hole in the bedroom while you jet set around the country, acting like a fucking movie star.

MINNIE: Don't talk about Mom like that.

KAT: No, this needs to come out, like a sickness, like puke, like a rancid infection—You two came here! Because you wanted to finally be daughters? What did you bring with you, huh? Love? Compassion? No! You brought all your SHIT with you!

MINNIE: When you're locked up with people, you're locked up with their habits—

KAT: Their whining and complaining—

VIVI: Their fucking mess.

KAT: The mess is in your head!

VIVI: Ya know, the roaches here in New York are worse than any in the world. You know that, right? Do you know why?

MINNIE: I never thought about it.

VIVI: People come to New York City from all over the world. And with them they bring their insects. Insects get into everything. So, you have all these roaches from all over the world mating with each other. They form this infallible roach. It's 100% American!

KAT: There's no roaches in my place. You keep it up, you're gonna will them here.

VIVI: What?!

MINNIE: Don't tell her that.

KAT: Law of attraction. G'head. Keep conjuring roaches.

(Another loud siren from outside. Vivi clasps her ears—)

VIVI: Fucking sirens!

MINNIE: It's nonstop.

KAT: It's called a pandemic.

VIVI: Should never travel when the planets are against you.

KAT: I love it when people blame their shit on rocks in the sky.

VIVI: You don't believe in anything, do you?!

MINNIE: Kat, why don't you check on Mom?

KAT: I just checked on her, she's fine.

MINNIE: Kat, please.

(Kat exits into bedroom.)

VIVI: I should've known not to come here, with her. She hasn't changed. And she calls mom a "black hole?"

MINNIE: The girl's burned out. She's been caretaking mom nonstop. It makes you crazy.

VIVI: My shrink tells me not to be so self-sacrificing.

MINNIE: This was for Mom. We weren't sure if we would ever see her again. We all wanted to take care of her.

VIVI: But who's taking care of us? We're stuck here now. Like some fuckin' crazy girl limbo. Can't leave if we wanted to.

MINNIE: Wherever there's a door, you can leave.

(Kat re-enters.)

KAT: She's fine. She's mumbling to her picture.

VIVI: It's called praying.

MINNIE: It's so wild, she's lost with dementia, but yet she prays so lucidly.

KAT: Yeah, she always did pray well.

MINNIE: She did the best she could with us.

KAT: Says you.

VIVI: I need another Xanax.

MINNIE: Wait and see if the one you took kicks in.

VIVI: It's not! Not with her around. She's like the iron dome. Pills don't have a chance.

KAT: Why the hell does she pray?

VIVI: 'Cause maybe, unlike you, she believes in something!

KAT: There's nothing left to believe! Go in there and take a look at her! She's forgotten everything! All she's loved, hated, places, people, you, me—done, dead and gone! In the end she just wants to go out and fucking play!

MINNIE: I wanna go see her.

VIVI: Mom?

MINNIE: Evelyn.

VIVI: Are you crazy?!

KAT: Not a good idea, Sis.

MINNIE: Just wanna see her one last time.

VIVI: You can't.

MINNIE: Don't tell me I can't.

KAT: You yourself said 700 people died today.

MINNIE: 731.

VIVI: It's a full-blown pandemic.

MINNIE: They're going to view her body one last time. I wanna go.

VIVI: No.

MINNIE: I'll be safe, quick, in and out, and I'll be back.

VIVI: And what the fuck will you bring back with you?!

KAT: If you go, I can't let you back in here.

VIVI: Don't say that.

KAT: We have a 93-year-old woman in the next room. A common cold could kill her, let alone—

VIVI: How can you be so selfish?

KAT: I'm serious, I won't let you back in here.

MINNIE: I don't wanna come back.

VIVI: Don't say that.

MINNIE: I don't wanna come back to my life at all. Not the life I was living. Ever since this whole thing started it put my mind in a whole different trajectory. Terrible things are happening out there but…I couldn't stop my life before. I didn't know how…I needed something to…stop it, to stop everything. To, to—

VIVI: Shut it all down?

KAT: Close the fucking operating system.

VIVI: What the hell are you saying?

MINNIE: It's gotta change. These lives of ours. We're all so unhappy.

VIVI: Thank God for pharmaceuticals.

MINNIE: No Band-Aids, Sis. Wounds are wide open.

KAT: *(Beat)* Get your mask, surgical gloves. Try to stay a few feet away from each other.

VIVI: Are you condoning this?

KAT: It was her friend, Viv. What kind of people are we if we can't walk through shit to say farewell to a friend?

VIVI: But, but—

KAT: But what?

VIVI: She's dead anyway.

KAT: This is not about the dead.

VIVI: What if she gets infected, what if she brings it back to Mom…To me…

KAT: How'd the rest of that poem go? The death one.

MINNIE: I don't remember a lot of it but…

"O God, I cried, give me new birth,
And put me back upon the earth.
Upset each cloud's gigantic gourd
And let the heavy rain, down-poured
In one big torrent, set me free,
Washing my grave away from me."

(Another loud siren is heard outside.)

GOLDEN RETRIEVER

by Louisa Burns-Bisogno

CHARACTERS

ANGIE	67, Female
SAL	68, Her Husband

(At Rise, Light in the junk-filled attic comes from a single bulb and from the open attic door. Boxes are open. Clothes and papers are strewn about. Angie has been frantically searching for something when Sal, her panicky husband, appears.)

SAL: *(Offstage)* Angie! Been lookin' for you. Grub Hub is on its way…

ANGIE: *(Barking like a dog)* Wuff! Wuff!

SAL: They'll be here in ten minutes.

(He enters the attic carrying a small gold gift bag.)

SAL: Ten on the button. And Zoom is scheduled so we feast with the family. Stop futzin around. Come on down.

(He approaches Angie. She turns on him growling…and threatening to bite.)

ANGIE: Grrrrrrr

SAL: What's with the rabid act?

(Angie goes back to searching through the suitcase.)

SAL: I hate to interrupt…but *(Yells)* what the hell are you doin' up here… barking? *(Calmly)* If you don't mind my asking?

ANGIE: Why does anyone go to an attic?

SAL: Riddles? Now? With lasagna and parmigiana on its way.

ANGIE: Why, Sal?

SAL: To hoard junk they shoulda thrown out in the first place.

ANGIE: Or to find a treasured memory.

SAL: Look later.

ANGIE: I'm not coming down without it.

SAL: The kids went all out. Reworked their schedules so we could celebrate together despite the fact they're thousands of miles away. Nothing can be more important…

ANGIE: *(Over)* Oh yes it can. I wanted to surprise you.

SAL: You surprised me alright. Growling on our Golden Anniversary. Threatening to take a bite out of my mask.

ANGIE: I got your attention.

SAL: So, what are you today? A bitch-on-freeze or a kooky spaniel?

ANGIE: You don't know how many times I wished I was the dog.

SAL: Me too. She doesn't make an issue over social distance. Jumps right on my lap.

ANGIE: I hear you all the time. "Good girl, Poochie. You're the best girl in the whole wide world. Love you, Poochie." You never say things like that to me.

ANGIE: Always the wisecracks…

SAL: It's not easy for me Angie…to express emotions.

ANGIE: Bull! You melt every time your furry pal cuddles with you on the couch.

SAL: She doesn't nag, "Give me the remote."

ANGIE: No…she hides it with her bones…and I get the blame.

SAL: She doesn't make me late when dinner's delivered. She beats me to the door.

ANGIE: So, feed the lasagna to her. She's the one you really care about.

SAL: Hey Angie…you're jealous of the dog.

ANGIE: Tell me Sal…what does that mangy mutt have that I don't?

SAL: Besides naturally golden blonde hair?

ANGIE: I'm serious.

SAL: Seriously…she isn't always moaning that with the lockdown everything's going to the dogs. Pooch is making the best of a bad situation.

ANGIE: It can't get any worse for us.

SAL: When bad times hit you used to cheer me on. Somewhere around ten years ago or twenty…you stopped.

ANGIE: I stopped because you stopped.

SAL: I stopped because…well, Poochie appreciates the odors I pick up in my line of work. You'd say, "Shower first." How do you think that makes a guy feel?

ANGIE: How does Poochie make you feel?

SAL: Can you handle the truth?

ANGIE: I'm a big girl.

SAL: I'll say.

ANGIE: I'll ignore that mean remark. The truth, Sal.

SAL: She makes me feel good. Never complains.

ANGIE: Why should she complain…. I wait on her hand and foot. Feed her two meals a day. Before COVID, I took her to the groom monthly to get coiffed and nails clipped. Can't remember the last time I had my nails done.

SAL: More complaints.

ANGIE: You complain. Every time I cook spaghetti.

SAL: You break it in two…that ain't authentic.

ANGIE: Oh, this is not about pasta, Sal. It's about intimacy.

SAL: Don't talk dirty, Ange. Not with the lights on.

ANGIE: For God's sake! I'm talking about sharing feelings. I feel like I died…but you never got around to burying me.

SAL: Could you be more specific?

ANGIE: You never talked to me. Did anything with me. You were always so busy with the business.

SAL: Hey Babe, I was busting my butt putting bread on the table. Paying off the mortgage…two times. Sending three kids to college.

ANGIE: Oh, yes…the kids. You were always too tired to talk to them too. That's why they all came to me with their secrets. "Don't tell Dad this." "Don't tell Dad that." Well, I never did. I kept it all in here

(She indicates her heart.)

SAL: What secrets?

ANGIE: I promised never…ever to tell. I swore I'd take their secrets to the grave. *(Throws her hands up in surrender)* Oh, what the hell! It doesn't matter anymore. Remember the time when John was so depressed?

SAL: Yeah, yeah…he was crying in his bedroom all the time.

ANGIE: He locked you out. Me he let in. Said I'd understand.

SAL: I understood. His girl broke their engagement.

ANGIE: She was pregnant.

SAL: They coulda married anyway. A five-month baby. Not that unusual.

ANGIE: It wasn't his kid.

SAL: That woulda been unusual.

ANGIE: And Danny…sweet, gentle Danny, so loving, so giving. Always did his chores faithfully. Shops for me even now. Remembers my birthday. Sends beautiful flowers…

SAL: *(Stunned by the realization)* Dan is gay?

ANGIE: No…that was Susie.

SAL: Our daughter a lezzie? You're killing me, Ange. Say it isn't so. No way! Can't be! She's been married 25 years. Has four kids. Does her husband know?

ANGIE: It was a college experience. Freshman year.

SAL: I slaved for Lesbo 101.

ANGIE: She was confused.

SAL: I'm confused. *(Takes a deep breath)* What secret did Danny keep from me?

ANGIE: None. That's the problem. It's not normal, Sal.

SAL: *(Sighs deeply)* Ah well…it's water over the bridge.

ANGIE: *(Correcting him)* Under the dam.

SAL: Whichever! The main thing. The kids turned out okay. You gotta give me some credit for that.

ANGIE: I put your name on the birth certificate…you want an Academy Award?

SAL: No! I want us to get the hell downstairs. Dinner's getting cold on the doorstep. We have exactly four minutes left to START the Zoom party in our honor. *(Lighter)* Hey, maybe it's good we don't show up. We were never orthodox.

ANGIE: What the hell do you mean by that?

SAL: Didn't we elope in the first place?

ANGIE: 'Cause my parents refused permission. Said it was just puppy love. That I was too young to marry.

SAL: Well, you're not a kid anymore.

ANGIE: More mean remarks. The other day…when my arthritis acted up…you said…"Why are you walking like an old lady?" You might have asked…are you in pain?

SAL: Of course…if you're walking like an old lady, you're in pain.

ANGIE: Oh, Sal we don't even speak the same language anymore.

SAL: I saw it on Dr. Phil. It's that…Mars-Venal thing.

ANGIE: Venus…you nut!

SAL: Nut? Me? I'm not the one howling in the attic. Who's forgotten that a certain husband invested in Grub Hub so a certain wife wouldn't have to cook on her special day.

ANGIE: My special day is just another 24 hours in quarantine. What a disappointment! I had planned the big '50' for fifty years. I even reserved the clubhouse.

SAL: The backyard woulda worked as well.

ANGIE: Not with over two hundred guests? John was flyin' in with the kids from San Diego. Danny was planning the menu. Sue was gonna take me shoppin' for a dress.

SAL: You didn't need another dress.

ANGIE: I needed it! I needed the big party. Surf and turf and a wedding cake.

SAL: Why waste the money?

ANGIE: Because we didn't have a wooden nickel the day we got married. I wore my poodle skirt and old sweater so the folks wouldn't suspect anything was goin' on. I took the bus. Was so nervous I missed my stop. Ran a mile back to the Church. I could hardly catch my breath to say I do. The only thing special that day was…It's got to be here someplace.

SAL: It hasn't been all bad, Ange. We had some good times, remember?

ANGIE: Not too well. I've felt…undesirable for years.

SAL: I tried. Even got Viagra.

ANGIE: The Viagra. I remember getting ready for bed…and you said… "Big Daddy will be up and running tonight." What happened, Sal… you never made it to the starting gate?

SAL: It's a long story.

ANGIE: We have time.

SAL: *(Checking watch)* Two minutes.

ANGIE: The short version.

SAL: Just as I was opening the prescription bottle…I noticed the leaky faucet. So I got down to turn off the water under the sink… figuring I'd fix it in the morning.

ANGIE: And…

SAL: As I pulled myself up I hit the Viagra bottle and another bottle on the counter. Pills spilled all over the place.

ANGIE: And…?

SAL: I gathered the pills up, but my eyes aren't so good anymore. Put some back in your bottle…but I must've read wrong. 'Cause I took two Vs… and got plenty of Zzzs.

ANGIE: You musta took MY Ambiens, Sal. I was about to take one when you announced the night of my life. So, I set them aside.

SAL: You always forget to tighten the cap.

ANGIE: So, it was my fault?

SAL: A relief to know it wasn't mine. This explains why I couldn't do it. No matter how many pills I took.

ANGIE: Now I know why I was so horny. Couldn't sleep for a month.

SAL: Ships in the night…

ANGIE: Two Titanics.

SAL: You wanna know a disaster? Right now, the entire Marano family is signing in from all around the country. In-laws and outlaws. Our three kids, six grandkids…not to mention a number of old friends. They're all in the Zoom Waiting Room wondering if we decided to skip the whole mishegas and finally get divorced. They've been taking bets on it for years.

(Angie starts looking in the trunk again.)

ANGIE: Thank God! Jesus, Mar,y and Joseph…I found it.

SAL: What? What?

ANGIE: My tiara…from when I played Queen Isabella in the high school play. I snuck it into my purse…and wore it when we married… fifty years ago today. I didn't have my family or friends to support me. No flowers, satin dress or billowy veil. No Venetian dessert table. This tiara was the only thing that made me feel like a bride on my wedding day.

SAL: *(Pulls tiara from Angie)* You are not going to wear that piece of crap again.

(They struggle for it.)

ANGIE: Wuff…Wuff…Grrrrrrrrrr…

SAL: *(Proffering the gift bag)*Down, girl, down! I got you a goodie.

(Angie grabs the gift bag and looks into it.)

SAL: I was gonna give it to you online. With the whole crowd watchin'. A romantic touch.

(Angie tosses the old tiara aside and pulls out an elegant gold and rhinestone tiara. She puts it on.)

ANGIE: Oh, Sal. You remembered after all these years. *(Reaches into the bag…)* Wait a Goddamn minute! What's this? A rhinestone dog's collar?

SAL: For Poochie…but it means nothing…I swear.

(Angie slips the dog collar around her wrist like a bracelet.)

ANGIE: You gonna promise to love, honor, and cherish me again, Sal?

SAL: Sure Angie…but I draw the line at scratchin' behind your ears.

THE AFFLICTION
by Coleman

CHARACTERS

MAN
PERSON ONE
PERSON TWO

(At Rise, an office. A Man stands, petrified. Person One enters, finding Person Two staring at the Man. At first it appears Person Two is also Petrified.)

ONE: *(Startled)* What the hell! I thought you were…

TWO: No. Not me. Him.

ONE: *(Examining the Man)* You're sure?

TWO: He hasn't moved.

ONE: How long has he been like this?

TWO: He was like this when I got here. That was around eight, eight-fifteen.

ONE: Have you called anyone?

TWO: No.

ONE: Good. The fewer people who know about this the better.

TWO: What do we do?

ONE: Nothing for now. He might come to.

TWO: He might, but he probably won't. Most people who…

ONE: Let's not get ahead of ourselves. We just have to wait and see what happens. The important thing right now is to keep it quiet.

TWO: Shouldn't we let his family know?

ONE: Why? It's not like they can do anything about it. They'll know soon enough. Meanwhile…

TWO: Meanwhile, what?

ONE: The first thing we need to do is lock the door and pull the shades down.

TWO: Isn't that a sure sign? That's like announcing what's happened.

ONE: Hmm. I suppose you're right. What do you suggest?

TWO: Maybe we could cover him with something?

ONE: He's in the middle of the room. It's not like he wouldn't be noticed.

TWO: We could move him. To the store closet, maybe.

ONE: We have a store closet?

(Two nods.)

ONE: You move him. I'm not going to touch him.

TWO: We could use the dolly.

ONE: Good idea…We have a dolly?

(Two exits, returns with dolly.)

TWO: Here. I'll back it up to him, you lean him into it.

(Two backs the dolly up to the Man. One starts to push on the Man, then realizes what he's about to do.)

ONE: Hell, no! I'll hold the dolly. You lean him into it.

TWO: I'm not going to touch him.

ONE: I'm sure as hell not going to touch him.

TWO: Use a book or something.

ONE: A book?

TWO: Yeah. I'll hold the dolly. And you, grab that book and push it against his chest.

(They perform the actions as indicated. The Man is now leaning back into the dolly. Two struggles to bear the weight.)

TWO: Help me!

ONE: No way.

(Two, struggling, has slowly lowered the dolly to the ground.)

ONE: That's not good.

TWO: You were no help.

ONE: What did you expect me to do? If I touch him…

TWO: I know, I know. I could have used a little help.

ONE: You could use going to the gym. He's not that heavy.

TWO: The gyms are all closed. Like everything else.

ONE: What do we do now?

TWO: Well, whatever we do, we can't stand still.

ONE: Stand still?

TWO: Yes. That's what causes it.

(Two has started moving—walking in circles, waving his arms, lifting one leg at a time, doing silly walks, etc.)

TWO: That's what they think. When you're exposed to the Petrification, you have to keep moving for at least 24 hours. It doesn't always work. Some people get petrified anyway, but most of the time, movement prevents…

ONE: Do you have any idea how silly you look?

(Two keeps moving.)

ONE: Where did you hear that nonsense?

TWO: Don't you watch the briefings?

ONE: I stopped watching them right after this thing started. Too depressing.

TWO: You should watch them.

(Two has grown more frantic in his movements.)

TWO: You should start moving. I'm telling you…
ONE: Moving.
TWO: Up to you.

(Slowly, One starts to move, a bit at a time.)

ONE: This is ridiculous.
TWO: I don't want to get this thing.
ONE: You think I do?
TWO: The way you're moving, you're not trying very hard.
ONE: I have a constitutional right to stand still.

(One steadfastly stops moving.)

TWO: Really?…Have it your way.

(One stands still. Two keeps moving. His movements are increasingly creative and increasingly annoying to One. One watches Two, apparent from modest turns of his head, eyerolls and sighs, until eventually, One stops moving and is petrified. It is clear from the expression on his face, that One is petrified of being petrified. Two pauses for a moment, inspects One, exits, returns with two cloths or blankets. He drapes one over the Man, the other over One. All the while he makes erratic and increasingly creative movements. Two admires his work, does a little dance, turns off the lights, and exits.)

HOME OFFICE
by Liz Coley

CHARACTERS

JANEY	A mom with two at-home telephone jobs
DON	Her husband, a financial adviser, new to working from home
JEFFY	Eight-year-old boy, offstage
EMMA	Ten-year-old girl, offstage

SETTING

During the pandemic. A home with two makeshift home offices in adjacent rooms. The wall between them.

(At Rise, two makeshift home offices in adjacent rooms can be minimally indicated. Janey has three iPhones. Don has one. They can almost hear each other through the wall. Two children, ages 8 and 10, are offstage. We can imagine them standing right outside the parental doors. At rise, Janey is making a list and reading a separate list loudly enough to be heard through the door. Don is on the phone.)

JANEY: Jeffy. Victorious.

DON: No, of course I understand you're worried.

JEFFY: Victorious: V-I-C-T-O-R-I-O-U-S.

DON: That's appropriate. But things will improve.

JANEY: Emma. Congenial.

EMMA: C-O-N-G-E-N-I-A-L. Are we almost done?

DON: Much sooner than they're predicting. Count on it.

JANEY: Done with spelling. Now it's math. What do you think about spaghetti.

EMMA: Again?

DON: Let's see what Friday's close brings, shall we?

JEFFY: Spaghetti: S-P-A-G-E-T

EMMA: There's a silent H, dummy.

JEFFY: I'm not a dummy!

JANEY: Kids! Shh. No yelling. Daddy's at work. *(To self)* Spaghetti. Four boxes. No. Better make it six. And six bottles of Ragu.

JEFFY: Oh! I know! Shpagetti: S-H-P-A-G-G—

DON: Surely not everything. Not now. Think of the fundamentals.

EMMA: No no no! Spaghetti: S-P-A-G-H-E-T-T-I!

JEFFY: Really?

EMMA: Really.

JEFFY: MOOOOOOM! Do you really spell spaghetti with an H?

JANEY: What? Yes, sweetie. After the G. Like laugh.

JEFFY: Spaffeti? Spaffetti, Mom? But we don't say spaffeti.

JANEY: It's not logical, Jeffy. You just have to remember it.

DON: I know it doesn't seem logical. But remember, if you sell at the bottom you are locking in—

(Janey's phone rings. The mystical sounding ringtone.)

JOE: The losses. You'll be carrying them forward for…

JANEY: Scoot, you two! Math worksheets time. Mommy has to do her own work.

(She glares at the doorway until the coast is clear.)

JANEY: Hi. I've been expecting you. You've reached Melissima at the Astral Hotline and I'm here to help you. I can already sense you are worried. About a love done. An elder, per—Oh, your sister.

DON: No, of course I understand you're worried. What if we move 25% into cash. Will that…

JANEY: You have some regrets, don't you? Things left unsaid. Things preying on you. Keeping you awake at night

DON: You have to be able to sleep. Yes, whatever that takes. A clean slate. All right. All right. Yes, Frank. All right. This line is recorded for your protection. Do I have your authorization to proceed with complete liquidation of the account?

JANEY: She's your only sister. She's ready to forgive you…I can assure you. Even though you voted for him—reach out. Today. A clean slate. Before it's too late.

DON: Okay. And we'll be in touch when things turn around?

JANEY: Yes, you can turn this around. Now go. I don't want to keep you on the line. It's eight dollars a minute, you know.

DON: Okay. That's done, then. You take care. Stay healthy.

(Don hangs up.)

JANEY: We're agreed then. Call her. You take care. Stay healthy.

(Janey hangs up. Deep breath. Then the momentary peace is broken.)

EMMA: Mom! Jeffy pulled my hair!

JEFFY: Did not.

EMMA: Then explain why my head feels like it's bleeding!!!!

JANEY: Emma. Sweetheart. You're my big girl—please, please be my big girly. You have a very strong head. It's not bleeding.

EMMA: How do you know? You can't even see it.

JANEY: I'm Madame Melissima, remember? I see everything. And why are you fighting instead of doing math? Ten o'clock is math work book time. Please help your brother with his times tables.

EMMA: Ugh! Okay.

JEFFY: I don't need help, Mom. She's not my real teacher.

(Janey's phone rings—the other phone, with a sexy ringtone.)

JANEY: Okay. She's not your real teacher. Please just—do math.

(She makes waving away gestures to the kids before she answers. Checks to make sure the coast is clear.)

JANEY: *(Sexy voice)* Well, hello sugar plum.

(Don's phone also rings. He answers.)

DON: Coastal Investing, Don here. Oh! Hey, Stanley! What can I help you with today?

JANEY: Is this Reggie?

DON: Some buy orders? I like a contrarian! You know, we haven't funded your IRAs for this year yet.

JANEY: Of course, I recognized your num—your voice, sweet pea.

DON: This is a great time to be buying. How much are we looking at?

JANEY: Your deep, penetrating voice. You know I hear it in my dreams. You know what kind of dreams I'm talking about? Do you, sugar plum?

DON: Loading up the wagon! Smart man. Let's start with cost averaging some of your blue chips…

JANEY: Dreams where I wake up hot and slick, sugar. And I'm holding you. And I imagine you're holding me. Your hands are—

EMMA: Mom! Mom, I don't get how to do these stupid powers! Ex-po-nents?

JANEY: *(Aside)* Oh, God. *(To Reggie)* Can you…can you please hold a second? I mean, hold me, squeeze me, and whisper sweet…yes, like that. *(To Emma, yelling)* I'm working, Emma. It's just multiplying over and over that many times.

EMMA: What? How do I do it negative three times? That's physically impossible.

JANEY: *(Aside)* Negative three? *(To Emma)* Ask your father. He's the number guy.

EMMA: But his door is closed!

JANEY: *(To Emma)* Just knock. Then go in and wait quietly. *(To Reggie)* Tell me more. Whisper and caress my—

EMMA: There's twenty-five questions! And I don't get any of them! Not even number one. Which is supposed be the easiest?

JANEY: Did you even read the chapter?

DON: Home Depot is looking like a strong buy. Let's say…

EMMA: It's too hard!

JANEY: *(To Emma and accidentally to Reggie)* Don't whine. It's not that hard. *(To Reggie)* Oh. Sorry. Yes. It's hard. So hard. *(To Emma and accidentally to Reggie)* You're supposed to be my big girl. *(To Reggie)* My big boy! Big man! Sorry. Really? Oh, well okay. Reggie, you're supposed to be my big girl…*(Aside)* What is happening?

JEFFY: Should I find a Kahn Academy for her?

JANEY: Yes, please, Jeffy. If you think it will help.

EMMA: I want a human teacher! I can't teach myself. This sucks!

JANEY: You know I can't be at the table with you. Go see your father. And don't say "sucks."

EMMA: He'll get mad.

(Janey makes a call on her other phone.)

DON: Just one second, Stanley. Can you hold? It's my wife on the other line. Some crisis at home.

JANEY: Don. Don. I need some help here. I'm sending Emma over.

DON: But can't you—

JANEY: It's math.

DON: Righty-o. As soon as I'm done earning a commission.

JANEY: *(To Don)* Thank you, honey. *(To Emma)* Go on. Daddy's expecting you. *(To Reggie)* Where was I? Are you still touching—? Reggie? Hello? Damn.

(Janey rests her head in her hands for a moment of peace.)

DON: Sorry, Stanley. Back at it. What do you think about adding to the AT&T while everyone is reaching out and touching someone? *(Laughs)* The safe way.

(Janey's phone rings. The psychic line. She gathers her strength to answer, eyes closed.)

JANEY: Hello. I've been expecting you. You've reached Melissima at the Astral Hotline and I'm here to help you. I can already sense you are worried. About a loved one.

JEFFY: *(Heard through the door and phone)* Hi, Mommy. Are you okay?

JANEY: *(Confused about whether to use phone or not)* Sweetheart. Why are you calling me? Why are you calling me on this number?

JEFFY: Because I need to know the future.

JANEY: Oh, sweetheart. I know this is tough, and we're all having to be very strong and adaptable.

JEFFY: But are you going to be okay?

JANEY: Yes, I promise. I'll be okay.

JEFFY: How do you know?

JANEY: Madame Melissima knows all.

JEFFY: Then why did you let that lady cough all over you? Didn't you know—

JANEY: I was just Mommy then. Not Melissima. I didn't know she was sick.

JEFFY: Oh. Okay. I miss you.

JANEY: I miss you too. But we'll be together in three more days. And I'll give you the biggest hug in your life. Hey, is Daddy teaching Emma about exponents?

JEFFY: Um. I'm not supposed to tell.

JANEY: Not tell? What? Wait. Let me look into the astral ether. I can sense…I can sense she's watching Tiger King again. Instead of doing her math.

JEFFY: You're amazing!

JANEY: *(Eye roll)* Yes, I am. It's not exactly appropriate…but I can sense that you want to watch with her.

JEFFY: Can I? Please, please?

JANEY: Okay. But both of you, no excuses, math after lunch.

JEFFY: I'm getting really good at making Easy Mac. Want some?

JANEY: Yes, I do. At noon. Now you two go occupy yourselves while I wait for more customers.

JEFFY: Okay. Bye, Mom.

JANEY: I love you. *(Aside)* Even at eight dollars a minute!

DON: Thanks, Stanley. I feel good about the future too. You take care. Stay healthy.

(He disconnects. Still holding his phone, he calls out.)

DON: Emmy? Emmy, you need some homework help? Emmy?

(At the lack of answer, he shrugs. And pauses. And dials. Janey's sexy phone rings. Again, she sighs, girds her loins, and answers without looking.)

JANEY: *(Using the voice)* Well, hello sugar. Welcome to the Hot line.

DON: Hi.

JANEY: Honey! Don! Why are you calling me on this number?

DON: I had this need to reach out and touch someone. You.

JANEY: Three more days.

DON: I know. I know. But…I miss you. Can we…can you…pretend?

JANEY: *(Using the voice)* Oh, sugar. Can you feel me? Can you feel me running my fingers through your hair? Can you feel me touching your cheeks? Brushing your lips? And now I'm kissing you. And no one, no one is wearing anything at all. Not even a mask.

DON: Not even a mask.

COVID COHAB
by Richard Lyons Conlon

CHARACTERS

COURTNEY	Late 20s-50s (you know, adult)
CHARLIE	Late 20s-50s (you know, adult)
HBO ANNOUNCER	You know what they sound like
MALE TV NEWS ANNOUNCER	
FEMALE TV NEWS ANNOUNCER	

Important Note: This is a very short play made up of very short scenes. It needs to play fast. The blackouts between scenes should only be a few seconds. So, no set or costume changes. It should be played with just three or four chairs. Props should be minimal with the majority being mimed by the actors.

SCENE 1

(At Rise, Courtney is alone in the living room of a small apartment. She pops the cork on a bottle of champagne and pours out a flute. She is feeling celebratory. She sits back in a chair, feet up. Makes an air toast.)

COURTNEY: For better and for worse. *(Thinks, reconsiders)* To a new life. Freedom.

(She pulls a framed wedding picture out of a drawer and removes the photo. Ceremoniously, she either burns it or tears it into tiny pieces. Then she sits back again to luxuriate in her new singleness. A slight moment of relaxation before she hears keys in the door. It opens. Charlie steps inside with two or more suitcases, briefcase, backpack, and more.)

COURTNEY: What are you doing?

(Charlie shrugs, closes the door.)

COURTNEY: What the hell do you think you're doing?
CHARLIE: I don't know. What's it look like?
COURTNEY: You can't.
CHARLIE: Not my choice, Courtney.
COURTNEY: You can't be here.

(He sheepishly shrugs.)

COURTNEY: We agreed. Everything is settled.
CHARLIE: Yeah, well, now it's unsettled.
COURTNEY: You're supposed to be at Kevin's.
CHARLIE: Kevin suddenly remembered his mom has an immune system.
COURTNEY: Then go to a goddamn hotel.
CHARLIE: They're all shut down.
COURTNEY: Oh my God!—What about the papers!
CHARLIE: Papers? What? Papers?
COURTNEY: The freaking papers! You're getting served at Kevin's address.
CHARLIE: I think the cops have bigger problems than serving—
COURTNEY: Well, you can't move back.
CHARLIE: You think I want to?
COURTNEY: You can't!
CHARLIE: Didn't you hear the Governor? We're in a lockdown. We are locked…down.
COURTNEY: You gotta find some place to go.
CHARLIE: What about your sister's?

(She stares at him.)

CHARLIE: I mean, why don't you go to your—
COURTNEY: We agreed. I stay, you go.
CHARLIE: Circumstances have changed.
COURTNEY: Not the most important one.
CHARLIE: Hey, I don't want to be here. There's nowhere else to go.
COURTNEY: You always wanted to see Italy…
CHARLIE: Whoa. That is just too dark. Even for you.
COURTNEY: Yeah, well, I'm feeling pretty damn dark right about now.
CHARLIE: Remember, I'm the one who volunteered to leave.
COURTNEY: So, leave.
CHARLIE: You're the one who volunteered to fuck your coworker.
COURTNEY: You're an asshole. (*Pause*) You can't stay.
CHARLIE: Courtney, I got nowhere else to go!
COURTNEY: You—! Just—! You are not staying!

(Blackout.)

SCENE 2

(Charlie's on the couch with the TV remote. Courtney's in a chair turned away, headphones on, working on her laptop. A little time has passed.)

CHARLIE: So, how much toilet paper do we have? *(No answer)* Courtney? How much—
COURTNEY: I thought I had enough. For me.
CHARLIE: Well, you can't know that for sure, can you? Not anymore?

(She gives him a death stare.)

COURTNEY: Why didn't you get your own apartment?

CHARLIE: I was. Kevin's was just a stopgap. So I could take my time. *(Trying to lighten the mood)* Hey, you want to watch something? Binge? That's what everybody's doing to get through—

COURTNEY: Watch whatever you want. I'm trying to work. Just keep it down.

(He clicks the remote: the theme to Game of Thrones.)

COURTNEY: No, no, no! Not *Game of Thrones*!

CHARLIE: Come on, you loved Game of Thrones—you said you wanted to watch it again.

COURTNEY: That was before I realized what a misogynistic, rapey, adolescent, torture-fantasy it was.

CHARLIE: I thought that's what you liked about it.

COURTNEY: Not funny. There's a million shows on.

CHARLIE: What do you wanna watch?

COURTNEY: I'm working.

CHARLIE: Oh, wait. Here we go.

HBO ANNOUNCER: And now, the HBO feature presentation: *Contagion.*

(He instantly looks hypnotized by the TV. She looks and is hypnotized, too. She slowly moves closer for a better look. Blackout.)

SCENE 3

(Courtney is on the couch, blankly staring at the TV. Charlie is working on his laptop. After a moment, he coughs. She glares at him. He coughs a little more.)

COURTNEY: Jesus, cover your goddamn mouth.

CHARLIE: Oh, right. Sorry.

COURTNEY: I swear, if you give me the virus, I will literally kill you.

CHARLIE: Don't worry. We're young. Strong. We're basically immune.

MALE TV ANNOUNCER: More reports are coming out about COVID-19 striking younger people.

CHARLIE: Yeah, with compromised systems.

FEMALE TV ANNOUNCER: Including young, strong, healthy young people.

(Courtney has a spray can of Lysol and starts spraying Charlie, who jumps up to get away.)

CHARLIE: Hey! What the hell?!

COURTNEY: Yeah, what the hell, indeed.

(Blackout.)

SCENE 4

(Both are on the couch, blankly watching TV.)

HBO ANNOUNCER: And now, the HBO feature presentation: *Outbreak.*

(They both lean in, mesmerized. Blackout.)

SCENE 5

(A little time has passed. Courtney and Charlie are on separate conference calls, each wears a headset. Their laptops are on TV trays, facing away from each other. Each one-sided conversation goes back and forth. They each find it harder to hear and have to get louder. Soon,

they're basically shouting into their headsets at the same time.)

COURTNEY: Hello? Courtney's here.

CHARLIE: Is everybody on the call?

COURTNEY: It is weird, working from home.

CHARLIE: Bill, you work remotely all the time.

COURTNEY: Well, let's get to the brief. Does everybody have it in front of them?

CHARLIE: So, Bill, if nothing's changed for you, why do you say you won't make your numbers this quarter?

COURTNEY: Xternity Cable's social media campaign, detailing how Xternity is helping their customers during this worldwide pandemic.

CHARLIE: *(Over his shoulder to Courtney)* You don't have to say "worldwide."

COURTNEY: *(To Charlie)* Shh…I'm on a call.

CHARLIE: *(To Courtney)* "Pandemic" means it's "worldwide".

(She flips him off, sternly.)

COURTNEY: We want to say Xternity cares, that we're here to help…

CHARLIE: Nothing's changed for you, dude.

COURTNEY: Hah, no, Beth, you really think Xternity Cable would suspend monthly payments? Yeah, fat chance in hell.

CHARLIE: So, what if your customers aren't doing business? You are.

COURTNEY & CHARLIE: Could you repeat that? It's a little hard to hear in here.

COURTNEY: No, Xternity is only saying they're going to help. They're not really going to help.

CHARLIE: As long as you've got phone numbers, you can make calls.

COURTNEY: I don't know. By providing quality entertainment to take their minds off the pandemic?

CHARLIE: I don't know. Because once this is over, they'll be ahead of everybody else?

COURTNEY & CHARLIE: *(To each other)* Hey, can you please keep it down over there?

(Blackout.)

SCENE 6

(Courtney is in a deep conversation on the phone. Charlie, on the other side of the room, listens.)

COURTNEY: *(On phone)* I'm coming home—right now…It's only four hours…I've got to see Nanaw… Mom! Please, if she's already got the virus, then I can't give it to her…You're sure?…You're sure she feels okay?…Well, hell, we're all quarantined now, aren't we?… Let me know if there's any changes…I love you, too.

CHARLIE: Nanaw?

(She nods, somewhat teary. He moves to her, hesitantly.)

CHARLIE: But the symptoms are just light?

COURTNEY: *(Shakes her head no, tears really start)* For now! But she's got it, Charlie! The virus. My Nanaw is sick!

(Charlie tries to hug her. She pushes him away.)

COURTNEY: Get away from me.

CHARLIE: Courtney! I'm sorry. I love Nanaw, too.

COURTNEY: *(Stares at him)* No! You don't get to love her anymore.

(Blackout.)

SCENE 7

(Charlie is laying on the couch, flipping through channels. Courtney comes in the front door, breathing hard. She's been jogging. Sniffing, a bit of a cough.)

CHARLIE: I can't believe you go out jogging. And without a mask.

COURTNEY: Running. And they said it's safe. Just maintain the six feet.

CHARLIE: Sounds like you caught it.

COURTNEY: I always do this after a run. You know that.

CHARLIE: Well, just stay clear of me. Besides, you always stink after jogging!

(She's pissed, jumps on top of him on the couch, and breathes in his face.)

CHARLIE: Ugh! Get off of me! *(Pushes her off, jumps up)* I can't believe you did that! You're a psycho! You're—just stay away from me.

COURTNEY: Stay away from you? Dammit, Charlie, that was my plan! To stay as far away from you as—

(Her phone rings. She sees who's calling.)

COURTNEY: Oh, shit. Oh, shit.

(Takes a breath, answers it.)

COURTNEY: Hi, Mom.

(Blackout.)

SCENE 8

(Courtney and Charlie sit apart on the couch, looking a little haggard. Time has passed. Quarantine is taking its toll. The apartment is littered with dishes and fast-food containers. They are staring blankly at the TV. They react to what we hear from the TV.)

FEMALE TV ANNOUNCER: Here's something to help us all get through Quarantine 2020.

MALE TV ANNOUNCER: The New York City Health Department has issued a helpful and healthful new report on living with the coronavirus.

FEMALE TV ANNOUNCER: Sex and Coronavirus Disease 2019 answers questions like, "But can you have sex?" and offers "tips for how to enjoy sex and avoid spreading COVID-19."

(Courtney and Charlie show interest, try to hide it.)

MALE TV ANNOUNCER: Something we're all interested in, right, Maureen? Helpful tips include: "*You* are your safest sex partner."

(Charlie and Courtney both nod: "That's a given.")

FEMALE TV ANNOUNCER: According to the report: "Masturbation will not spread COVID-19"—Gavin—"especially if you wash your hands before and after."

(Charlie and Courtney again both nod: "That's a given.")

MALE TV ANNOUNCER: "As well as any sex toys."

(Charlie and Courtney look around: "Who? Me?")

FEMALE TV ANNOUNCER: "The next safest partner is someone you live with."

(Charlie and Courtney: disturbing, though potentially good, news.)

MALE TV ANNOUNCER: "Having close contact—including sex—with the person sitting next to you is recommended over outside play."

(Charlie and Courtney: disturbing…arousing? They edge closer to each other?)

FEMALE TV ANNOUNCER: "Kissing can easily pass COVID-19. Avoid kissing anyone who is not part of your small circle of contacts." So, Gavin: no long, hard, deep, hot, passionate kissing.

COURTNEY: *(Jumps up with remote, clicks off TV)* Okay. Nothing we need to hear.

CHARLIE: Yes, thank you. Unnecessary information, I think.

COURTNEY: Well, I suppose it was helpful—up to a point.

CHARLIE: Right. I mean kids could be watching. There's no school, for Christ's sake.

COURTNEY: You know, it makes sense. Keep sex contained among people already exposed to each other.

CHARLIE: Of course.

COURTNEY: For some people, that could be a viable option.

CHARLIE: Definitely, there are people that would work for.

COURTNEY: You know what's ironic? The only thing we really had going for us was sex.

CHARLIE: The only thing?! Yeah, okay, you're right.

COURTNEY: And yet, here we are. Locked down…just the two of us.

CHARLIE: With the NYC Health Department telling us we should—ya know—each other.

COURTNEY: But we just can't do that.

CHARLIE: I know. We just…can't.

(Both look up and straight ahead. Blackout.)

SCENE 9

(Courtney is lying on the couch, staring blankly at the TV. The door opens and Charlie enters quickly, clutching a four-pack of toilet paper. He is disheveled.)

CHARLIE: It's a madhouse out there. Ya' hear me—a madhouse!

COURTNEY: You get the TP?

CHARLIE: I had to fight off three other maniacs. This is the last in town.

COURTNEY: That's all you got? Christ, we need way more than that!

CHARLIE: Did you hear what I said? The world's gone crazy.

COURTNEY: Did you buy a gun?

CHARLIE: No, of course I didn't buy a gun!

COURTNEY: Not that we need one. It's just that—

CHARLIE: Right. It's just, you know, in case.

COURTNEY: I was only kidding, you know. I would never want a gun in here.

CHARLIE: I'm so glad to hear you say that. I hate guns. And all the gun places are closed.

(He collapses on the couch. Both stare blankly at the TV.)

HBO ANNOUNCER: And now, the HBO feature presentation:

World War Z.

(They move slowly toward each other, put their arms around each other, their eyes still glued to the TV.)

SCENE 10

(Courtney on the phone. Charlie stands a few feet away, waiting for news.)

COURTNEY: Mom? Just say it…Shit!

CHARLIE: Shit? Is she…?

COURTNEY: *(To Charlie)* ICU! She's in the ICU. *(Back to phone)* Well, when can she get one?…The respirator, Mom! When will she—?! What do you mean? If she needs it—…No, Mom, wait. Mom! *(Mom's hung up. Courtney speaks, in shock:)* She needs a—they don't have any fucking respirators. They don't have—! *(Goes to Charlie who wraps her up in a hug)* Charlie, how can they not have any goddamn…? *(After a full hug, she slowly pulls away)* Well, shit, I'm going. I've got to go.

CHARLIE: Home? You're going—?

COURTNEY: I've got to be there. I'm going right now.

CHARLIE: Courtney, you can't.

COURTNEY: Hell, yes I can.

CHARLIE: You can't do anything for her. You can't get near her. Or your parents.

COURTNEY: I'll wear a mask, gloves. I'll stand outside their house. In the goddamn street if I have to! Charlie, I have to go there! *(Looks at him)* You understand that, right?

CHARLIE: Yeah, sure, I guess if you have to. *(She moves on, to get ready)* You gotta do what you gotta do.

COURTNEY: *(She stops)* Is that it?

CHARLIE: What?

COURTNEY: You're not going to come with me, are you?

CHARLIE: Well, no. I don't think it's the smart thing to do.

COURTNEY: I thought you'd—. I could use your help. I could really use—

CHARLIE: I don't think *you* should go.

COURTNEY: You said you loved Nanaw!

CHARLIE: Yeah, but…there's nothing you can…

(She just stares at him.)

CHARLIE: Hey, it's not like you and I are…you know. Anymore.

COURTNEY: *(Stares at him for a few moments)* Right. Yeah. That makes sense. Just, uh, typical. *(She exits to pack a bag)* It's not like we're people. Anymore.

CHARLIE: Courtney.

(He sits back, second-guessing his decision. Picks up the remote and clicks.)

HBO ANNOUNCER: And now, the HBO premiere presentation of… *Marriage Story.*

(Charlie stares blankly at the TV.)

CHARLIE: Fucking HBO.

THINGS CAN ONLY GET BETTER
by Sean Crawford

for Ramona

CHARACTERS

GRACE	A woman of any age
STU	A man of any age

SETTING

March, 2021. A living room. Sofa, center, facing audience.

(At Rise, a sofa, center. Grace and Stu on the sofa. The sound of pacing footsteps upstairs.)

GRACE: Let's say you had to.

STU: I don't.

GRACE: If you did.

STU: Why would I?

GRACE: Matter of life and death, let's say. This is now a matter of life and death.

STU: It's not, though. It's just another dinner.

GRACE: But it'd be more SATISFYING…

STU: If it was what?

GRACE: If it MATTERED, Stu. Things always matter more when they MATTER.

(Stu looks at her, then at the ceiling.)

GRACE: So, you don't care?

STU: About what?

GRACE: ANYTHING?

STU: How'd we get from one thing to anything?

GRACE: I'll decide myself.

STU: *(Still looking at ceiling)* She just never stops. Day and night. *(Looks at Grace again)* I don't care what kind you get.

GRACE: WE. Not me. WE get.

(The sound of walking above them escalates. Stu looks at her throughout without blinking.)

STU: I also don't care what toppings WE get.

GRACE: I'll order mushroom.

STU: *(Stands)* So you get the one I hate most??

GRACE: Said you don't care.

STU: *(Looks to ceiling again)* Because I have a lot on my mind, Grace.

GRACE: You've had ONE thing on your mind. For WEEKS.

STU: (*Starts pacing around)* Why can't she meet some guy…

GRACE: *(Stands)* MONTHS!

STU: …ask her to move in with him…

GRACE: We don't know if she likes guys…

STU: Is there really NO ONE willing to live with her? Not one person anywhere??

GRACE: We don't know anything about her.

STU: *(Stops, counts on one hand)* Jerk. Selfish. Bipolar.

GRACE: Okay.

STU: Heavy-footed. Inconsiderate. Want more?

GRACE: No

STU: Because we would need my toes.

GRACE: I get it. She has…problems.

STU: She's a lunatic, Grace. Call a spade a spade.

GRACE: So, you can't focus on pizza toppings? For a few seconds because someone ELSE has problems??

STU: I want you to confirm this is crazy.

GRACE: What?

STU: This. *(Points to ceiling)* That.

GRACE: She's not a THAT. She's a person.

STU: Well, that's what I want. You to affirm out loud what I just said.

GRACE: AFFirm or CONfirm? They're different things—

STU: BOTH. I want BOTH and for you to say that I'm…

GRACE: Right? You want me to say you're right again, right?

STU: No, I want to feel like I'm not crazy.

GRACE: She lost her JOB, Stu.

STU: A YEAR ago.

(Grace sits, takes a breath.)

GRACE: Look. I agree she's a bad neighbor.

STU: She told Chris she'd stop pacing LAST SUMMER.

GRACE: And he can't evict her during COVID.

STU: *(Walks to her)* It's MARCH. Did you know it's March again??

GRACE: Yes.

STU: *(Kneels before her)* We were talking about this LAST March.

GRACE: Honey YEAH. I was HERE. Then and now. And nearly every minute in between.

(A pause. They look at each other. The pacing above gets louder. Stu clasps his hands in prayer and drops to his knees in front of her.)

STU: Why can't you just SAY this is crazy when it's so OBVIOUSLY crazy and your husband so clearly NEEDS you to say it's crazy?

GRACE: Adjectives don't really change anything.

STU: *(Rests head in her lap)* Who can pay rent in Boston for a year with no job?

GRACE: We can't.

STU: I'm serious: Who can do that?

GRACE: People with generational wealth?

STU: I thought for sure she'd be homeless by now. I've been praying so hard for it. *(Pause)* And for forgiveness.

GRACE: We just don't know anything about her…

STU: It's like thirty grand a year to live here…

GRACE: And we can't go up there and talk to her…

STU: THIRTY GRAND A YEAR. *(Angry at the thought)* I mean, what the…

GRACE: We can't talk to ANYONE in person…

STU: *(Stands)* How is Jacob Marley paying all that??

GRACE: Please don't get agitated again.

(Stu starts pacing all over the stage.)

STU: I'm not agitated, I'm just…

GRACE: Pacing?

STU: FED UP.

GRACE: *(Stands)* You're fed up with pacing so you're…pacing?

STU: No, I'm fed up with my wife not having my back.

GRACE: What is that supposed to mean?? *(No answer; he keeps pacing)* Well?? What the hell is that supposed to mean, Stu?

STU: I told you what I wanted.

GRACE: Tell me again.

STU: No.

(She starts following him as he paces, trying to get in front of him.)

GRACE: We've argued about this so many times I don't even know what we're saying anymore.

STU: It was two minutes ago, Grace.

(She grabs his shoulders, stopping him long enough for her to get in front of him. They are right behind the sofa, center.)

GRACE: What's this I don't have your back stuff? You've never said that to me before.

STU: You just keep taking her side all the time.

GRACE: How? She's not even here.

(The footsteps become even louder; with now the sound of furniture being shoved, scraping the floor above. Stu grabs one of the sofa's cushions, squeezes it, leans forward until face-to-face with Grace, and whispers:)

STU: She's ALWAYS here.

GRACE: *(Whispering also)* Why'd you put a cushion between us?

STU: Why do you always take her side?

GRACE: *(Places head on cushion, looking out at audience)* It's not that I'm taking her side. It's that I know she has no one. Or probably has no one. And I know that she's probably lonely.

(Stu walks to an upstage corner, taking sofa cushion with him. He lies on the floor, facing the ceiling. The noise above stops.)

STU: Well, you're a better person than me, Grace. *(Rests head on cushion)* I want her out on the street.

GRACE: No, you don't. I know that you don't.

STU: Of course, I do.

GRACE: No, you don't. That's not the man I married.

STU: Of course, I don't. *(Takes deep breath)* I'll change the way I react to it. I won't respond to crazy with crazy.

(She grabs the other cushion and joins him on the floor upstage.)

GRACE: See, that's all I've been saying all along. You said it better than me.

STU: What?

GRACE: That all we control is how we react.

STU: I have no idea what I said.

GRACE: Not in so many words but still.

STU: I just wish it could stay quiet like this.

GRACE: All we control is how we react... *(She takes his hand)* As long as we keep that in mind... *(They smile at each other)* Things can only get better.

(They kiss. A few happy moments in silence. Then a woman's scream is heard upstairs, followed shortly after by the sound of the same woman sobbing uncontrollably. Grace and Stu look at each other, no longer smiling, as if frozen in place. Lights fade down as the sobbing grows louder.)

QUARANTINED!
by Phil Darg

CHARACTERS

STACY	20-25, Female; aspiring theatrical director; wants to "take charge" of everything—and she often does; Theatre student at NYU
JOHN	20-25, Male; aspiring musician/composer; tends to be a bit lazy and self-serving; Theatre student at NYU
KEVIN	20-25, Male; aspiring writer/playwright; somewhat depressed and deliberately detached; has a bleak and cynical view of life; Theatre student at NYU
MICHELLE	20-25, Female; aspiring actor/singer/dancer; always needs to perform—even if it's just to display her own exaggerated emotions; Theatre student at NYU

SETTING

March-April, 2020; An apartment in New York City, shared by all four characters.

(At Rise, a living room/shared space of a modest Manhattan apartment. Stacy, Michelle, John, and Kevin are all present.)

ALL: *(delivered straight out)* Day one . . .

(Beat. The lights shift.)

STACY: Great—we're finally all moved in…Couldn't stand my old roommates any longer. I know it's weird to move in together like this in the middle of the term, but I thought...Well, we're all NYU Theatre students, if we live together, we can support each other.

MICHELLE: Totally, Stacy? You go girl! *(Singing, sounding kind of like Oprah Winfrey)* Support!!!

KEVIN: Okay, let's take it down a notch, Broadway girl—

JOHN: You're a really great singer, Michelle.

MICHELLE: I know...thanks, John.

STACY: We've got like...the perfect combination here. I'm a director, Michelle sings—

MICHELLE: And acts, and dances—

STACY: John plays and composes music—

JOHN: Yes, I do—

STACY: And Kevin—

KEVIN: "Kevin surveyed his new roommates carefully...Would they prove to be as disappointing as the last set? Only time would tell—although his familiar sense of despair and feelings of hopelessness increasingly began to grow."

STACY: And—as you know—Kevin writes.

KEVIN: Yeah. A writer. At least, that's what I keep telling myself...writer, author, playwright...unable to get a single play published or produced...so...life's good.

MICHELLE: Oh, Kevin—you're hilarious!

KEVIN: Hilarious...That's what I was going for...

STACY: We should all collaborate on a new project...We could come up with something fresh.

JOHN: Sounds good to me. I've got my keyboard set up already.

MICHELLE: Perfect! My own personal, in-house accompanist!

JOHN: I'd love to play for you, Michelle.

STACY: I say we start the creative process right away.

KEVIN: "Kevin felt his sphincter tighten. There was something about Stacy that made him tense."

STACY: Haha...

MICHELLE: I'm totally up for anything! Just tell me what you want me to do: sing, act, dance –

KEVIN: Right now, I'd like you to put a cork in it.

MICHELLE: Just let me check my phone first. *(Looking at her phone, beat)* Hey guys…there's something big on the news…New York—"state of emergency?!"

STACY: What? Let me see.

(Beat as they all check their phones, etc.)

JOHN: It's that Coronavirus thing again. So sick of hearing 'bout that.

MICHELLE: "Shelter in place?" What does that mean?

STACY: Oh my God . . . They just closed the university . . . everything's going on lockdown.

SONG #1: "Quarantined!"

KEVIN: She's right—everything's closing. We s'posed to stay put…We can go out for groceries—but that's about it—and we're all supposed to stay six feet away from each other.

STACY: Social distancing.

MICHELLE: Oh, my God! I am not good at that! I'm a very social person!

STACY: We've been quarantined!

ALL: (4x) I DON'T WANNA
I DON'T WANNA
BE IN QUARANTINE!

STACY: They want to flatten the curve.

MICHELLE: What does that mean?

KEVIN: It means that they want us to self-isolate to prevent the spread of COVID-19.

STACY: Exactly. Lessen the pandemic so that the hospitals can deal with sick people.

MICHELLE: But...I've got things to do...

ALL: (4x) I DON'T WANNA

I DON'T WANNA

BE IN QUARANTINE!

JOHN: Damn...I just got a text from work. I've been laid off. No work and no money. Great...

STACY: They're saying that COVID-19 is really contagious—and it can be *fatal.*

MICHELLE: Well, I'm a millennial. That means I'm perennial...I'm not going to get sick—

KEVIN: Anyone can get it. The mortality rate is over two percent.

STACY: Everybody has to stay in! You're all going to shut up and do what I say! Self-isolation starts now—and that means you, Michelle.

MICHELLE: Arrr...I can't just put my whole life on hold!

ALL: (4x) I DON'T WANNA

I DON'T WANNA

BE IN QUARANTINE!

QUARANTINED!

(Pause. The lights shift.)

ALL: *(Delivered straight out)* Day two...

SONG #2: "Goin' Viral"

JOHN: Whoa...the stock market just tanked...

STACY: Guys, this thing is serious. Hundreds of people are dying every day.

KEVIN: Wolf Blitzer said millions could get sick...

JOHN: We might all be goin' bye bye...

MICHELLE: Oh my God!

KEVIN: PETRIFIED BY CORONAVIRUS

FEAR OF GETTING IT—IS A REAL MINUS

COMING IN FAST—LIKE—STRAIGHT OUTTA WUHAN
MORTALITY—RATES AT—TWO PERCENT—OOH, MAN!
ALL: VIRAL—WE MIGHT BE GOIN'
VIRAL—PLUMMETING DOWN A
SPIRAL—WE MIGHT BE GOIN'
VIRAL—PLUMMETING DOWN A
KEVIN: HOLE FROM WHICH THERE IS NO RETURN
MARKET'S DOWN THE DRAIN—YOUR MONEY'S GONNA BURN
SEEN IT ON THE CCN—WITH HOST WOLF BLITZER
WORLD ECONOMY—IS NOW ON THE FRITZER
ALL: VIRAL—WE MIGHT BE GOIN'
VIRAL—PLUMMETING DOWN A
SPIRAL—WE MIGHT BE GOIN'
VIRAL—WE MIGHT BE GOIN'—BYE!

(Pause as Kevin and Stacy exit. The lights shift.)

JOHN & MICHELLE: *(Delivered straight out)* Day three…

JOHN: Oh…you're in here…Sorry. I was just looking for a place to be alone.

MICHELLE: Me too. This apartment isn't very big, is it?

JOHN: No…*Uh*—my nose itches…

MICHELLE: John—what're you doing? Don't touch your face! You can get Coronavirus that way.

(Music cue.)

JOHN: You…you really care about me that much?

MICHELLE: Yes! Don't touch your face.

JOHN: What if I touch…your face?

MICHELLE: W-what…?

SONG #3: "Can I Touch Your Face?"

JOHN: CAN I TOUCH YOUR FACE?
MUST WE STAND APART?
WILL THIS VIRUS—MAKE US LONELY OR SHOULD I MAKE A START?
MICHELLE: Oh…John…
JOHN: CAN I KISS YOU NOW?
SHOULD WE TAKE A RISK?
BEEN SO ALONE-AH—SINCE THIS CORONA
I WANT TO FEEL YOUR LIPS
Michelle, I know we've only been stuck here for three days, but…I think I love you!
MICHELLE: Oh my God…

(John kisses Michelle and she then starts to sing.)

MICHELLE: YOU JUST TOUCHED MY FACE
JOHN: Uh huh…
MICHELLE: AND YOUR LIPS MET MINE
JOHN: They did…
MICHELLE: MY HEAD IS SWIMMING
WITH UNCLEAN GERMS THAT I'LL
WASH WITH TURPENTINE
JOHN: Oh…
MICHELLE: BUT THERE'S SOMETHING ELSE
JOHN: Oh?
MICHELLE: THAT I FELT AS WELL
JOHN: Really?
MICHELLE: I FELT A FEELING—SO DEEP WITH MEANING—
THAT I THINK I CAN TELL

BOTH: (3x) LOVE
THIS IS LOVE
THIS IS LOVE
THIS IS LOVE
I THINK THAT THIS IS LOVE!

JOHN: Michelle, will you…"go" with me?

MICHELLE: Um, we can't go anywhere. We're under quarantine—remember?

BOTH: CAN I TOUCH YOUR FACE?
MUST WE STAND APART?
WILL THIS VIRUS—MAKE US LONELY OR
WILL IT STIR OUR HEARTS? OUR HEARTS!

(Kevin enters.)

KEVIN: Hey guys, I—STOP! What're you doing?! Don't touch each other!

MICHELLE: We're in love…Kiss me, John!

JOHN: But Michelle, my germs –

MICHELLE: I want your germs…*inside me…*

(Beat as John and Michelle passionately kiss, embrace.)

KEVIN: *Really* sorry I walked in just now…

(Pause as Stacy enters and the lights shift.)

ALL: *(Delivered straight out)* Day five…

STACY: They've shut *everything* down…Times Square is empty…

MICHELLE: *(Looking at her phone)* Oh look, there's a really funny toilet paper meme…

JOHN: Hey Michelle…wanna make out?

MICHELLE: Um…no…don't think so…I think maybe we should see

other people…

JOHN: There's only four of us here—and I'm pretty sure Kevin's not your type. What's wrong?

MICHELLE: It's not me—it's you.

JOHN: What do you mean?

MICHELLE: I mean…deodorant much?!

JOHN: Oh…but I thought…it was love—something special—just between us.

KEVIN: "It wasn't love," Kevin replied—doing his best to sound authoritative. "It was selfish, spontaneous biological attraction—hastened by heightened emotional circumstances and a lack of viable partner options." Hey…that wasn't too bad. I should write that down.

STACY: Kevin's right…Real love is something you do…for others.

(Pause. The lights shift.)

ALL: *(Delivered straight out)* Day seven…

(They are all sitting about listlessly. Suddenly, the sound of applause and cheering is heard in the background.)

JOHN: What's that?

STACY: It's coming from outside…Everybody's…cheering.

(They all rush to the window and look out. Beat as Michelle checks her phone.)

MICHELLE: They're applauding the health care workers! They're doing it every night at 7 P.M.

(Beat as they all look at each other.)

STACY: C'mon! Let's do it!

(Michelle, Stacy, and John cheer/applaud loudly out the window, etc.)

KEVIN: "It was then that Kevin realized that he was the last sane person on Earth…"
STACY: Get over here!

(Kevin joins them—but cheers less exuberantly. The lights shift.)

ALL: *(Delivered straight out)* Day eight. Seven P.M…

(Michelle, Stacy, and John cheer/applaud loudly out the window, etc. Kevin joins them—but cheers less exuberantly. The lights shift.)

ALL: *(Delivered straight out)* Day nine. Seven P.M…

(Michelle, Stacy, and John cheer/applaud loudly out the window, etc. Kevin joins them—but cheers less exuberantly. The lights shift.)

ALL: *(Delivered straight out)* Day ten…

SONG #4: "Monotony"

JOHN: I'm bored…
MICHELLE: Anyone wanna play *Pictionary*?
STACY, KEVIN, & JOHN: No.
STACY: Want to work on something creative?
KEVIN, JOHN, & MICHELLE: No.
KEVIN: What's for dinner?
STACY: Macaroni and cheese.

(Kevin, John, and Michelle groan in disappointment.)

ALL: *(Delivered straight out)* Day eleven…
JOHN: I'm *so* bored…
KEVIN: What's for dinner?
STACY: Macaroni and cheese.

(Kevin, John, and Michelle groan in disappointment.)

ALL: *(Delivered straight out)* Day twelve…
JOHN: I'm *soooo* bored…
KEVIN: What's for dinner?
STACY: Macaroni.

(The music ends. Beat as they all look at Stacy.)

STACY: We're out of cheese…
KEVIN: "Kevin surveyed his roommates closely. He wondered—if this thing went all 'Donner Party'—which one of them would be eaten first…"
MICHELLE: You will…you'll be eaten first…we already took a vote…
STACY: *(Checking her phone)* Oh my God…I just got a text from my Mom…My grandma's in the hospital! She was having trouble breathing, so they took her in…now she's on a ventilator…
MICHELLE: Oh, Stacy…I'm so sorry…
STACY: If she dies…I won't even be able to say goodbye to her…

(They all look at Stacy sympathetically, and then the lights shift.)

ALL: *(Delivered straight out)* Day thirteen…
STACY: Guys, we're low on supplies. I made a list. We're almost out of

food…and toilet paper.

MICHELLE: …Gross…

KEVIN: "One of us has go to the store," thought Kevin—praying that it wouldn't be him.

JOHN: Well…I don't have any money—so it can't be me.

(Beat as they all look at John.)

STACY: Yes, it can. It'll be your contribution. You can use my credit card.

JOHN: …Fine…

STACY: Wear a raincoat—and put up the hood. It'll cover you pretty well. *(Handing John some gloves and a mask)* Here—take these. Wear them the whole time—don't take them off until you get back.

JOHN: I'm gonna look like such a dork…

STACY: Stay at least six feet away from anyone else. Just get what's on the list. Make it fast—and when you get back, here's the process: gloves, mask, coat—off. Leave them in the hall. Anything you bring in—set on the table. Then, you wash up—twenty seconds scrubbing those hands…hmm…actually, maybe you should take a shower—

MICHELLE: Never a bad idea—

STACY: Don't touch anything he brings back! I'm going to sanitize every item—then, I'll wash up.

KEVIN: Okay…that's the plan…

(Pause. The lights shift.)

ALL: *(Delivered straight out)* Day fourteen…

KEVIN: Hey…um…where's the toilet paper you bought…?

JOHN: The store was out. I couldn't get any. We only have one roll left.

(Beat.)

STACY: We'll have to ration it.

KEVIN: What? Are you kidding me?!

STACY: We have to work together on this.

KEVIN: This isn't the kind of collaboration I thought we'd be doing…

STACY: Six squares a day per person.

KEVIN: "And that was how Stacy got Kevin in the end…"

MICHELLE: Ewwww! Gross!

KEVIN: If you think I'm going to get by on six squares of toilet paper a day…

STACY: I'll give you a choice: you can either use less toilet paper…or start recycling it…

KEVIN: I'll use less…

STACY: Good choice…

(Pause. The lights shift.)

ALL: Day…?? *("What day is it, anyway?" "How long has it been now?" etc.)*

MICHELLE: It's weird. I don't even know what day it is…Monday? Saturday?

JOHN: It's Wednesday.

KEVIN: It doesn't matter…Every day is exactly the same…

STACY: *(Reading from her phone)* It says here that feeling anxious and depressed is normal for this situation.

KEVIN: Well…whadya know? I'm finally normal…

MICHELLE: Nothing is normal…the only thing that helps me through this is…Andrew Cuomo.

JOHN: I knew there was someone else…

MICHELLE: *(Reading from her phone, quoting Andrew Cuomo)* "New York loves everyone. That's why I love New York. It always has, it always will. And at the end of the day, my friends, even if it is a long day—and this is a long day—love wins." *(Beat—looking at the others, very emotional)* Love wins…

STACY: He's right. Love wins…all those health care workers risking their lives to save ours…That's love…Grocery stores staying open so that we can eat…that's love. Staying in this apartment for weeks so we don't infect other people…that's love.

MICHELLE: So…how long are we going to be here?

STACY: Nobody knows…It could be a long time.

KEVIN: It seems like it's been a long time already…

JOHN: I wish this thing was over…I just want to…actually hug someone.

(Music cue.)

STACY: It won't last forever…it can't…One of these mornings, we'll wake up, and the sun is going to shine down on all of us…and then we'll know…it's finally over…and there'll be no more distance between us…just love…because we'll know how important it is…to have people near us…

SONG #5: "Daybreak (This is Love)"

STACY: SOME DAY SOON FROM NOW
WE'LL LOOK OUT AND SEE
A NEW SUN RISIN'—IT'S NOT SURPRISIN'
TO SAY WHAT IT WILL MEAN
AND BY THEN WE'LL KNOW THAT IT'S DONE AT
LAST NO MORE LONGIN'—FOR SOME BELONGIN'
WE'LL HOLD EACH OTHER FAST

ALL: (3x) LOVE
THIS IS LOVE

THIS IS LOVE

WE'LL KNOW THAT THIS IS LOVE!

STACY: Look out the window…it's almost spring…It's pretty cloudy right now, but…it won't be that way for long.

STACY: SOME DAY SOON FROM NOW WE WON'T STAND
APART WE'LL HAVE EACH OTHER—OUR SISTERS—
BROTHERS AND THEY WILL FILL OUR HEARTS

ALL: (*3x*) LOVE
THIS IS LOVE
THIS IS LOVE
WE'LL KNOW THAT THIS IS LOVE!
(*3x*) LOVE
THIS IS LOVE
THIS IS LOVE WE'LL
KNOW THAT THIS IS LOVE!
IT'S LOVE!

(The lights fade out.)

JOSH'S VOICE
by Jared Eberlein

(At Rise, Josh, a high school senior, is alone onstage.)

JOSH: Sometimes I'll be sitting around with a group of my friends or in a class, or go to some assigned student workshop, when it never fails. Some well-intentioned, but maybe trying-too-hard-to-be-cool adult joins in the conversation and says, "I can't believe this has been going on for an entire year." And my immediate reaction is usually, thanks a lot for the reminder. And my reaction after that is usually backed up by some of kids who are rolling their eyes, like "we're gonna have to talk about the same thing we're always talking about, but instead of being real, we'll have to do some weird spy language version, because the grown-ups are looking for constructive comments not truth. *(Then)* I really do feel for the kids who look like no one's asked them for months how they're doing. You can tell who they are. They want to break-down but feel like no one'll be around to pick up the pieces if they do. Then: *(Playing the scene, in a "grown- voice")* "Anyone want to share?—What you feel like it's taken you to get through this—Whatever you want to call the last twelve months. A year, a lifetime, a pandemic...pandemonium." –There's the wordplay teachers think its super cute to use. I try to just look down and away, I pull my bangs down as far over my eyes as possible and wait for the gaze to pass me by. *(Playing)* "How about you?" "Me?" "Yes." *(Then)* Okay. I proceed to tell the group my whole life story, stupid kindergarten crushes, near-death experiences and all, and then...I end on hopeful note. And I think that's the thing I'm most nervous to share. My hope. It's rough for people right now. And I know that. And I feel it. But I know my friends and I—and the millions of people like us—aren't done. We're not down or out or finished. So, I hope. And I feel ridiculous sometimes. And of course, I don't want to be laughed at or seem naive. But—*(Then)* If there's anything we want to do or be and we haven't gotten to yet, maybe hope it's awful to talk about. Maybe Mr. Pandemic-Pandemonium-Dad-Joke-Teacher-Dude, knows it too and that's what he's looking for someone to be brave enough to share. Who knows?

YOU MADE ME LOVE YOU SOMETIMES
by Joel Fishbane

CHARACTERS

VIVETTE	30s, Black
GILES	30s, White

(At Rise, Summer, 2020. Mid-pandemic Vivette and Giles are a mixed-race couple lounging on a couch, watching Judy Garland sing "You Made Me Love You" from The Broadway Melody of 1938.)

VIVETTE: Ugh, we have to change this.

GILES: It's a classic.

VIVETTE: It's disgusting.

GILES: Judy Garland was genetically incapable of provoking disgust.

VIVETTE: I didn't say she was disgusting. It's the scene.

GILES: She's writing to Clark Gable. "You made me love you." It's adorable. I have loved this scene for years and nothing you will ever say can make me change my mind.

VIVETTE: She's an underage girl who they hypersexualized by having her sing a song of desire to a man twice her age.

GILES: Well, when you put it like that…

(He turns off the movie. They sigh.)

GILES: So now what?

VIVETTE: Netflix?

GILES: I finished it.

VIVETTE: You can't finish Netflix. It's a bottomless pit.

GILES: Oh, there's a bottom. I have found it, and I will never be the same.

VIVETTE: Disney Plus?

GILES: Watched it.

VIVETTE: Prime?

GILES: Done.

VIVETTE: Pornhub?

GILES: We'd wake the kids.

VIVETTE: We could be quiet.

GILES: When have we ever been quiet?

VIVETTE: Maybe we can start. It can be our kink. We were looking for one.

GILES: Is quiet a kink?

VIVETTE: Everything is a kink.

GILES: I can't believe you ruined Judy Garland. Maybe that should be our kink. You stomp on all my youthful passions, but, you know, you do it in heels.

VIVETTE: I'm sorry I ruined it for you. I think too much. On my first day of acting class, my teacher warned us we would never be able to enjoy things again.

GILES: We need to find something you can't criticize.

VIVETTE: It doesn't exist.

GILES: Football.

VIVETTE: Too violent.

GILES: Monopoly.

VIVETTE: Promotes capitalism.

GILES: Poker.

VIVETTE: Gambling is an addiction.

GILES: Jogging.

VIVETTE: Dull.

GILES: Watching a sunrise.

VIVETTE: Duller.

GILES: The laughter of a newborn baby.

VIVETTE: Babies only laugh when they shit themselves.

GILES: You really are unbelievable.

VIVETTE: I know. It's a bit of a gift.

GILES: Well, the COVIDemic has us trapped. Maybe this is what we should do without time. Create something new you can love.

VIVETTE: Humans are incapable of creating new things.

GILES: Not this again.

VIVETTE: Obsolescence is a myth.

GILES: A myth, I know. Typewriters are obsolete.

VIVETTE: They used a QWERTY keyboard, which we all still continue to use on our computers, even though it's wildly inefficient.

GILES: Radio drama.

VIVETTE: Now on podcasts.

GILES: Vaudeville.

VIVETTE: What do you think YouTube is? Everyone is just uploading their act.

GILES: Cassettes, records, eight-tracks.

VIVETTE: You used to spend money on them and now you spend it on Spotify. It's been the same business for a hundred years. It's all about selling you a song that you won't remember a year from now. Never underestimate the comfort of an old habit.

GILES: Why do I feel like I was just insulted?

VIVETTE: People stay in marriages for years. There has to be a reason.

GILES: I think they call it love.

VIVETTE: Love doesn't last.

GILES: Now I know I'm being insulted.

VIVETTE: Put aside the emotion. I'm trying to express an idea. Love transforms and evolves. What we have now isn't what we had then. It's morphed into, I don't know, benign familiarity.

GILES: You make us sound like a tumor.

VIVETTE: There is no such thing as "new." We are a culture of reboots, remakes, and repeats. We don't want the new.

GILES: I'll remember that when I go into work. They'll ask me for my new ad campaign, and I'll tell them to use the old ones. You know. For the familiarity.

VIVETTE: I can't believe you have to go into work.

GILES: Pandemic protocols are in place. Lots of masks and Plexiglass.

VIVETTE: Still, when Mitch told me they'd called you all back, I was like "Whaaa?"

(Vivette gets a notification on her phone.)

GILES: Advertising doesn't work long distance. We need to be in the room. Brainstorm, bounce ideas, call out each other's bullshit. You won't believe how many miracles happen over a ham sandwich—

VIVETTE: —oh my God.

GILES: What??

VIVETTE: *Oh, my Goddamn—*

GILES: What? What?

VIVETTE: Remember when I auditioned for the Australian company of *Hamilton*?

GILES: Sure. They turned you down.

VIVETTE: Well, they just changed their minds. That's what I'm talking about! They, oh my God, they want me to fly down—

GILES: You mean when it reopens—

VIVETTE: I mean now. Well, next Friday. Australia is open. I just need to quarantine for two weeks when I arrive.

GILES: Well, that's—

VIVETTE: I know—

GILES: —the stupidest thing I've ever heard.

VIVETTE: Not how I was going to finish the sentence.

GILES: They can't just reopen. It's a pandemic. By definition, it's worldwide.

VIVETTE: Australia has been open for weeks. I go, I get tested, I quarantine, it's fine. Megan's been doing it, and she says it's been great. I won't just be the swing. I'll be an understudy.

GILES: So, what, you want to pick up and leave?

VIVETTE: It's for Eliza…

GILES: And who takes care of the kids? Especially now that they're trapped at home?

VIVETTE: *(Singing)* Ooh, I do, I do, I do, I do…

GILES: How long would this be?

VIVETTE: Six months.

GILES: On the other side of the world.

VIVETTE: Can we afford a nanny?

GILES: Some person who comes in and out every day, bringing in the virus and God knows what else?

VIVETTE: It's fine. You just need to bring them into the bubble.

GILES: It's not that. After the renovations last year and the surgery…

VIVETTE: That can't be right.

GILES: It's right. You're going to have say no.

VIVETTE: You did not just say that.

GILES: We can't afford to both work and pay for childcare.

VIVETTE: I'm back in six months.

GILES: And if they extend?

VIVETTE: Well, sure, but, by then, the whole COVIDemic will be over and done.

GILES: That is grotesquely optimistic.

VIVETTE: They said by the fall—

GILES: When the plague hit Shakespeare's time, they closed the theaters for two years. The Spanish flu lasted just as long.

VIVETTE: That was before modern science.

GILES: Modern science is helpless against the stubbornness of human pride. You saw all those spring breakers running around without masks? Governors reopening? People blissfully ignoring science? People want to think they're immortal and they lie to themselves until they believe they are. And big business lets them because it helps the bottom line. That's probably what's happening in Australia. I'll bet it's not some paradise. You'll probably get COVID the moment you touch down.

VIVETTE: You really want me to say no.

GILES: I just don't think it's safe.

VIVETTE: Megan said—

GILES: Megan believes in crystals and vagina rocks. I'm telling you, this thing is not ending anytime soon. We can't afford to have illusions. And what if there's a second wave? You want to be trapped in Australia, away from the kids?

VIVETTE: I mean, no, but…

GILES: Right. Glad we settled that.

VIVETTE: Settled what?

GILES: You know, the thing.

VIVETTE: Did I miss something?

GILES: We discussed it and you're staying.

VIVETTE: Giles, this is the biggest thing I've ever been offered. I'm not turning it down so you can go figure out the best way to sell people processed cheese.

GILES: Cheezy-Whip is an authentic cheese experience—

VIVETTE: So what? I stay home and you go to work? Is that what you're saying?

GILES: Lots of people do it.

VIVETTE: Just like good old days. Make America sexist again.

GILES: Don't start. I told you: we can't afford to both have jobs.

VIVETTE: But I'm the one who has to quit?

GILES: You're not quitting. You're just not taking work. You're, like, going on hiatus.

VIVETTE: I don't want to go on hiatus. You go on hiatus.

GILES: I would, but I'm in the middle of this project…

VIVETTE: Convenient.

GILES: You can still do your auditions. You said it's all self-tapes now. If you need to take a day off every now, if you get a job, you know, a day on a little film or something I will—

VIVETTE: I got a job. I have been offered a job. I'm saying yes.

GILES: Don't you dare send that text.

VIVETTE: Oh, Lord, protect me from the stubbornness of pride.

GILES: What's that?

VIVETTE: It's not human pride we're fighting. It's masculine pride.

GILES: That's not what this is.

VIVETTE: If you had to go to Australia, you would go.

GILES: That's different.

VIVETTE: I'll bet it is. You don't want to be a house husband.

GILES: This isn't about the battle of the sexes, Billie Jean King, so get off the tennis court.

VIVETTE: I understood absolutely none of that reference.

GILES: I would love to be a house husband. I would love to live off of you. I am all for equality. But right now, I make more than you.

VIVETTE: This is the offer.

(She shows him the email on her phone.)

GILES: For *theatre?*

VIVETTE: For *professional* theatre. Anyway, it's got the travel costs and stipend worked in and they're offering me a little extra, so I'll hustle my big talented butt down there. I told you: this is the real thing.

GILES: I mean, it's an impressive paycheck, but still…

VIVETTE: Let's flip a coin.

GILES: What?

VIVETTE: Fifty-fifty chance. Since you believe in equality, it doesn't matter which of us works, right? Heads I stay, tails I go.

GILES: I'm not…fine. Always comes up heads anyway.

(Vivette flips the coin. They look at it. She smirks.)

GILES: Best two out of three?

VIVETTE: You'll make a great house husband.

GILES: The thing is, I have these responsibilities—

VIVETTE: Which are more important than mine—

GILES: I am the marketing director for the entire—

VIVETTE: This is Eliza. This is Hamilton.

GILES: Putting emphasis on words doesn't do what you think it does.

VIVETTE: Go to hell, Giles.

GILES: Keep it down. You'll wake the kids.

VIVETTE: Can't do that. Then you might have to deal with them.

GILES: What is that supposed to mean?

VIVETTE: Nothing. I need to—I'm going to take a bath—

GILES: I deal with the kids.

VIVETTE: Playing video games with them is not dealing with them.

GILES: I help with their homework.

VIVETTE: You got every answer wrong.

GILES: I told you, it's the new math. What the hell is with that anyway? Why do we need new math? Numbers don't change.

VIVETTE: I wake them up. I make their meals. I deal with the school, I take them to swim practice—

GILES: You're better at those things than I am.

VIVETTE: You don't need talent to take someone to a swimming pool.

GILES: You know how I get around chlorine.

VIVETTE: I think you secretly like it.

GILES: No, really, it gives me a rash.

VIVETTE: I meant having a housewife. You hate when I get work. Every time I get a job, you get grouchy, as if it's some imposition.

GILES: Stop this. I am your biggest fan.

VIVETTE: When I'm not working. When I don't get the part, you are right there for me. Always so supportive. There, there, you say. You'll get 'em next time, tiger. Oh, you love those moments, don't you? I'm the failure and you get to play the big strong man, making all my little problems go away.

GILES: Are you plugged into a parallel world? What marriage have you been having?

VIVETTE: And then the moment I get work, the moment I get one of my "little" jobs, you suddenly become difficult. "Oh, Vivette, its 'impossible' to move a meeting around!" "I can't possibly pick them up at school!" "You want me to take them where?"

GILES: I am busy. I am a busy man.

VIVETTE: Yes. A busy man. And you think that makes all your problems so much more important.

GILES: I didn't say that.

VIVETTE: You were going to.

GILES: You don't know what I'm going to say. And you don't know my life. Do you know what it's like for me? My problems are important, not that you ever ask about them. Do you know why I have to fall all over you when you don't get a part? Because you become the little engine that couldn't. "I think I can't, I think I can't, oh woe is me. I'll never get work, never." I have to sit there and pull you back from the ledge every goddamn time.

VIVETTE: Now you're just being mean.

GILES: And when you do get the part, it's even worse. You come home and I have to listen to every little detail about what happened on set or what happened in rehearsal. It's like you just relive it or you won't believe it really happened. So, yes, I don't want you going to Australia because you know what will happen? You will call me every night and give me a report about how you tripped backstage or the idiot in the front row was on his phone or, horrors, that you hit an A-flat when it should have been an A and you're so embarrassed. You know what? I do like it when you don't work. At least then I come home and all your stories are about the kids, which is something I actually care about. *(Pause)* That didn't come out the way it was supposed to.

VIVETTE: You want a redo? Sure, let me just get the Time Stone out my Infinity Glove—

GILES: It's actually a gauntlet—

VIVETTE: I know what it is, movies are my thing, you arrogant prick. But I guess you forgot since you don't actually care when I talk to you.

GILES: It's not like you're any better. It's not like you're super interested in my stories—

VIVETTE: I'm interested—

GILES: What campaign am I working on? Go on. What campaign have I been slaving over for months?

VIVETTE: The cheese thing.

GILES: The cheese thing was last year.

VIVETTE: Really?

GILES: You know that if you ever looked past the next audition.

VIVETTE: And you can't see past the next ad campaign.

GILES: Well, you won't have to worry about that anymore.

VIVETTE: What does that mean?

GILES: It means they fired me.

VIVETTE: They—

GILES: Pandemic downsizing. And because I botched the insurance account. That's the thing I was working on which you didn't remember.

VIVETTE: Giles. I'm—but you said they'd opened the office again?

GILES: You were talking to Mitch. He said something and then I had to go along with it. I was hoping I'd find other work and then I could just tell you I'd switched.

VIVETTE: Then what was all that nonsense about me needing to stay? We need the paycheck…

GILES: And I will get one.

VIVETTE: You don't have to. I have a job now. So, what the hell is this?

GILES: It's just…if I get a job, it will still be more for more money, so my original argument holds.

VIVETTE: Yes. If you get a job. Which you might now. When were you going to tell me any of this? When we were on the street or were you just going to causally mention it when we were lining up at the food bank?

GILES: I was hoping I wouldn't have to mention it.

VIVETTE: Masculine goddamn pride.

GILES: Yes, that's right. It was all pride. But I haven't exactly cornered the market on it, so don't get all superior on me.

VIVETTE: I resent that.

GILES: Resent it all you like, you narcissist.

VIVETTE: I am not a narcissist. You're a narcissist, you pimple!

GILES: Am I a narcissist or a pimple?

VIVETTE: You're a walking case of syphilis, is what you are.

GILES: Least I'm not a sellout.

VIVETTE: Bowel obstruction.

GILES: Vomit licker.

VIVETTE: House husband.

GILES: Understudy.

VIVETTE: Better an understudy in Australia than a house husband filing for divorce.

GILES: You don't mean that.

VIVETTE: No?

GILES: So, this is what it comes down to. Love really is dead. Familiar. Just not so benign, are we? Might as well cut it out before we rot.

VIVETTE: You don't know what it's like. You haven't gone on a job interview in years. I go on them every week. Every audition is just me giving people another chance to look at me and say no. I thought they hated me. I got to the final rounds, and they just said No. Without an explanation. Then, all these weeks later, they thought of me. Of all the actors in the world, Jerry thought of me.

GILES: Of course, they did. You're a treasure. You're not just a talent, Viv. You're the real deal. I knew it the first time I saw you.

VIVETTE: You liked me because I was playing a stripper.

GILES: I believe it was a burlesque dancer. See? I pay attention. And you sang that song. *(Dancing and grinding)* "You gotta have a gimmick, if you're gonna get ahead…"

VIVETTE: Promise you will never do that again. You really think I'm talented?

GILES: You know I do.

VIVETTE: Then swallow your pride.

GILES: It's not just that. The virus…

VIVETTE: That's bullshit. We could die of the virus the next time we go shopping. I don't buy it. Come on, Giles. What is this really about?

GILES: I think I'm a bad father.

VIVETTE: You…

GILES: That's why I let you do everything. You're better at it then I am. I see the kids. They respond to you.

VIVETTE: I never know what I'm doing with them.

GILES: Well, it doesn't show. Must be all that acting. If you leave me alone with them, it'll be like throwing us into a horror flick. And not one of those good ones where the horror is a metaphor for social commentary. This would be a splatterfest.

VIVETTE: Oh my God. You're really scared of them.

GILES: Every time we're alone, it's like I'm in a slasher flick. Only they're the killer and I'm the nubile virgin who isn't getting out alive.

VIVETTE: You might want to rethink that metaphor.

GILES: They terrify me.

VIVETTE: They terrify me, too.

GILES: But you still know what to do. You keep them in line, you remember their appointments. You were the one who knew to have the Talk. I'd never have thought of that.

VIVETTE: The Talk?

GILES: The thing about the cops and how they need to be careful because, you know…

VIVETTE: Because black boys are more likely to be shot than white ones?

GILES: You see? You knew you had to have that conversation. It didn't even occur to me. And how would I even talk to them about it? You know how to protect them. I just know how to teach them to reset the Xbox.

VIVETTE: I don't know how to protect them. If I knew how to protect them, I wouldn't have to have the Talk. The whole point of the Talk is because I know I can't protect them. They don't warn you about this when you're a parent. Reverend tells us to go forth and multiply, but he doesn't tell us that it means we're going to be scared every day of our lives.

GILES: You really think that?

VIVETTE: Every day. But you know what scares me the most? That someday they are going to be sitting on some therapist's couch complaining about all the ways I screwed them up.

GILES: Well, that's…oh my god.

VIVETTE: I know.

GILES: I never even thought of that.

VIVETTE: And now you will never stop. There I go, crushing all your hopes. But relax: since you're never around, all their problems will be about me.

GILES: God, do you think they're going to hate us?

VIVETTE: I'm the wrong person to ask. I'm an artist. I spend all day surrounded by people who hate their parents.

GILES: Advertising execs are no better.

VIVETTE: Do you hate your parents?

GILES: Only when they visit.

VIVETTE: Do you think they'll hate me if I leave?

GILES: Well, my mother will be judgmental, but—

VIVETTE: The kids. I'd be abandoning them.

GILES: They're young, they'll get over it.

VIVETTE: But will you? Will we?

GILES: Eliza is, like, a good part, right?

VIVETTE: It's the lead.

GILES: You should have opened with that.

VIVETTE: I thought you knew. We've seen the show.

GILES: I don't like anything that doesn't star Judy Garland or my wife.

VIVETTE: The truth comes out.

GILES: You really want to go?

VIVETTE: For this, for this chance? Yes.

GILES: There are things to consider.

VIVETTE: My insurance will cover us. We should be able to make it work.

GILES: The sex will be hard. Guess Zoom will be our kink.

VIVETTE: It's too weird.

GILES: You really need to turn off that critical brain.

VIVETTE: Not sure I can.

GILES: Maybe we're impossible to change.

(She sends the text. Then she turns on the TV. Judy Garland comes in singing "You Made Me Love You.")

GILES: Really?

VIVETTE: Consider the brain turned off.

(They watch the movie.)

GILES: This is good. Sitting here with you. It's…
VIVETTE: Comfortable.
GILES: Benign. And familiar. I'm going to miss you when you go.
VIVETTE: But you'll be here when I get back, right? Right?

(He takes her hand and kisses it. As the lights fade, we distinctly hear the lyrics from the old song: "You've got the brand of kisses that I'd die for.")

SPLITTING BUTTERNUTS
by Bonnie Milne Gardner

CHARACTERS

BLEEDER	20-50s, any gender. Casual dress
SCRUBS	20s-50s, any gender. Medical top and pants

SETTING

Outside emergency room entrance. No benches or places to sit except one chair for Scrubs. Nearby is a large black trash bin marked "Hazardous Waste." A line of yellow tape surrounds the stool. One red and one black circle painted on floor outside tape.

(At Rise, Scrubs sits on a stool, wears gloves and a face shield, holds a clipboard with tongs attached. Bleeder enters, with a towel-wrapped hand and a small Chinese food takeout box. Bleeder quickly heads for the entrance door. Scrubs stands to block the way.)

SCRUBS: Good evening!

BLEEDER: Hello. Emergency entrance?

SCRUBS: Yes, it is.

BLEEDER: Thanks.

SCRUBS: Hey, wait!

BLEEDER: Why?

SCRUBS: Please stand on the red circle. I need to ask you just a few—

BLEEDER: But I'm bleeding!

SCRUBS: This will only take a minute. No building entry till you clear this list of—

BLEEDER: *(Approaching Scrubs)* What? I can't hear what you're—

SCRUBS: Stay BEHIND the yellow tape! On the circle, please. Entrance will be granted after these questions are answered.

BLEEDER: Oh. Okay. See, I was trying to cut open a big butternut squash, and it slid off the—

SCRUBS: Question one: At any time in the last fourteen days, did you leave the country?

BLEEDER: Uh, no.

(Scrubs makes a check after Bleeder's answer. Scrubs will do the same for each upcoming question.)

SCRUBS: Question two: Did you come in contact with anyone who's been out of the country?

BLEEDER: No. Um, it's really deep.

SCRUBS: Just a few more. Three: Have you displayed coughing, fever, or shortness of breath?

BLEEDER: No. But right now, I'm bleedin' like a stuck hippo.

SCRUBS: So, no symptoms. In the last twelve hours, did you ever once touch your face?

BLEEDER: Well, I, uh—

SCRUBS: Or forget to sneeze into your elbow?

BLEEDER: Maybe…

SCRUBS: Did you properly destroy all used tissues and condoms?

BLEEDER: The hell…?

SCRUBS: On average, how many times a day do you wash your hands?

BLEEDER: Um, let's see…

SCRUBS: Between ten and fifty? Fifty and a hundred?

BLEEDER: Maybe…six? Listen, I'm starting to lose the feeling in my—

SCRUBS: Do you participate in any of the following: Tailgate parties? Barber shop quartets?

BLEEDER: No.

(Bleeder groans.)

SCRUBS: How about goat yoga?
BLEEDER: For the love of all that's HOLY!
SCRUBS: Hey, I'm just doing my job. Here's the entry form.

(Scrubs takes tongs out, puts the paper in it, and holds it up for Bleeder.)

BLEEDER: So, we're done?
SCRUBS: Yes. Thank you for your patience. You may enter.
BLEEDER: Finally.

(Bleeder picks up the takeout box. Scrubs puts up a hand to stop.)

SCRUBS: Wait! What's in that box?
BLEEDER: Oh, come ON…
SCRUBS: Put it down on the black circle, please.
BLEEDER: Okay. Why?
SCRUBS: No outside food in the patient area.
BLEEDER: What?
SCRUBS: I must record the item and then discard it in the bin marked "Hazardous Waste."
BLEEDER: It's not waste!
SCRUBS: Sorry, that's the policy. Any outside contamination—in the bin.
BLEEDER: You don't understand.
SCRUBS: Yeah, I know—world's best Crab Rangoon. Everyone tries to sneak in contraband. Then I get blamed. So out it goes.

(Scrubs uses tongs to grab the box.)

BLEEDER: No, WAIT!

SCRUBS: Listen. Do you want to see the doctor or not?

(Scrubs takes the box, opens bin.)

BLEEDER: STOP! It's my finger!!

SCRUBS: What?!

BLEEDER: *(Holds up bandaged hand)* In the box. My finger. On Ice.

SCRUBS: Well, that's a new one. Nice try, but I'm not buyin' it.

BLEEDER: Dude, you ever tried to split open a butternut? It's a bitch.

SCRUBS: Okaaay, maybe I'll just try a taste of this award-winning Chinese.

BLEEDER: No, no, no, no…

SCRUBS: So, what's today's special? Peri Peri Chick—Ahhh!!

(Scrubs opens the box, gasps, drops it. Bleeder grabs it.)

BLEEDER: Like I said. Finger. Now, outta my way, pea-brain.

SCRUBS: STOP. Give me your entry form.

BLEEDER: Why?

SCRUBS: *(Grabs the form with tongs, searches clipboard for a different form)* Back on the red circle, please. That, um, severed body part? Requires a different assessment.

BLEEDER: Are you kidding??

SCRUBS: This "pea-brain" is just following standard procedure. Question one…

BLEEDER: Listen, I really am feelin' lightheaded. Can't this wait? Just let me in.

SCRUBS: Of course. You are cleared to enter. The box is not.

BLEEDER: But, without the finger, what's the point? C'mon, Scrubs, just open the door, for me and the box.

SCRUBS: As soon as you complete these questions, Butternut.

BLEEDER: Seriously?! The ice is starting to melt!

SCRUBS: Hey. RULES, you know? I could lose my job. *(Looks around fearfully)* Even my license.

BLEEDER: Okay, okay. Get on with it.

SCRUBS: Question one: Which hand is it?

BLEEDER: This one.

SCRUBS: Left. *(Makes a check)* Question two: Which digit was it?

BLEEDER: The middle one. You know, right here.

SCRUBS: Nice. What type of instrument, uh, severed the body part?

BLEEDER: Chef's knife—a big one. Can we hurry this up?

SCRUBS: At any time in the past fourteen days, did the instrument leave the country?

BLEEDER: Leave the—huh?

SCRUBS: Or come in contact with anyone who had left the country?

BLEEDER: It just sits in the butcher block.

SCRUBS: At the time of dismemberment, was anyone else present?

BLEEDER: I live alone.

SCRUBS: Right. So, no one else was injured?

BLEEDER: Just me, Scrubs. For now.

SCRUBS: We'll just put "No." Next question: The instrument used in the injury, was it sterile?

BLEEDER: Well, washed. Um, Dawn Ultra?

SCRUBS: Was it ever used in a bar fight?

BLEEDER: Wha—? No.

SCRUBS: By a taxidermist?

BLEEDER: Grr-oss!

SCRUBS: So, again, "No." Next question: In the past month, have you experienced an increase in sadness or depression?

BLEEDER: Pretty damn depressed right now.

SCRUBS: So, "Yes?"

BLEEDER: No.

SCRUBS: Good. Do you have feelings of anger towards the severed body part?

BLEEDER: My finger?

SCRUBS: And could this injury have been intentional?

BLEEDER: What is your PROBLEM?

SCRUBS: I told you, it's policy. Just. Following. Orders.

BLEEDER: Like a sadistic, heartless, TOAD! How can you buy into this crap!?

SCRUBS: HEY. Last week they fired the CNA I took over for. No warning. *(Whispers)* All the poor lady did was fast-track a Grubhub guy with an inflamed hernia.

BLEEDER: My whole arm is inflamed.

SCRUBS: His intestine had ruptured the abdomen wall.

BLEEDER: So? I've got my effin' finger in a takeout box!

SCRUBS: And I've got chronic fatigue syndrome, plus overdue rent, two kids on the spectrum, and a Dad on disability. I can not lose this job.

BLEEDER: *(Sighs)* Yeah, okay. Sorry, sorry. Listen, how much longer?

SCRUBS: Just a couple more. Promise.

BLEEDER: All right. *(Winces)* Ow. Listen, can I at least sit down somewhere?

SCRUBS: Of course you can, but that requires a different assessment. *(New page)* Question one…

ACT WITHOUT WORDS

by Valerie Gramling

An empty stage. The floor is marked off in six-foot squares with masking tape.

A enters from the right and stands in the middle of a square (CR) facing the audience. After a few minutes, B enters from the left and stands in the middle of a different square (CL) facing the audience. There is an empty square between them.

After a moment, A sneezes. B looks at A, surprised. B walks towards A, but when B reaches the edge of the square, a warning siren sounds. A moves towards B, but when A reaches the edge of the square the siren sounds again. A and B try to reach each other, but each time a part of their body crosses the edge, the siren sounds.

A and B stand facing each other, trying to connect.

The theatre begins to shake. Suddenly, the square in between A and B erupts, spewing debris everywhere. The shaking grows stronger; lighting instruments fall from the grid, pieces of the ceiling fall on the ground. Fire and smoke come out of the hole in the center of the stage, filling the theatre. Giant, nightmarish creatures begin to emerge from the hole, shrieking and running amok throughout the theatre. They crash into the walls, which begin to crumble as the entire theatre is destroyed by waves of explosions.

A and B continue to stand in their squares facing each other. Silence. Still in their squares, A and B clasp hands. Silence. Darkness.

MEMBERS ONLY
by Joe Gulla

CHARACTERS

FEBO	Late 50s, Gay Italian American, works in "Private Sanitation"
DENNIS	Late 50s, Noted New York playwright

SETTING

Dennis' Apartment in Chelsea, New York.

(At Rise, Lights up on Febo. He is lying in an adjustable bed. Head propped, he is surrounded by an empty picture frame and some electronic devices: remote controls, iPad, iPhone.

Febo is sporting Italian American sleepwear: white tank top, black briefs, two gold chains and a pinky ring. The bed sits awkwardly in a well-appointed living room. Modern, stylish...money is clearly involved.

Febo's been in bed all day. He is restless. One of his legs rests above the sheet covering him. He checks his iPhone. Taps on it a bit. Then, tosses it back on the bed. Next, he picks up the picture frame. Stares at it. Turns it around. Tosses that too.

From the bed, he catches himself in a mirror offstage right. He poses a little. Flexes a bicep. He attempts to do something with his hair. Runs his fingers through. Some tousling. He attempts to place some behind his ear.

Dennis enters from stage left. He is carrying a bag of Chinese food. He is dressed comfortably: slacks and a loose, button-down, linen shirt.

A medical mask dangles from his neck. He catches Febo fixing his hair.)

DENNIS: Now, that's bed head!

FEBO: Bed head? More like, quarantine head! Or "won't settle in place" head.

(Febo smacks his head and hair.)

DENNIS: Every hair out of place…head! Especially the ones that are badly in need of a 'touch up'…head!

FEBO: *(Smiles and shoots back)* Dick head!!!

(Dennis sits in a chair near the bed. He begins removing various Chinese takeout boxes. He pauses and becomes wistful.)

DENNIS: *(Waxing nostalgic)* Ah…remember "head"?

FEBO: *(Playing along)* Head? Ah, yes…head! The gift YOU never wanted to give…but always wanted to get!

DENNIS: *(Matter of fact)* This was discussed early in the relationship. "Head" was YOUR department!

FEBO: *(Laughs)* MY department?!

DENNIS: Febo, my dear, yes! As "Department Head" of the "Head Department," you did great work. Some would say you were a "head" of your time! In fact, I'll say it, baby! You gave some damn good head!

FEBO: Well, The "Crown Jewel" in my Dad's kick ass porn collection was always *Fellatio Follies 4*! Those porn chicks taught me everything I know!

DENNIS: *(Still organizing food)* I'm impressed and thankful for the girls…and even more impressed and thankful for the alliteration. Take this! You need the soup!

(Dennis hands Febo one of the Chinese takeout soup containers.)

FEBO: *(Taking the food)* Um, I noticed that someone. I can't imagine who…ripped a photo out of my cute and expensive picture frame?

DENNIS: *(Clearly not innocent)* Who would do such a thing?

FEBO: Not sure, but the police…not me…are implicating a famous playwright.

DENNIS: *(Correcting)* A NOTED playwright!

FEBO: Well, a noted and famous playwright!

DENNIS: *(Serious)* There was a guy…wearing a certain jacket…during a certain time…in that photo!

FEBO: *(Robotically)* I never loved him. I love you. Come here!

DENNIS: Don't joke!

FEBO: I'm not!

(Dennis gets closer to Febo. He leans over. He attempts to kiss him. Febo puts his arms up and makes a cross with his fingers.)

FEBO: Mask! Six feet! Purell! What the fuck are you doing?

DENNIS: I miss you! I need to kiss you! Touch you!

FEBO: Jesus, Dennis! You're sounding very "Hallmark meets Lifetime meets Harlequin Romance!"

DENNIS: Harlequin Romance?! You really are an old man!

FEBO: One year older than you! And, uh, award-winning playwrights tend to be very distinguished! You'll always seem older, Den! Blame it on your Tonys!

(Dennis dons a medical mask. He applies hand sanitizer.)

DENNIS: As opposed to garbage men! Because you guys are known catnip to the youth market!

FEBO: *(Can't help but laugh)* Catnip!!!! Jesus…and, um, you know damn well, I'm in "Private Sanitation"!

DENNIS: All of that makes me nervous! Always has! Does the mafia really exist? Don't answer that!

FEBO: Get over here!

DENNIS: You just told me to mask up.

FEBO: So, you could come over here, you douche!

DENNIS: Why is it so sexy when you call me a douche?!

FEBO: COME HERE!

(Dennis walks over and sits on the side of the bed. He holds Febo's hand. They hold hands for a few beats. Then, Febo slowly reaches up and grabs Dennis' neck. Dennis is resistant at first, then yields. Febo pulls Dennis' head to his. Their face masks touch where their lips are. Febo's hand moves up and holds the back of Dennis' head. He holds it in a somewhat sexually dominant way. Then, Dennis reaches out and holds Febo's head in the same manner. They are both holding the back of each other's head. Both masks meet at their mouths. They freeze in this position. It is quiet and moving. If the masks were not between them, they would be in a passionate kiss. There is strength, union, and commitment in their pose. Slowly, Dennis begins to tear. Next, he is crying, yet he stays in position. Febo holds his head tighter. Dennis is audibly weeping now. His head rolls to Febo's chest. He continues to cry. Dennis is positioned awkwardly on the bed. Febo holds him. Febo begins to get emotional, but fights it…)

FEBO: The fuck?!

DENNIS: *(Trying to gather himself)* Shut up!

FEBO: What the hell?!

DENNIS: Shut up! Eat your cold sesame noodles!

FEBO: I suck at using chopsticks when a grown man is weeping right in front of me!

DENNIS: No, You just suck at using chopsticks! Period. There's a fork in there.

(Febo digs out a fork and begins to open the cold sesame noodle container.)

FEBO: What's with you? We have a ton of Xanax you know!

DENNIS: I'm scared.

FEBO: Scared? Of what?

DENNIS: You're sick!

FEBO: Um, I know! It sucks! I feel like shit!

DENNIS: I don't like seeing you this way! This is all freaking me out!

FEBO: The Corona stuff?! It's sucky! But I'm fine! You don't have it! Thank God! And we are "taking precautions!" Unfortunately, we have experience dealing with plagues! Last time we wrapped THAT head!

(Febo points to his crotch!)

FEBO: This time we wrap THIS head!

(Febo points to his face!)

FEBO: We got this!

DENNIS: Not funny in the least! Baby, you actually have it! COVID! It's scary! This is serious business!

FEBO: I'll be fine! I'm not THAT sick! Let's be real!

DENNIS: You don't know you'll be fine! No one knows anything! Some people have NO symptoms. Some people drop dead, Feb!

FEBO: You seriously think I am going to die from this?! Check out these quads! They ain't goin' nowhere!

(Febo presents his leg to Dennis. He flexes his quads and calves.)

DENNIS: Feb, I am serious. People DO get very sick!

FEBO: I know! I know! But I don't have that strain.

DENNIS: Strain?

FEBO: There's different strains. Levels. I've been learning about this. I am not just sitting here bingeing *The Comeback.*

DENNIS: I LOVE The Comeback! Levels?

FEBO: Yes! Levels! For instance, I'm easily a "Tom and Rita Hanks" level…bordering on an Idris Elba! They all coughed a little. They took a few naps and then they posted some Instagram photos in quarantine. They're all fine!

(Dennis looks at Febo in disbelief.)

DENNIS: *(Deadpan)* Oh, okay, I feel better now!

FEBO: *(Reaches for Dennis' hand)* I'm serious! I feel fine! Don't be scared!

DENNIS: I'm even more scared now!

FEBO: Stop! Why?

DENNIS: I didn't realize your pandemic information resource was the *Wendy Williams Show*!

FEBO: Dennis, listen, I'm going to be okay. I really am. And I know why you're in this overly caring…overly concerned…Mother Theresa state!

DENNIS: "Mother Theresa state"?! What the fuck?!

FEBO: Noted playwright says "fuck"! This is an awesome day in quarantine!

DENNIS: Seriously, Feb! What are you talking about!

FEBO: *(Slowly)* Dennis. Hubby. My man. We have been together for thirty-seven long years and, yes, I am not counting my two-year hiatus with the "Members Only" jacket model…because, as you constantly remind me…

FEBO & DENNIS: Those years did not exist!

FEBO: But the bottom line is: we're together a long time! I am a Gay Italian…from the Bronx. I know what guilt is. And you got it bad!

DENNIS: You have no idea what you are talking about!

FEBO: I do, babe! I was there for you when you were diagnosed.

DENNIS: *(Unsettled)* C'mon, shut up…

FEBO: I was. I was there! I loved you! I'm still loving you! And, um, I continued to love you DURING the "Members Only" jacket model time!

DENNIS: That's debatable!

FEBO: It's not! The couples therapist said so! I have paperwork! I'm trying to make a point, Dennis!

DENNIS: Eat your wonton soup, Feb!

FEBO: You don't owe me anything!

DENNIS: I know that. Feb, c'mon, eat…

FEBO: You. Don't. Owe. Me. Anything!

(There is a long pause. Dennis stares at the floor.)

FEBO: I honestly don't remember helping you, baby! I know I did some stuff for you! I did what I could. You were scared. We were all scared! The details escape me now 'cause, honestly, the only thing I remember is: I DID NOT WANT YOU TO FEEL ALONE! I knew what it was like to fell alone! To feel like no one gave a shit…to barely be noticed until…well, until a fuckin' plague showed up! What a public relations tsunami! AIDS! They see us now! No more being ignored! How perfect! Our time to shine! "Hey Grandma, I'm gay! Oh, and yeah, I'll be dead any minute!"

DENNIS: Feb…

FEBO: Ignore the fags…erase the fags! How convenient!! Now we can!!!! I remember, Dennis!

DENNIS: Calm down, Feb!

FEBO: *(Becoming emotional)* We were all fuckin' terrified! And we barely knew what to REALLY be afraid of! What type of ugliness the actual illness and death would bring! When you tested positive, Dennis, I was not afraid of you going blind! Shitting your pants! How you'd suffer! I barely understood what could come! How bad it could be! No, honestly, I was simply freaked out by someone I loved being alone…FEELING ALONE!

(Febo breaks a bit. He starts to cry but tries to stifle tears.)

FEBO: I JUST DIDN'T WANT YOU TO FEEL ALONE!

(Dennis walks to Febo. Dennis hugs Febo. It is a long embrace.)

FEBO: *(Coming to)* Six feet! C'mon! Step back, bitch!

(Dennis and Febo separate.)

FEBO: So, seriously, Dennis, that's really all I did! And, honestly, it didn't feel like much! So, let this go! Ya hear me?! I'm gonna be fine! Stop coddling me and feeding me. You're making me fat! Give me a fucking medal for something else! Award me for giving killer blow jobs! I deserve that medal! I give awesome head!

*(Febo takes an MMA Heavyweight Champion stance. His hands

and arms are outstretched. He walks around the stage greeting his invisible public. Dennis applauds, and then just stares, his love for his husband printed on his face. Febo continues his victory lap.)

FEBO: BEST HEAD! FEBO ANNUNZIATA! NOBEL PRIZE FOR BEST BLOWJOB?!! FEBO ANNUNZIATA! PULITZER PRIZE FOR SUCKING…AND SWALLOWING!!!

DENNIS: Gotta be, Febo Annunziata!

FEBO: *(Slower)* Yep…Febo Annunziata. Husband of noted playwright, HIV Positive Role Model, coulda easily been a "Members Only" jacket model…Dennis Carolan!

(Dennis and Febo are on separate sides of the stage. Two very different men…always. A beat.)

DENNIS: I love you! I hate how this fuckin'…yeah, I said it again… pandemic…This fucking, soul-killing pandemic is triggering me! You WERE there for me! I won't let you forget it! I will make sure you are in as little discomfort as possible while you have this thing. It's my duty. My honor! I'll wear masks and Saran Wrap and drown myself in fifty different hand sanitizers because, at the same time, I am someone who should seriously NOT contract this damn thing…high risk that I am!

FEBO: DEJA MOTHER FUCKIN' H-I-"VU"POSITIVE!!!!!!

(Beat.)

DENNIS: Promise you won't get more sick! I need you to promise!

FEBO: Tom and Rita…I told you! Worse case: Idris Elba.

(Beat.)

DENNIS: I honestly couldn't live without you!
FEBO: You got my heart by the fucking balls!

(Febo and Dennis stare at each other from afar. They want to connect, so they don their medical masks. They walk to each other and assume the head holding pose from earlier. The lights begin to dim. In shadow, they pull down their masks and kiss passionately.)

PANDEMIC BIRTHDAY CARD
by Alli Hartley-Kong

CHARACTERS

RICH   Late 70s or early 80s

SETTING

April, 2020. Inside a nursing home in northern New Jersey

(At Rise, Rich is fiddling with the computer, from which we see him as if he is on a video call. Rich leans over in and out, pressing buttons.)

RICH: Hello— is this on? Greg said there'd be a blinking red light in the— oh. Yes. I guess this is on. Shit. Oh, I wasn't supposed to say that while it's recording. You can edit this right? Just delete this. Okay, so I'll press the button again—

(Rich stops, pokes at the screen. He smiles, thinking he is just starting the reading.)

Okay. Okay, I pressed it again, blinking red light, great. Hi Cole! Happy birthday! You're eleven! I know this isn't probably how you imagined Grandpa wishing you happy birthday but—I think this is working better than…than that FaceSpace thing we tried the other day— You know what's funny? If anyone walked by in the hallways, they'd think I'm talking to myself— *(Miming "cuckoo" face)* Huh—did that make you laugh? I guess we're all a little crazy now. Your dad said some of your friends from school are going to drive by your house and wave, so at least you'll get to see some people today, even if it's six feet away. That'll be fun, right? Not the same, I know. But it'll be something different…

This whole thing is so strange. You know what it kind of reminds me of? Have you ever heard of President Kennedy? He was president, and then he got shot. Well, on that day, that very minute— Grandma and I were on an airplane going to Hawaii, our first trip together. We were up in the air—underneath us, the country had changed, but we didn't know, we were so happy on the plane, it was the best day of our lives, we were going on vacation! And then we landed—oh my god! The President is dead! It was terrible, people were crying, nobody knew what to do. We just wanted to get back on that plane, just back it up to a few hours before, and go home to our friends, to the way life had been. But we couldn't. Our lives were never the same again, but over time we adjusted. And that's what we will do now.

Your dad told me you heard about the two people upstairs who died, and you were scared for me. Cole, I'm so thankful just knowing you are thinking of me, but don't be scared. I'm not scared. And you know why I'm not scared? I got a guardian angel up in heaven, watching over me. I got Grandma.

Do you remember Grandma, Coley? You were seven when she died…You probably remember her as some sick old person in a bed. But she wasn't always like that. When she could talk—oh my god, she would talk! You couldn't get her to stop talking sometimes! Yap-yap-yap-yap-yap! You remind me a lot of her, Cole. You have her inside you. She taught me my favorite saying. *When the going gets tough, the tough get going.* I remember that, when I'm scared.

When Grandma died, I thought—well, this is what my life is like now, no more happy days. But I was wrong. I miss her every day— I wonder what she would be doing, if she was alive during this. Probably making masks. Boy, this whole thing might have been a lot easier if she was in this room with me. But I have to remember—even though she's gone, I still got good days. I'm still happy most of the time, just like you're gonna be happy after this, no matter what happens. Cole, remember the last day we saw each other? You and Dad took me to lunch. After lunch you wanted us to go to that place to drive those—those midget cars, what do you call them nowadays? Go Carts? I was kinda tired that day, so Dad suggested we do it some other time. If I had only known what was coming—I would have said "sure, let's go!" I might have even taken a lap or two around the track myself! Wouldn't that have been funny? But we didn't know then…Oh, Cole. I miss you. Being a grandpa is the best thing that ever happened to me.

This is tough, Coley. But that's life, and we have no choice but to go through it. So, for your birthday, here's a special message from me—and from your grandma. I'm just sorry she got to miss out on watching you grow—but I'm staying here, safe, so I can see you when this is all over. So, here's the message—from me and grandma. Say it with me, I know you know it—*when the going gets tough, the tough get going.*

Happy birthday, Coley. I love you. I'll see you soon.

(Rich ends the video.)

ZERO SUM GAME
by Daniel Ho

CHARACTERS

ANDREW	Top-left Screen
CATHY	Top-right Screen
BETH	Bottom-left Screen
DAVID	Bottom-right Screen

(At Rise, screen up on Andrew and Cathy.)

ANDREW: *(Over his shoulder)* Honey, I'm going to go online for a few minutes. You going to be okay?

CATHY: *(Over her shoulder)* Yeah, sure. I'm going to talk to my Mom.

(They both face the screen. Screen up on Beth and David.)

BETH: Hi.

ANDREW: Hi.

DAVID: Hi.

CATHY: Where were you?

DAVID: I had to wait for Beth to go away. Not a lot of places to hide nowadays. Can't make up another trip to the home office.

CATHY: Where is she now?

DAVID: She told me she's reading. How are you?

BETH: How are you?

ANDREW: Where's David?

BETH: I don't care about David. How are you?

ANDREW: I'm fine

CATHY: Can Beth hear us?

DAVID: No. She's in the other room. Talking to her Mom. We're alone.

CATHY: Oh, the usual. Bored. Restless. Tired. Feeling useless.

DAVID: No more lectures?

CATHY: Graded my last paper. I'm relieved. Trying to teach kids how to make a better life for themselves when the whole world is ending.

BETH: How are you, really?

ANDREW: I told you. I'm fine.

BETH: Don't talk to me like my husband. I have David for that. Let's talk like two people who love each other.

DAVID: I'm fine, actually.

CATHY: That's good. Andrew's the same.

ANDREW: I'm miserable. Which would be no problem, but I have to deal with Cathy's misery on top of my own.

CATHY: It's tough. For everyone. But unlike everyone else, we seem to be getting by.

ANDREW: Of course, I can't tell her I'm miserable.

BETH: Why not?

CATHY: We sit on the couch and put on two or three movies. It's very peaceful.

ANDREW: If I watch one more movie, I'm going to smash my head through the television.

DAVID: I love movies. Beth had us get rid of cable so it's a lot of reading.

BETH: I've been reading a lot of relationship books.

CATHY: What does she read?

DAVID: No idea.

BETH: And they all talk about the importance of communication.

ANDREW: Sounds great, but if I tell her how unhappy I am, we'll get into an argument because she'll try to be happy, and I can't be happy and she feels like she failed and all of a sudden it's my fault.

DAVID: At least it keeps her quiet.

CATHY: I'm sorry.

BETH: I'm sorry.

ANDREW: And the worst part is we'll be upset with each other but I can't even escape by taking a walk. I'm stuck inside with her.

CATHY: Actually…honestly, I think something's bothering Andrew, but he won't tell me.

BETH: Does she know about us?

DAVID: Does he know about us?

ANDREW: Just that we're friends.

CATHY: We're all one big circle of friends.

BETH: Well of course he knows that. He introduced us.

CATHY: It's so sordid.

BETH: What's wrong? Does hearing that bother you?

DAVID: Maybe love shouldn't be measured by wholesomeness.

CATHY: Maybe there's a reason for that. This isn't going to work, you know.

ANDREW: I mean, where is this all going, anyway?

BETH: Nowhere. Literally nowhere. Nobody is going anywhere. Flies in amber.

ANDREW: Flies in amber don't get divorces. Sorry, does hearing that bother you?

DAVID: Maybe this is fine. Did that occur to you?

CATHY: Lying to my husband while the man I love is somewhere else with someone else? No, it never occurred to me that this is fine.

BETH: So, what do you want to do?

DAVID: We can't do anything else.

ANDREW: We can't do anything.

BETH: Where is she now, anyway?

ANDREW: Talking to her Mom. I told you that.

CATHY: And that's why this is killing me. I can't live with him anymore I can't. I know he's miserable and I know he hates me, and he won't say anything so it just sits there and we just fester in this apartment and I just want this to end so I can take a walk and get away from him for an hour.

ANDREW: It would be easier if I didn't want her to be happy.

BETH: Oh my God, you still love her.

DAVID: Do you love him?

CATHY: Yes.

ANDREW: No. It's not love. I just want her to be happy. Just not with me.

DAVID: I still love Beth.

BETH: I hate David.

CATHY: What?

ANDREW: What?

BETH: He makes me unhappy.

DAVID: It sounds weird, but I still do. She just wasn't. . . isn't making me happy.

BETH: I have one life and it's being wasted because I'm not happy. He's not killing me, but he's wasting my life. Why wouldn't I hate him?

ANDREW: He's a good guy.

CATHY: You're a good guy.

BETH: Yes. And that's what makes this so painful.

DAVID: Thanks. But that's what makes this so painful.

ANDREW: In all fairness to David, nobody's happy right now.

BETH: I'm happy. Here. With you. I'm happy now. Does that tell you anything? Because it's telling me everything.

DAVID: I mean I don't get it, sometimes she seems perfectly happy. Sometimes she's absolutely glowing, and I try to figure out what I did right. And I think I have it figured out…make dinner, give her a hug, clean the dishes. Then I do it again and she gives me the death stare. It's all a guessing game. I wish I knew, except…

ANDREW: Are you?

CATHY: Except you might not want to know the answer. If you're guessing, there's hope. There's still pain either way, but you have hope.

DAVID: Yeah. Hope. That I might be able to salvage a marriage that makes me miserable. Then I could be happy. And then I would have to leave you. So, I'd rather guess. That way no one wins but no one loses.

CATHY: And nobody gets what they want.

DAVID: I get both.

ANDREW: Do we stay in love, or do we do the right thing?

CATHY: You want both?

BETH: Don't make me hate you too.

DAVID: Sorry, between the two of us, who do you hate really?

BETH: That's the problem when you let someone close. Five serious relationships, and just when they mean the world to me…once you get close you can see the baggage.

CATHY: Hold on, let me check on Andrew. *(Turning and shouting)* Andrew? Andrew?

(Beth hears Cathy and she instinctively ducks below the screen. Andrew turns to answer her.)

ANDREW: Yeah, what?

CATHY: You okay in there?

ANDREW: Why wouldn't I be…I'm fine.

CATHY: You sure?

ANDREW: *(Snapping)* Yes!

(Andrew turns back to the screen, disgusted with himself. Cathy turns slowly back to the screen, upset.)

DAVID: Does he talk to you like that a lot?

ANDREW: Relax. She's not here. She's just checking on me.

BETH: How dare she? No wonder you bit her head off.

ANDREW: I don't know why I snap at her like that sometimes.

CATHY: Sometimes. I don't know why.

BETH: If I were your wife I'd call you out and give you a piece of my mind. Actually, that is what I do. And here you are with me.

DAVID: Beth is the same way with me. Always giving me a piece of her mind, it's like I'm in a perpetual oral exam.

BETH: It's the guilt. Or the self-hatred. You can't have one without the other.

CATHY: I don't know why he gets mad at me.

DAVID: He's just stressed.

CATHY: Couples are supposed to lean on each other in times of stress.

DAVID: Maybe you're not a couple.

CATHY: This sounds a lot like the conversation that led to this mess. And look where we are now.

DAVID: That was mean.

BETH: Is your self-pity going to take long? I might need to grab another bottle.

ANDREW: You have one.

BETH: This one's starting to bore me. I'm in the mood for something light and sparkling.

ANDREW: Doesn't suit you.

CATHY: It's not just Andrew. I'm stabbing Beth in the back.

BETH: Touché.

ANDREW: Why are we doing this?

(Cathy touches the screen, as if she can reach David. David does the same, as they make an attempt to hold each other.)

BETH: You can live a miserable life and be bored, or live a miserable life full of excitement.

ANDREW: Cathy isn't boring.

BETH: I never thought so. But I don't have to eat her Fettuccine Alfredo every Wednesday.

ANDREW: She's actually perfect. Smart. Caring. Intuitive. Great legs.

BETH: Great legs only get you so far.

ANDREW: I knew she was perfect when I married her. I thought her being perfect would make me happy. How is it not making me happy?

BETH: How are you making her happy?

ANDREW: You think she's not happy?

BETH: Where is she now?

ANDREW: In the other room.

BETH: Have you ever noticed you're both busy at the same time for the same amount of time? It's enough time for us to have an affair. Enough time for anyone.

(Andrew turns his head.)

ANDREW: Cathy? Honey?

(Cathy responds to Andres, but keeps her eyes locked on David.)

CATHY: Yes?

ANDREW: Are you…Do you want me to get you anything?

CATHY: I'm fine.

ANDREW: Okay…I love you.

CATHY: *(Still looking at David)* I love you.

DAVID: You love him.

CATHY: Yes.

BETH: Isn't this nice. People outside are dying by the thousands, and here we are playing this game as the world is dying. Because we just want our own happiness. How beautiful. How selfish.

CATHY: We need to end this.

BETH: I should get going.

ANDREW: Where are you going?

DAVID: I can't.

BETH: Same as you. Nowhere.

CATHY: I have to.

BETH: You've lived your lie this long. You can hold on for a little longer.

ANDREW: Which part of my life is the lie?

BETH: Depends. Who are you talking to right now?

CATHY: You do make me happy. I have moments being happy. With you. Love makes people happy, and for a while I forgot what that felt like. And I owe you for that. But the difference between love and life is love doesn't care about consequences.

DAVID: So, you want me to stay trapped with a woman I don't want to be with to live a life I hate. That's the choice you're making?

CATHY: There is no choice right now.

ANDREW: I should get going, too.

BETH: Go where? We're all stuck.

ANDREW: I need to spend time with Cathy.

CATHY: I don't want to be with Andrew either. We'll make the most of it. Put up with each other while we smile. And then when this is over, life can move on.

DAVID: Why not now?

CATHY: You want me to ask for a divorce then spend the next six months locked up with him?

BETH: Did you just fall in love all of a sudden?

ANDREW: I can try.

DAVID: And what about us?

CATHY: We helped each other ask the question. But neither of us is the answer.

ANDREW: You know, I keep thinking about how all of us met and you and Dave at the wedding and whittled up to us…

DAVID: Can I at least see you tomorrow?

BETH: Don't think about that. It's irrelevant. We're here now. We're doing this now. People meet and they have a magical moment, and they think that moment will carry them till death do us part. But we can't go to our favorite restaurants now or recreate that romantic walk in the park. It happened then. We don't know when things will move on, so there's no future. We're stuck where we are and that's all we have now, and we have to deal with it now.

ANDREW: So, what have we got?

BETH: Good night, Andrew.

(Beth's screen goes black.)

ANDREW: Hey, I lost your picture. Can you still hear me?

CATHY: I don't know. Good night.

(Cathy's screen goes black. David's screen goes black.)

ANDREW: Hello? You still there? Hello? *(Beat)* Hello?

AFTER THE PLAGUE
by Charles L. Hughes

CHARACTERS

JORDAN	A young involuntary shut-in
TAYLOR	Her Friend
ELLIOT	A Mannequin

SETTING

Jordan's apartment and the immediate outside.

(At Rise, the set is divided between Jordan's apartment and the outside by a door and wall in a way evocative of a prison fence. The outside facade of the apartment, bright and welcoming, starkly contrasts with the small, sparse, disheveled interior. Jordan, unkempt and unhinged, sits in a chair near the door. Elliot, a mannequin that has been garbed heavily under thick layers of clothing so as to be almost unrecognizable as such and wearing sunglasses and a medical mask, is arranged nearby.)

JORDAN: *(To Elliot)* Hmm? What was that? Oh. Yes. Thank you. *(Beat as Elliot speaks some unheard words)* No, no, I couldn't possibly. That's very sweet of you though.

(Taylor approaches the front door and knocks. She's the same age as Jordan, but visibly more put together.)

TAYLOR: Jordan? Hello? It's Taylor. You in there…guess that's a stupid question. Umm, so since…yeah…how are you?

JORDAN: What the hell was that? Who's there? UPS guy? Are you knocking now?

TAYLOR: It's me. Taylor. Your friend?

JORDAN: Friend? You? You hearing this, Elliot? Can you believe this—*(Unheard by us, Elliot interrupts to chastise)* you're right. Language, there could be children out, for all I know. What? *(In response to another of Elliot's unheard comments)* Jesus, El, that's worse than what I was gonna say. You have issues.

TAYLOR: Jordan? Are you with someone?

JORDAN: Ha! With someone. Just me and Elliot. *(To Elliot)* No offense.

TAYLOR: Elliot?

JORDAN: Yep, Elliot. Good ole Elliot.

TAYLOR: Who's Elliot?

JORDAN: *(To Elliot)* Can you believe it? She forgot us both.

TAYLOR: I didn't forget you, Jordan. You know I'd never—

JORDAN: You're right. People don't forget things ON PURPOSE. That's just ignore-ance. Ignorance? Ignoring-ance? Pretending inconvenient people don't exist.

TAYLOR: That's not what happened. Can't you just open—

JORDAN: Oh, you aren't afraid you'll catch the scary death bug? Sure you don't want to leave to me to die, alone, again?

TAYLOR: You weren't going to die.

JORDAN: Could have, for all you cared.

TAYLOR: It was a matter of public safety, but it's over—

JORDAN: Is it? You never know. The invisible demons might still be floating through the air, the pathogenic creepy-crawlies wriggling under my floorboards as we speak. *(To Elliot)* No, I'm not being too harsh.

TAYLOR: Wait, Elliot…that department store, before it closed you bought a mannequin—

JORDAN: She's a mannequin-American. Says right here, made in Michigan.

TAYLOR: Jordan, you know that Elliot, that she isn't…?

JORDAN: Isn't what? Willing to abandon me? To shun me, like a leper? To ghost me like my name's Casper? All because of one sneeze on a dusty day?

TAYLOR: It was—

JORDAN: A matter of safety. Oh, go learn new song and dance.

TAYLOR: I tried texting—

JORDAN: Ha! She says like a gal can keep up a data plan when she's fired, sorry, given extended leave for public health reasons. Ha! Haha! Good one, Elliot.

TAYLOR: Jordan, I think you might need help.

JORDAN: Why?

TAYLOR: Because Elliot isn't, she isn't…she's not a real friend. You know that right?

JORDAN: Well, excuse me for making do with what I had. And who are you to judge the quality of my friends?

TAYLOR: I mean she's not a real—human—friend. You should see someone—

JORDAN: Oh, sister, that train left the station three long months ago.

TAYLOR: Look we were, are, worried about you. Let us help.

JORDAN: We? Us?

TAYLOR: Yeah. Me, Bob, Judy, Keith, Jenny. We all want to be there for you.

JORDAN: Right. Finally. But you're the only one here now.

TAYLOR: I, we thought—

JORDAN: One at a time? Just to be safe?

TAYLOR: No, no, we know it's—

JORDAN: Three months. Three God-forsaken months, Taylor. *(Turning and "listening" to Elliot)* That's right, when the atheist says God-forsaken it means something! Three months alone.

TAYLOR: How was I supposed to—

JORDAN: Letters! Sticky notes on the door! Smoke signals! Anything. Anything but the silence!

TAYLOR: I didn't know.

JORDAN: Because you couldn't look at a screen and press a button, or because you wouldn't risk a seventy-percent recovery rate? Was I not worth those odds to you?

TAYLOR: That's not fair, there was a lot of contradictory information.

JORDAN: So that WAS it, huh?

TAYLOR: No, I mean, it was…so much was going on.

JORDAN: I wouldn't know. I was here. By myself.

TAYLOR: You mean…the whole time?

JORDAN: Mostly. I tried going out for walks. People avoided me then too. Neighbors started spraying down the railings on the stairway after I'd leave. Apparently, they sent out a community warning about the walking-infected. Not that I would know. Again, no data, no Wi-Fi, because, no job. No friends. All for a sneeze and some goddamn shakes.

TAYLOR: The risk was—

JORDAN: Life's a risk. Every day, it's a dangerous business, going out your front door. Tolkien. *(To Elliot)* Yes, I know, I'm paraphrasing. We can't all have the damn book memorized.

TAYLOR: But I'm here now. I'm here for you now, Jordan.

JORDAN: Yes, you are. Now that it's all clear, and I know how much you care. How much you trust me. How little.

TAYLOR: Jordan…

JORDAN: Go home, Taylor. Have fun with Bob and Judy and Urkel and whoever our supposed friends were. Leave me and Elliot alone.

TAYLOR: You don't need to be alone anymore.

JORDAN: Anymore? Really? God, you're such a…go away. Don't start pretending to worry now. We'll be fine.

TAYLOR: You expect me to believe that?

JORDAN: You did before. All evidence to the contrary be damned.

(Taylor, visibly conflicted, appears to try and conjure a convincing refutation, but ultimately submits and walks away.)

JORDAN: She's gone. She really left. I know, I know, Elliot. But I really wanted to be wrong. It's just you and me now. You and me.

(Delivering her sole line in the play, Elliot speaks in an ethereal voice. Ideally, this recorded line should be clear but as ambiguously a realistic voice as possible: maybe Jordan really is hearing voices, or maybe it's a breeze or a creak of the floor or some chime or an appliance or alarm that only sounds just enough like a human voice for the mind to fill in the blanks.)

ELLIOT: Goodbye.

(Gradually but quickly, Jordan descends into hysteria during the following lines, culminating in clutching and violently shaking Elliot.)

JORDAN: What's that? Speak up, Elliot. Elliot? Elliot?! I know you can hear me, Elliot, answer me! Elliot! Don't leave, not you, no, no, answer me, you bastard! Speak to me! I can see, I can see you! You're with me! We're in this together, aren't we! Aren't we? Huh ?! *(Beat)* Elliot?

HENNY PENNY
by Andra Laine Hunter

CHARACTERS

APRIL	Female, fevered and sweaty
LEON	Male, a sexy cowboy
HOMER	Male, a preacher with some "rooster-like" qualities to him; in fact, if #45 and a rooster somehow reproduced, it would be Homer

SETTING

Spring, 2020. April is on this Zoom from a room with a bed in it in New York City. Leon shows up from the wide, open plains. April and Leon reach out to Homer when they need him. He comes from a holy place to offer comfort.

Important Note: The "bocks" in the script are chicken noises. Homer and April get more "chicken-like" as the play proceeds. Leon has always been a possum. We just don't notice it right off.

(At Rise, April is in bed, struggling.)

APRIL: Fire ants from the deepest pit of a bottomless hell're bitin' me all over! I'm H-O-T hot, baby! Whooooooooo!

(April bolts out of bed. She's drawn to the computer screen through which we are viewing her, mesmerized by it, like a moth to a flame. We see she doesn't look too good: kinda sweaty, kinda glassy-eyed; there's a wild look to her. She stares into her screen and whispers.)

APRIL: I think the Lord speaks a little louder with ever rise a my temp'rature. *(The chime that tells you someone's in the waiting room sounds)*

Hear that? Angels're singin' me home to glory.

(April studies the screen as Leon appears. He's a cool drink of water if there ever was one. April smiles at him.)

APRIL: Wisteria's bloomin'.

LEON: Always does, this time a year.

APRIL: Like the purple soul of spring. You been around these parts before?

LEON: One box looks a lot like another.

APRIL: I thought I was in some kinda box. I think I got a fever.

LEON: C'mere.

(Leon presses his hand to the screen, and April presses her face against her screen.)

LEON: Burnin' up. Feel it right through the glass.

APRIL: Shit. That's bad, right?

LEON: Real bad, darlin'.

APRIL: Are you here to git the chickens put up?

LEON: *(Taking off his hat in mourning)* It's a big flock, ma'am, and…a possum got three of 'em.

APRIL: No! Which three?

LEON: I got the rest put up nice and tight.

APRIL: Not my blue-egg layer?

LEON: How do you tell by lookin' at 'em what color eggs they lay?

APRIL: By the ear lobes.

LEON: Well…I mean, you know…it's hard to say, Miss.

APRIL: Just look at the ear lobes, dammit!

LEON: I'm tryna put this delicate, ma'am: Weren't really no earlobes left to look at. You catch my drift?

APRIL: Nonononononono…

LEON: You wanna say a few words?

(April nods, brokenhearted. No chime; Homer just appears.)

HOMER: Yea, though I peck thru the Valley a the Shadow a Death—The Shadow which covers all earthly landscapes—even the green pastures with the still waters 'n pools of sunshine where peckin' is most fruitful are in the Shadow a Death, bock, you see, and taxes, for it is in Death's Shadow alla us chickens must lay our eggs. Notably, the blue eggs.

APRIL: Not the blue eggs!

HOMER: The blue eggs must adorn the path from coop to Paradise, laid and layin' in the Shadow a Death, just like the rest of us: That's how God wrote the bible.

LEON: Amen!

HOMER: But here—at this moment—we find ourselves in the lowest, darkest deepest—the valley of the shadow of death, ya see; down, down: the deepest darkest earthly doom we can face, yet we are not afraid! Oh, no.

APRIL: Amen!

LEON: Amen and hallelujah!

HOMER: For the Lord is with us. His rod and His staff—our sure, certain knowledge He wields them—gives us comfort. For the truth is, someone must beat our enemies off us, 'n it's the rod and staff does that. For the truth is, even when we lie down in the green pastures, by the still waters, we are yet in that looooong shadow: —yet and yet and ever on. There's never a time while breath is drawn that out of death's shadow we have gone.

LEON: A preacher 'n a poet!

APRIL: But how do you tell—

HOMER: B-bock! And so, we must know the rod and staff, like hands on a clock keep time for us; they tick away the hours, circlin', circlin', till we at last emerge from death's shadow, victorious! And we see the landscape unshaded, in color, as we never could while we were standin' in the shadow. God restores our vision, you see—

LEON: Amen!

HOMER: —in death.

LEON: Couldn't a said it better myself, Preacher!

HOMER: Peyton. Peyton Homer Winslow, bock-bock, the Third, but you can call me Homer. What ails that little Chicken there?

APRIL: I got a fever. I think it's bad.

HOMER: Oh, Lord!

APRIL: And a possum got three a my sisters, bock, in the night.

HOMER: Not the blue-egg layer?

APRIL: You said it, Sir.

HOMER: Amen. God rest that blue, egg-layin' heart. But, bock, your feathers're ruffled: I b'lieve there's more you haven't breathed on yet.

APRIL: Oh, you're lookin' right inta my bock bock heart, Preacher.

HOMER: Tell me, Henny Penny.

APRIL: I feel a cold, sharp weight apressin' on my neck.

HOMER: Is it that bock-bock devil lust that's got you in his fiery talons? That cowboy there's menace-hot. Iffin' I swung that way, even I might find m'self—

APRIL: No…it's…well, if the rod and staff beat our enemies off us, then maybe I'm somebody's enemy, and bock! I don't even know it, and I got beaten off 'em with the rod and staff, bbbbb-bock!

HOMER: Bock, bock! A profundity amidst profundities: Bock! How do we know if we're the enemy gettin' beat, or the rod and staff sore from deliverin' blows?

APRIL: 'Xactly.

HOMER: Leon? Bock! Thoughts?

LEON: *(Stroking his whiskers)* You wanna know what I think? A cowboy like me?

HOMER: A bock, bock, b-ooock!

LEON: There's a golden, shinin' Axe in the sky.

(April climbs up on her chair.)

APRIL: I think I see it!

LEON: It swings back 'n forth like the Pendulum of God's Clock—

APRIL: Why, I'm afloatin' away off into the sky towards it!

LEON: *(Tenderly, to April)* Fly, Hen; I won't let you float away! *(Back to business)* You left that out, Preacher Man: the Rod & the Staff are the Hands of God's Clock, but the golden Axe is the Pendulum.

HOMER: *(Singing)* Keepin' time, keepin' time. The Lord is keepin' all our time.

LEON: The Lord wields His Rod 'n Staff, but it's one certain Angel delivers the Blows of the Axe.

HOMER: Bock! Bock! Here I am!

APRIL: My wings are strong! I'm goin' up, up, up!

HOMER: I lay my neck on the bock, bock stump to await that angel's golden blow—

LEON: I see it there, Homer. And though I salivate at the sight a your stretched-out Neck on that rough and bloodstained Stump, it ain't your Neck I was sent to caress.

HOMER: No?

LEON: Naw, Sir, not this time. Chicken Little?

APRIL: Bock! Bock! Bbbbbbock!

LEON: You ready to come home to roost?

APRIL: Bock! Boooock! I done floated off! It's like my bock bockety wings're workin' better 'n ever before!

LEON: Little Chicklets often feel their wings a'stretchin' to new spans when I come around.

APRIL: It's a powerful feelin', b-bock!

LEON: Yes, Chicky: that's the Axe.

APRIL: Oh, it's beautiful! Can I touch it?

LEON: Best to let it touch you.

APRIL: It'll give me that unshaded vision, right?

HOMER: Now hear me, Chicken Little: *(Singing)* Your own wings alone won't take you further than the sky. And where you gotta go is where only souls can fly.

LEON: Keep on singin', Preacher Man.

(Homer keeps singing his song. Leon swings his golden axe. A thump, and April jumps off her chair.)

APRIL: Ow! I done hit the sky, just like you said, Preacher!

HOMER: Cock-a-doodle-doo!

(Leon holds the Axe in view of the camera.)

APRIL: Bbbbbbbbock! Bock! B-bock! Bock bock bock bock!

HOMER: Heeeere, chicka chicka chicka chicka.

LEON: Come to shelter, Henny Penny: the sky's fallin' all around you.

HOMER: For when the Heavenly chimin' calls thee to stretch thy Neck on the rough and bloodstained Stump, thou shalt fear no evil, for it's an Angel's golden Axe that comforts thee.

APRIL: Bock?

(Leon motions, and April lowers her head, stretching her neck in front of her computer screen. April makes (or a sound effect plays) the little purring noises that chickens make. The sound of an axe. A release of breath. A rooster crows. The screen shows, "This meeting has been ended by the host.")

APRIL SHOWERS
by Caytha Jentis

CHARACTERS

MAN	30s or 40s
WOMAN	30s or 40s

SETTING

A Day in April, 2020; a Park Bench.

(At Rise, we see an empty park bench in a desolate park. An ambulance siren is heard. After a little time, a Man wearing a mask sits on the edge of the bench. Lost in thought he stares out and takes in the unusual stillness. After a long minute, a Woman in a mask sits down at the opposite end of the bench. She stares out too. After a long beat—)

WOMAN: *(With a shiver)* It's still so cold.
MAN: I know. Out like a lion, right?
WOMAN: And deserted.
MAN: I know.
WOMAN: But it's April.
MAN: April showers bring May flowers.
WOMAN: It's almost May.
MAN: Is it?
WOMAN: It's just so cold. Like death.

(Beat.)

WOMAN: First time I'm out since…Since…since…the 'sheltering at home' lock down.
MAN: I've been going out…for walks…Long walks. And toilet paper!

(They both laugh awkwardly.)

WOMAN: Yeah. Toilet paper. And Purell. Of course. Tylenol. But we have it delivered. And then left outside.

(Another siren.)

WOMAN: Those sirens…They are haunting.
MAN: Damn sirens.

(Another silent moment.)

MAN: I didn't know if you were coming.
WOMAN: I didn't either.

(He stares at her while her eyes remain forward.)

MAN: I'm glad you did.
WOMAN: I needed to get out.
MAN: Me too. *(Beat)* How's Jonathan?
WOMAN: Jonathan's…Good. Working from home. Me too. But I always did.
MAN: Of course. The kids?
WOMAN: Schooling from home.
MAN: Mine too. Of course.
WOMAN: Of course.
MAN: Not easy.
WOMAN: Nope. Not easy at all.
MAN: Nothing is.
WOMAN: Yup. Sucks.
MAN: Totally.
WOMAN: Everything does.

MAN: Emily, you know, has ADHD.

WOMAN: That's gotta…

MAN: Suck…Yup.

WOMAN: Jonathan's mother is now living with us.

MAN: That's gotta…

WOMAN: Suck! Yup.

(Another awkward laugh.)

WOMAN: She's very scared.

MAN: Aren't we all?

WOMAN: Yes. Of course. We all are. And vulnerable…She's driving me nuts!

(Another laugh.)

WOMAN: How's…

MAN: … Jane…well…you know, she's a nurse. So…

WOMAN: Essential.

MAN: Very.

WOMAN: Does she—

MAN: —No. No. Pediatric oncology.

WOMAN: Of course. I knew that. My brain…

MAN: Her mother died.

WOMAN: Oh. No. I'm so sorry. I had no idea.

(For a moment, she contemplates comforting him, but stops.)

MAN: It's all right. You wouldn't. Know. She was very old and had dementia. She was in one of those…nursing home.

WOMAN: Oh. Those sound so awful. On the news. I am so, so sorry. How is Jane?

MAN: Fine. Fine. She's…resilient. You know, a nurse. Takes care of others. Takes care of herself.

WOMAN: Right.

MAN: We did one off those virtual funerals. It was weird.

WOMAN: I can't even imagine.

(Another moment to digest. Another ambulance siren.)

MAN: I've been furloughed.

WOMAN: Oh. I'm sorry.

(He shrugs.)

MAN: Don't be. Getting stimulus checks…

WOMAN: That's good.

MAN: It is. I needed a break. I meditate. Now.

WOMAN: You meditate?

(Long beat.)

MAN: Know anyone who…

WOMAN: Died?

MAN: Yes.

WOMAN: No. But my friend's husband was in the hospital for a couple of days. Pneumonia. Was really scary. Still not, you know…fully recovered. He was…is…a marathon runner. Was training for Boston…Boston strong…

(She sighs.)

MAN: I didn't know if you were coming.

WOMAN: You said that.

MAN: You haven't answered any of my texts.

(For the first time, she looks over to him for a moment and then looks straight ahead. She sighs.)

MAN: I'm glad you came.

(He inches a little closer to her on the bench.)

WOMAN: Stop. I probably shouldn't have. They just don't know how…

(He moves back. He looks at her longingly.)

WOMAN: And please stop…staring at me.
MAN: It's not transmitted through the eyes.
WOMAN: I know. That's not what I meant.
MAN: I miss you.
WOMAN: I…
MAN: I want to touch you. I need to touch you.
WOMAN: No. You can't. *(Beat)* Anymore.

(That word is like a knife in the heart to the Man.)

WOMAN: Jonathan washes everything. The food. Our shoes. The dog. Disinfects…And then disinfects some more.

(She holds up her hands.)

WOMAN: My hands are raw from sanitizer.
MAN: Are things good with—
WOMAN: —Yes! Yes! Very. Just a little controlling. It's understandable.

MAN: It wasn't before.

(She ignores this.)

WOMAN: Stop. We are a pod. We do family dinners. We say Grace and actually mean it. We don't want to get it.

MAN: Of course. No one does. I get it.

WOMAN: I do love him. And my family. And what I have. Gratitude.

MAN: Gratitude. I know. *(Beat)* I love you.

WOMAN: Don't say that.

MAN: I can't help it.

WOMAN: *(Pleading)* Please. I just can't…go there. Now.

MAN: We were supposed to go away together.

WOMAN: I know. I know.

MAN: I still have the tickets.

WOMAN: No. Get rid of them. Get a credit. It was wrong. It was bad. A different time. A different life. Fortunately, no one got hurt. You deleted all the photos.

(He doesn't respond.)

WOMAN: What if you get sick? Intubated?

MAN: Stop.

WOMAN: Delete them! Please. I have too much stress already. This has to go away.

MAN: But it's all I have to remember. When I'm alone. I'm alone…a lot.

WOMAN: Delete them!

(It's silent. She looks over at him. He nods.)

WOMAN: Look. I have to go. Jonathan will worry. Wonder. Plus…we all just need to be "safe."

MAN: I get it.

(He puts up his elbow. She stares at it, and then gets up. She looks at him lovingly perhaps for the last time. She exhales and turns. His elbow still held up…She turns back and sits down next to him. She puts out her elbow to touch his. It's a moment in time. He starts to breathe a little faster from her touch and melts into it. She too feels the connection. After a moment, she begins to breathe a little heavier as she erotically gyrates her elbow into his.)

WOMAN: I miss you, too.

REMEMBER
by Kathleen Kaan

CHARACTERS

SARAH
MARYANNE

SETTING

New York City, 2020, during the COVID pandemic. One small apartment on the Lower East Side. One apartment on the West Side.

(At Rise, two women are talking on the phone.)

SARAH: Hello.

MARYANNE: It's me. What are you up to?

SARAH: What do you think? How about you?

MARYANNE: I'm trying to get my ass up and do something productive. I should exercise.

SARAH: Good luck.

MARYANNE: I just joined this DailyOm thing. Twelve exercises—one each day.

SARAH: Does it work?

MARYANNE: It can't hurt. I gained weight since this pandemic. I have to do something.

SARAH: I guess.

MARYANNE: The best thing about it is that they send me these special "thoughts" every day.

SARAH: What thoughts?

MARYANNE: Well, the first one I got was entitled "Intent."

SARAH: Intent. What does that mean?

MARYANNE: It means "When we live with intent, we own our actions."

SARAH: Own your own actions. That says a lot.

MARYANNE: You'll love this…ready…"Enjoy your Age."

SARAH: Fuck that one. Tell me another.

MARYANNE: How about "Knowing when to let someone go." Believe me, I read that one over and over again.

SARAH: What a bastard.

MARYANNE: It is what it is.

SARAH: How are you doing?

MARYANNE: I'm not crying every day.

SARAH: You're strong, MaryAnne.

MARYANNE: I'll get over it. Someone will come into my life. I just can't give up on that.

SARAH: I don't want to think about love.

MARYANNE: Why would you say that?

SARAH: Because deep down I know I'll never have anyone. It's too late for me.

MARYANNE: That's not true.

SARAH: I just hate this isolation.

MARYANNE: I know. It's awful.

SARAH: I talk to myself out loud every day. I'm so lonely I'm having conversations with my plants.

MARYANNE: Stop it.

SARAH: It's true.

MARYANNE: You're so funny.

SARAH: Yeah. A bundle of laughs. That's me alright. You know what I've noticed since this pandemic?

MARYANNE: What?

SARAH: People talk about the challenges facing families, kids, seniors. You hear it every day on the news.

MARYANNE: That's true.

SARAH: No one mentions people that are single and alone. It's like we don't exist. We're forgotten.

MARYANNE: We just have to be strong…What else can we do?

SARAH: My apartment is so tiny. Never thought about it before. Two lousy windows overlooking the side of another building. I never realized it was so dark in here.

MARYANNE: You should go out and take a walk.

SARAH: I'm afraid to go out.

MARYANNE: It's just a little walk.

SARAH: I don't want to go for walks alone. It makes me feel worse.

MARYANNE: Did you get tested?

SARAH: No. You?

MARYANNE: Twice.

SARAH: I don't know why I need to get tested. Living in New York nothing is open. What the hell is the difference at this point.

MARYANNE: They're talking about a vaccine. That's hope.

(Silence.)

SARAH: Whatever.

MARYANNE: Wouldn't you take it?

SARAH: I guess.

MARYANNE: You're just in a bad place that's all. *(Silence)* Let's think of the good old days.

SARAH: What are you talking about…2019?

MARYANNE: You still have your sense of crazy funny. Okay, let's talk about shopping for clothes?

SARAH: I haven't worn a thing except my sweatpants for almost a year.

MARYANNE: I know, but that will change. Don't you miss going into Saks and trying something on before you buy it?

SARAH: Nothing is the same anymore.

MARYANNE: Boy, do I miss Macy's beauty counters.

SARAH: Nobody's looking at me anyway.

MARYANNE: I do it for me. I don't want to lose myself. I just can't lose myself.

SARAH: We're different, MaryAnne. You said you wouldn't judge. Isn't that right?

MARYANNE: Yes. Anything you want.

(Silence.)

SARAH: I don't want anything anymore.

MARYANNE: Sarah, close your eyes. Remember how the trees changed color in the Fall?

SARAH: Okay.

MARYANNE: And the crunchy sound of the leaves when you walked in the park.

SARAH: I'll miss the Fall.

MARYANNE: I miss the ocean. I loved just sitting on the sand and watching the waves come and go.

SARAH: Yeah.

MARYANNE: I miss so many things. Don't you?

SARAH: Not really.

MARYANNE: Do you remember what it's like walking in the snow?

SARAH: Yeah.

MARYANNE: I think it's going to snow next week. I can't wait.

SARAH: I don't see much out of these windows. Just the brick wall of the other building.

MARYANNE: Are you on Zoom? It's a life saver for me.

SARAH: I don't do Zoom.

MARYANNE: Then we'll do Zoom together. You can get dressed up and we'll have a virtual party. How's that sound?

SARAH: Sure.

MARYANNE: We'll have dinner just the two of us. It will be the highlight of the day.

SARAH: I'm drinking too much. That's my highlight. I could open a God damn liquor store with all the wine I have.

MARYANNE: Drinking can get you even more depressed. That's according to my shrink.

SARAH: I don't have a shrink.

MARYANNE: It's important to talk to someone during this mess, Sarah.

SARAH: What's the point?

MARYANNE: Believe me, it can help.

SARAH: Why do you keep asking me if I Remember this, if I remember that?

MARYANNE: They're nice memories. That's all. Sarah, tell me what's going on. I just know something's wrong.

SARAH: I haven't been feeling very well lately.

MARYANNE: Please, you have to get tested.

SARAH: I feel there's not much time left.

MARYANNE: Try not to think like that.

SARAH: I'm frightened.

MARYANNE: Oh, sweetie. Don't be. I'm here.

SARAH: I don't go out of the house.

MARYANNE: What are you talking about?

SARAH: I'm tired of it all. No job, no family, no nothing.

MARYANNE: You have friends that care. I care.

SARAH: I'm sorry, MaryAnne.

MARYANNE: What are you sorry about? What are you saying?

SARAH: I can't live like this anymore.

MARYANNE: I'm coming over.

SARAH: Don't.

MARYANNE: Put a mask on and I'll have a mask on and we won't stay close to each other. We'll be safe. I promise.

SARAH: Don't come.

MARYANNE: I'll order some food and you've got the wine. It will be like old times.

SARAH: Not this time, MaryAnne. I gotta go.

MARYANNE: No wait. Just talk to me a little while longer.

SARAH: That's just it. I have nothing to say anymore.

MARYANNE: Wait! Do you remember the parties we used to have? We'll have them again. I promise.

SARAH: Okay.

MARYANNE: Do you remember when you met that cute guy at the bar in Soho? The musician who bought us drinks all night. You remember, don't you? *(Silence)* He really liked you, Sarah. He really liked you.

SARAH: Gotta go now.

MARYANNE: It's fun talking about things we remember, don't you think?

SARAH: Sure. I remember…

MARYANNE: What, Sarah? What do you remember?

SARAH: I remember the blue sky. I would kill to see the sky again.

(Sarah hangs up the phone.)

MARYANNE: Sarah. Sarah? Are you still there? Answer me!

A VISIT DURING COVID
by Leon H. Kalayjian

CHARACTERS

STAN	25, Non-amazing and Average
FLO	55, Black and Feisty

(At Rise, Stan is in a tank top revealing non-amazing muscles. He sits on his couch, actively playing a video game. Flo walks in and stands next to the couch, holding a shoulder bag.)

STAN: What are you doing?…You're not wearing a mask. *(Still playing)* How…How…*(Puts the controller down)* How did you get in here? Who are you?!

FLO: *(Plops down next to Stan)* Relax, I don't have COVID and I'm not human.

STAN: What?

FLO: I'm your freakin' fairy godmother. *(Stan puts the controller down)* You got any Diet Coke?

STAN: *(Stands)* Get out! And why are you near me?

FLO: I don't have COVID. I can't get it. I'm not a human being. I'm here 'cause you're…

STAN: Get out. *(Heads to the door, opens it)* I don't know what you're thinking, or who you are, but you have no right to come in here, sit on my couch.

(Annoyed, Flo opens her shoulder bag, pulls out a snow globe-looking thing.)

STAN: No. Don't take things out of your bag. You're leaving.

(She sets the globe on a coffee table in front of the couch.)

FLO: My name is Flo.

STAN: Get out, Flo.

FLO: Come.

STAN: What is that? Put it back in your bag.

FLO: That's you in there. Come. Take a look.

STAN: *(Comes closer)* What is that?

FLO: You were getting me a Diet Coke.

STAN: That looks like me. That looks like an old me. *(Picks up the globe, looks at it closely)* I'm all gray.

FLO: Stanley Rosenstein, born July 9, 1996, raised in North Bergen, attended Central Valley Community College, no wife, no children, only four girlfriends in your entire life, and no dates for the last five months. Can you get me a freakin' Diet Coke?!

STAN: How do you know that? I did go on a date.

FLO: You walked into a Chipotle, saw Karen Hughes, and asked to sit with her. That's not a date, compadre.

STAN: Technically but…Diet Coke. I do happen to have that.

(He disappears into the kitchen.)

FLO: I know you do. You bought it at Pathway yesterday. Don't drop that crystal ball.

STAN: *(Offstage)* You saw me shopping at Pathway?

FLO: Yes. Jill Tobin got Elon Musk. Jeff Billingsley got Brad Pitt.

(Stan comes back with a can of Diet Coke.)

FLO: And I got you, babe.

STAN: Life's a bitch, isn't it?

FLO: Afterlife as well. No glass? Is this how you entertain otherworldly beings?

STAN: Right.

(He heads back to the kitchen.)

FLO: Never mind the glass. I saw how you wash glasses. I'll drink from the can.

STAN: Okay.

(He returns, hands her the can, holds a second can.)

FLO: Sit.

STAN: No thank you?

FLO: Thank you. Sit.

STAN: *(Looking at the globe)* I look terrible…so gray and sick-looking.

FLO: Well, that's the day you die.

STAN: I die? *(Slumps down into the couch, staring at the globe)* Really? What do I die from?

FLO: Cancer…seventy-one-years-old…No wife. One child. No savings. No health insurance, or you would have caught the cancer early.

STAN: Seventy-one? I'd be on Medicare, right?

FLO: Medicare in the year 2061 is for seventy-four-year-olds and up.

STAN: Why?

FLO: Money ran out. They kept raising the age. If you're born in the 2000s, you will have a fifty-percent deductible.

STAN: Where is my child? Is he in the snow globe too?

(He searches the globe.)

FLO: Blames you for the divorce. He lives in China so he didn't come back when he heard you only had a few days. He barely knew you anyway.

STAN: *(Stands)* This is a joke, right? Some sick joke. How do you get a moving picture in this snow globe?

(He looks at it from different angles.)

FLO: This is your twenty-five-year intervention. You get another at fifty, and you will get one at seventy-five if you live that long.

STAN: Yeah…thanks a bunch, Tinker Bell. *(Tosses her the snow globe)* David Blaine pulls keys out of his stomach with a coat hanger. You're gonna have to do better than this.

FLO: *(Stands)* Eighteen-years-old…Lamar Country Club…men's bathroom. What did you do with that industrial vacuum cleaner?

(She pops open her can.)

STAN: Oh…wow.

FLO: And you couldn't shut it off. The janitor raced in and pulled the plug. Were you trying to do liposuction?

STAN: How did you know?

FLO: So anyway, this is your intervention. Things don't have to go badly. You have choices. You don't have to wind up alone, dead, no money, forgotten.

(She sits.)

STAN: What do I do, Flo? How do I get out of this?

FLO: Oh, I don't know.

(She drinks her soda.)

STAN: But you're my fairy godmother.

FLO: I can hear your ideas and help you, but they have to be your ideas. I can't come up with these without your input.

STAN: Well, I'm really not in a good situation here. It isn't fair. I wasn't given a lot to work with.

FLO: Okay, so you work at Verizon. You've got an associate degree in marketing…You had 40,000 points and twelve health on that nonsense.

(She points to the television.)

STAN: I don't have to play video games. It's just, I'm home from the virus and I'm bored.

FLO: What about doing something to get ahead?

STAN: But I like Verizon.

FLO: You're not gonna be there forever. Think ahead.

STAN: I can be the manager if I'm driven but likable and not threatening.

FLO: You're not going to be the manager. You need a situation where you can control your destiny.

STAN: *(Rings his hand through his hair nervously)* Wow.

FLO: Is that a deal breaker?

STAN: I just can't think of anything I'm qualified to do. I mean, I know some marketing. I know cell phones. Sometimes I think maybe I can contact a new…a new Indian cell phone company and handle their marketing in the…the USA?

(Flo shakes her head.)

STAN: What?

FLO: Indians? Cell phones? Marketing…it's in their blood. They'll do that themselves. They're not hiring some newbie that vacuums his person.

STAN: Oh.

(Flo laughs.)

FLO: Hey, it's funny. Sue me.

STAN: The woman I marry…have I met her yet?

FLO: You don't have to marry her, you know.

STAN: Well, do I love her? Am I gonna love her at some point?

FLO: Yes, but it doesn't matter, 'cause you know how it turns out.

STAN: But I will love her, and she will love me.

FLO: Yeah.

(She drinks.)

STAN: Maybe that's good enough. Maybe the memory that I was once in love will be enough. It will help me go through the cancer.

FLO: That's not helping. And it's pretty dumb.

STAN: I have a son, right? What's his name?

FLO: *(Stands)* Why are you getting into all this? I'm telling you it doesn't have to go this way. I'm telling you there's options. You don't have to be a penniless bum. You have to make some choices. Some tough choices, and work hard, and—

STAN: Is it Phyllis? It's Phyllis, isn't it?

(He smiles.)

FLO: Stop it. Wipe that smile off your face. It hasn't happened yet.

STAN: I knew it. It is Phyllis. *(Opens his soda)* Is my son, really cute? Do I take him to go see Santa and walk him around the neighborhood on Halloween? Does he play an instrument? Does he play sports? Do I watch him score goals playing soccer?

FLO: You are impossible to work with.

STAN: You tell me I have a wife and son and I'm supposed to just forget about them?

FLO: He's not born yet. You haven't dated Phyllis. If you tell yourself now that you won't date her, none of this happens.

STAN: Okay. So, what do I do? What's my option? Open a restaurant?

(He stands.)

FLO: That's financial suicide. What do you know about restaurants?

STAN: Okay. Apply for a manager job at Boost? I could be the night manager at Walmart if I take their training course. I could try to flip houses…I don't have much credit, but maybe I can go halfers with my brother…or I can write pop songs and try to get someone talented to record one. I like movies. I can write a screenplay. *(Flo stares at him)* What?

FLO: Are you playing with me?

STAN: No.

FLO: There's people working songs all their lives, writing and making movies in film schools, people experts at renovating houses, and you're gonna just jump in and make money?

STAN: What can I do?

FLO: The world is changing. Take advantage.

STAN: How? I don't have money to invest. I could make YouTube videos.

FLO: Doing what?

STAN: Fun things. Going to museums and parties. Ball games… concerts.

FLO: There's a million hot girls shopping that now. Why am I gonna watch you when I could be watching a Kim Kardashian lookalike?

STAN: I don't know…I'm just terribly ordinary. I'm not talented…I'm not artistic. I got 1100 on my SAT's which isn't terrible but it's just enough to tease me into thinking I'm smart enough to go to college. I'm good looking enough to think I'm gonna get the girl. But you know what? That's a lot of people. I am so average… which isn't bad. So, what's wrong with some happiness? Some joy and pride before the whole thing blows up and I die a slow and painful death.

FLO: Okay.

(She heads to the door.)

STAN: Wait. Where are you going?

FLO: You will forget me and this conversation, but you'll still remember your motivation and the path you are taking, if that makes sense to you.

STAN: If there is a better option, I'm open to it. I just can't think of it.

FLO: You know the ugly girl at work.

STAN: What…Hillary Selman?

FLO: Her parents have a lot of money. Her father is a brain surgeon.

STAN: Why would I want anything to do with Hillary Selman?

FLO: 'Cause that's your only out. I wasn't supposed to tell you that, but it looked like you were going to choose going down in flames, and I don't like seeing that. If you date Hillary, she'll fall for you and she'll live her life thankful she has you. Verizon's going to close all their stores 'cause of COVID. They're selling phones on line 'cause everyone is limiting going out. People don't have money to keep upgrading phones. You're not gonna have a job soon. You have to move fast. Call your manager and get her phone number.

STAN: What's the rush? I can call her anytime. I mean, if I decide to call her.

FLO: Just call her today, if you please.

STAN: Flo? *(Looks at her, she doesn't meet his eyes)* Why did you choose today to see me?

FLO: 'Cause you're twenty-five years old.

STAN: I've been twenty-five for some time. I'm almost twenty-six. What happens to Hillary if I don't call?

FLO: How would I know? You presume too much.

STAN: Somethings gonna happen and you know.

FLO: Look, I can't say anymore.

STAN: She's gonna die from COVID if I don't call…How? Don't deny it. Your face says it all.

FLO: She's going to sign up for a clinical trial. She's going to let herself become exposed to see if an experimental vaccine works. It won't work for her. And she does this 'cause she has nothing really going for her and she wants to do something that's worthwhile. She's a good person.

STAN: But if I call, she won't do it. She won't do it 'cause a guy like Stanley is exceptional.

(He raises his hands triumphantly.)

FLO: *(Laughing)* Exceptional, with string bean arms and one-thousand Facebook friends.

STAN: SO, she can save the country from COVID, or she can choose me, and she chooses me.

FLO: You're more venal than Trump, you know that?

(She takes the crystal ball.)

FLO: Look at Stanley now.

(He looks into the ball, smiles.)

STAN: He looks pretty freaking happy.

FLO: I need that. *(She smiles, puts the globe back into her bag, zips it)* So, you're gonna be forgetting me in a minute or two. But you will know what to do. I have helped you form a purpose. You know what to do, right?

STAN: Thanks. And keep watching me.

(Flo leaves. Stan smiles as he closes the door, dials his cell phone.)

STAN: Hey, I was just saying to myself, I haven't seen Phyllis's lovely face in a long time…

A LYING TOGETHER
by Arden Kass

CHARACTERS

ELLIE	Mid-40s or 50s
ALAN	Mid-40s or 50s

(At Rise, Ellie and Alan wear what used to be called workout clothes, but is now known as a COVID wardrobe. A huge box takes up most of the stage.)

ELLIE: But we have a bed.

ALAN: You have a bed.

ELLIE: We sleep together every night in a queen-sized bed. In our aptly named bed-room.

ALAN: Not as together as we used to.

ELLIE: Because we're divorced now.

ALAN: Not officially.

ELLIE: We were just waiting for the papers, Alan, which are delayed "indefinitely." We're only living together because we're in the middle of a plague and I have nowhere else to live. Even if I had a place to move to, I'd get infected or infect someone I love or get fined for congregating with the movers. That's that the only reason we're still here together, in this house, sharing that bed—

ALAN: Your bed. The bed you brought with you when we moved in here.

ELLIE: You and I have spent one third of our lives in that bed, for twenty, no twenty-three years, including the years before we were married and even…when we were trying to have kids.

ALAN: This isn't easy for me, Ellie.

ELLIE: Oh. For me, it's the dream of a lifetime. Lying in bed watching you scroll through Tinder all night. Even with doctors' offices and banks shut down, it's reassuring to know a guy can still get a virtual booty call.

ALAN: Not just guys. I could show you plenty of—

ELLIE: No thanks.

ALAN: I'd rather have a live booty call—with my wife.

ELLIE: Ex—

ALAN: Not officially.

ELLIE: And no. No booty calls. We just share a bed now. It's too confusing otherwise.

ALAN: Not to me. I know exactly what I want. I want you. Every morsel of you.

ELLIE: Except you don't want to be married to me anymore. That was the first thing we'd agreed on in years, as I recall.

ALAN: I think I lied about that.

ELLIE: What?

ALAN: Or I was wrong. Or really confused.

ELLIE: That's absurd. You announced it to our therapist. And the arbitrator. And you had plenty of time to change your mind in between.

ALAN: People say things they don't mean. Especially in front of other people.

ELLIE: Nah. I've always known when you were fibbing. I would have felt it. And, P.S.: if the world is really ending, I want it on record that I didn't want to be married to you anymore, either.

ALAN: Maybe we were both wrong.

ELLIE: You seem poised for your next chapter. With your brand-new bed.

ALAN: This time could be a reboot for us. We could discover new things about each other…

ELLIE: Like I discovered that you live for phone sex.

ALAN: I don't have phone sex with them. I just lie there looking and imagining it.

ELLIE: To think, you used to lie there and fantasize about buying a home smoker.

ALAN: One of the things you used to say you loved about me was my…appetite. Was it true?

ELLIE: I don't see how that's relevant here.

ALAN: Being in that bed with you all these months, together but not together, I've had a lot of time to think about that…

ELLIE: Alan. You need to internalize this. This time last month, I would have been gone and into my own apartment. But now, even my realtor isn't really working. Not for renters. It's a total seller's market, and she's not wasting a second on one little apartment rental. So, the fact that you and I still get into the same bed together…it's a matter of circumstances and — I was going to say convenience. But it's not convenient. It's deeply, awkwardly, profoundly inconvenient, and humiliating, too.

ALAN: Have I been cruel to you?

ELLIE: I'm a captive! I'm stuck here, more or less at your whim, under a roof you now own. You could toss me out today if you got an urge to.

ALAN: I can't imagine myself doing that.

ELLIE: Well, could you have imagined this?

ALAN: Ellie. I'm in earnest. Let's start from the ground up.

ELLIE: Lettuces start from the ground up, not people. Or twenty-year marriages.

ALAN: Imagine making love for the first time, all over again. In the new bed.

ELLIE: Except that, as you so carefully pointed out, I have my own bed, already. A sturdy, attractive bed. With a fairly new mattress even, that we selected together. Actually, as far as I can tell, the provenance of our bed is not the real issue here.

ALAN: Maybe it's cursed.

ELLIE: Maybe, last September you chose to sleep with my physical therapist while I was away visiting my sister.

ALAN: You kept talking to me like I was the—the maintenance man around here. Not like I was your lover and friend and biggest fan.

ELLIE: Was I being unreasonable? Every single one of your projects was lying around here in a state of suspended animation. And so were you. That back door was boarded up for a year until I paid someone to finish it. We're required by law to have two viable means of egress, ya know? That's not my personal opinion—it's building code.

ALAN: I was busy, I was job hunting.

ELLIE: Imagining you were job hunting. God only knows what you were really hunting.

ALAN: Look, it doesn't matter now. Because now, for God only knows how long, here we are. Just you and me.

ELLIE: And your newly delivered bed. Which you've yet to successfully explain—

ALAN: How much harder can I try?

ELLIE: Harder. And don't even try to get me to help you put it together. Like all the IKEA stuff, and the flat pack sofa—

ALAN: In my whole adult life, I've never purchased a new bed, right?

ELLIE: This is so like you.

ALAN: What, to be a romantic?

ELLIE: To sail out and treat yourself to a new bed in the midst of a global catastrophe, simply because you have a desire —

ALAN: Did you see me "go" anywhere?

ELLIE: —and you can afford it, so why not?

ALAN: As it happens, I got a very good price on it. But did you see me "go" anywhere? Did you?

ELLIE: No, but I know how you operate. When we bought that last mattress, you grilled the poor saleswoman for three-and-a-half hours on materials, construction, flammability, recycle-ability, and then insisted we lie down and take a nap right there in the store. She was probably wondering why we didn't bring our coffeepot. And our sex toys.

ALAN: Well, humorous as that sounds, that's not how I did it this time. As you noticed, I've discovered the joys of the Internet. And UPS.

ELLIE: You ordered online? Wow. Miracles happen.

ALAN: Personal growth.

ELLIE: You must have been really desperate.

ALAN: Why is this concept so threatening to you? It's a bed. Four planks and a headboard.

ELLIE: I assume this new bed is for your bedroom?

ALAN: I still think of it as our bedroom.

ELLIE: Well, it's not possible to fit two queen beds in there, that's for sure.

ALAN: True.

ELLIE: And we turned the second bedroom into an office.

ALAN: We could put yours in there and turn it into an office/guestroom.

ELLIE: We won't be having guests anytime soon, according to Dr. Fauci. So maybe you're suggesting I go sleep in there?

ALAN: That's not at all what I'm—

ELLIE: ONE BEDROOM. TWO BEDS. What are you thinking, queen-size bunk beds?

ALAN: Suppose we take it apart, and—

ELLIE: What?

ALAN: Put it in the basement.

ELLIE: You want me to sleep in my old bed in the basement? Did I say humiliating? I meant mortifying.

ALAN: Babe, I—

ELLIE: Don't call me babe, right now.

ALAN: I didn't mean you should go sleep in it.

ELLIE: Sure, no problem. It's my bed, right?

ALAN: This is the dumbest conversation I ever—

ELLIE: Bad Ellie. Go To Your Bed. Now.

ALAN: Why don't we wrap it up in plastic and put it out in the garage for now.

ELLIE: What for?

ALAN: In case, I mean, when and if you move, which would be purely at your discretion, you can, ya know…

ELLIE: Take my damn bed with me when I go.

ALAN: I don't want to just dump it at the curb.

ELLIE: How gracious.

ALAN: You're not leaving me a whole lot of room here.

ELLIE: Oh, speaking of Lebensraum…I'll just make camp in the foyer.

ALAN: This is not a war, and I am not attacking you. I'm just—

ELLIE: Spreadin' out. Getting your space back.

ALAN: I am trying to get comfortable with my life. That's all.

ELLIE: By getting rid of anything that has ex-wife "cooties?"

ALAN: By trying to make it so I can sleep through the damn night without writhing in psychological and physical torment.

ELLIE: Oh, he's horny. My tiny violin weeps.

ALAN: Aren't you? Though, that's not the point.

ELLIE: Who cares? *(Beat)* I really envy your ability to compartmentalize.

ALAN: Get an engineering degree.

ELLIE: Now he gets a sense of humor.

ALAN: Just being rational for a minute here—What would be the downside of a little physical comfort? We're married. We're adults. Healthy, functional adults…

ELLIE: Gosh. How could I have overlooked all that? You know what? I'll go sleep in the living room, on the sofa. You can return your stupid bed tomorrow. *(Beat)* And don't unwrap the mattress or they won't take it back.

ALAN: I don't want them to take it back. I want you to sleep in it with me. And more.

ELLIE: Do you realize we've spent more time discussing your little impulse purchase than we have on anything else for the last eight months?

ALAN: Minus the eight million hours at the therapist. And your new apartment. Which you insisted that I help you research. Though you clearly knew I couldn't even stand buying cleaning products online.

ELLIE: We gave it our best for twenty years, Alan.

ALAN: I always think of you as more creative than this. More emotionally intelligent.

ELLIE: I'm going to pretend it's still this morning, and we've just awakened. The sun is coming in through the skylight, I'm noticing that the hair on your chest is starting to turn gray and, none of this ever happened. And then I'm going to go downstairs and play my flute.

ALAN: I love it when you play the flute.

ELLIE: So why did you wear headphones half the time?

ALAN: You practiced a lot.

ELLIE: Musicians do.

ALAN: Even the cat took cover sometimes.

ELLIE: Then she'll get exactly what she wants as soon as I can make it happen.

ALAN: I don't give a shit what she wants.

ELLIE: Or what I want apparently.

ALAN: You want something from me?

ELLIE: Maybe I did.

ALAN: Why didn't you just ask?

ELLIE: I did, for years. I asked you in the kitchen and the living room. I know I asked you in bed. The bed in question.

ALAN: Maybe I didn't hear. There was always so much noise in this house then.

ELLIE: Actually? This house has always been quiet. Too quiet, if you ask me. That's why I had so much time to practice flute. Because you quit talking.

ALAN: I felt like we were communicating just fine.

ELLIE: I don't mean physically.

ALAN: It was so beautiful and perfect with you. I can't even bear to think about it.

ELLIE: That is a lie. A manipulative lie. Obviously, you have been thinking about it. But think about this, too. When we first met, and even that time we drove cross country together, it was never that quiet. There were ebbs in the conversation, of course, which is to be expected. But not deadly outer space quiet. I know we were new to each other back then and we had so much to reveal about ourselves, but then it got very quiet, very fast. Like a steep drop-off in the curve, every month. If we'd kept going, we'd qualify as Zen monks.

ALAN: Zen monks with a hot sex life. *(Beat)* What if I felt like I had nothing left to "reveal?"

ELLIE: Oh, please. There's always something. Even if it's—an email from a long-lost classmate. A work anecdote…Unless your silence was hiding something.

ALAN: Like what?

ELLIE: Something you're not proud of. Or, something else you lied about that could hurt me. And cause you problems. Was there more?

ALAN: More what?

ELLIE: Just cough it up—there's nothing to lose now. Was there more of it?

ALAN: More of what?

ELLIE. More than my physical therapist.

ALAN: Oh.

ELLIE: Yeah. See, I could always feel it. Stop looking so—crumpled. Just level with me. Once and for all.

ALAN: *(A long beat)* Well—I guess…I guess we both expected that after a while someone else would be living here too, with us. Talking and laughing and playing…

ELLIE: So, what? You decided to hoard your best material till "they" arrived.

ALAN: I don't think I decided anything.

ELLIE: They told us definitively that that wasn't happening, and you declined to adopt. You didn't care, you said, "All I need is you." You swore. Then you grieved about it for ten years? Is that what you're telling me?

(She shoves him, to his shock.)

ELLIE: You fucking stupid fucking liar! You were angry about it all that time and you didn't say that to me?

ALAN: *(Dodging blows)* Did you ever ask? *(She hits him again)* Anyway, I probably couldn't have explained it even if I wanted to. There was so much noise, like I said.

ELLIE: How can a house be too quiet and too noisy?

ALAN: Friends, specialists, therapists, phone calls, cousins who watched one Ted Talk too many. Money, renovations, work, your Masters degree—

ELLIE: And, your business. Both businesses.

ALAN: True.

ELLIE: Like the Hindenburg and the Titanic.

ALAN: Then I finally land a job—and—they dump me.

ELLIE: They didn't dump you. They downsized. Like everyone else in America that year.

ALAN: Okay, fine. Maybe it did get a little quieter—right around then.

ELLIE: It was already plenty quiet. That just added reverb.

ALAN: Shh. Listen.

ELLIE: What? *(Looking around, scared)* What?!

ALAN: It's totally quiet now. There's nobody here but us and no one else is calling or dropping by. Even the mail person doesn't come up the driveway. Maybe it'll be like this for months. May be forever.

ELLIE: So?

ALAN: I'm talking to you. Are you listening?

(Pause. She listens...actively. Decides something.)

ELLIE: Just come clean, Alan. You had that bed on order for the moment. I walked out that door, but they couldn't store it anymore. Or maybe the store closed down. True?

ALAN: I didn't buy it just for me. It's for us.

ELLIE: Liar! You're such a liar! And a coward and a manipulator. You'll say anything to get me to have sex with you. I hate you. To be honest, I would rather sleep in the garage.

(Ellie smacks Alan, who falls back onto the big box. She storms off. Alan just lies there...Ellie returns, arms crossed and stands over him.)

ELLIE: You really bought this online? Sight unseen? Without analyzing it or trying it out?

ALAN: Why would I lie?

ELLIE: You, the man who won't even buy cat litter online. Why?

ALAN: No more hitting?

ELLIE: I can't promise.

ALAN: I started to hate our other bed. When I thought about us struggling in it for so long. So much pain.

ELLIE: That was almost ten years ago.

ALAN: I know. But after that there was something— a sort of absence that was a presence, too. *(He starts to cry)* I thought it would fade away. We had so much that was right and, and we were both so determined to make it feel like before. But almost every night, no matter what we did in it, no matter how amazing it felt, physically…Then I started worrying if it was the same for you. If you were angry and disappointed too and doing your best to fake it but didn't know what to say. But then this past month, Ellie, every night in your sleep, you curl up under my arm like a warm little bird. Exactly like you always used to do, before.

ELLIE: *(Dismissive)* I do not.

ALAN: Every night. But if I touch your face and you wake up, you practically vault off the bed.

ELLIE: Bullshit. Why haven't you told me that before?

ALAN: Because I thought you'd say I was lying. To get what I want. Like you just did—

(He cringes, ready to duck. Instead, Ellie straddles him on the box.)

ELLIE: *(Realizing)* You truly believe the bed is cursed?

ALAN: I couldn't believe you just didn't love me anymore.

(She kisses him. He kisses back. Instantly, they are immersed in awkward passion.)

ALAN & ELLIE: *(Mixed up)* Ow. Oh—sorry. Oh god. Careful—wait, uh— maybe on the floor—

ALAN: We do have two very comfortable beds.

ELLIE: Nope. I'm taking you at your word. From the ground up.

(They go back to what they were doing. Lights dim, then blackout.)

DELIVERY
by Greg Lam

CHARACTERS

SAM	18-25, Asian American, Chinese restaurant delivery guy, dressed to be out and about, wears a cloth mask over his mouth and nose
TOM	30s-40s, White, house owner, dressed to stay indoors

SETTING

The front porch outside of a house. There's a wooden front door behind a clear storm door.

(At Rise, Sam knocks on the front door. Sam is wearing a cloth mask over his mouth and nose, latex gloves. He holds a brown paper bag full of takeout food. He stands aside and waits for the homeowner to arrive. The door opens and Tom appears. Tom opens the front door but leaves the clear storm door closed.)

SAM: Hi there. I'm from Golden Dragon.

TOM: Hello.

SAM: You're Mr. Hastings? You ordered Chicken wings? Pork fried rice? Uh…

TOM: Yeah. You can just leave it there.

SAM: Oh, okay. We, uh, packed the extra duck sauce and fortune cookies for you there, too.

TOM: Thanks. Thanks a lot.

(Sam leaves the package by the door and steps back. Waits. Tom does not open the door to retrieve the food.)

TOM: Well?

SAM: I'm sorry?

TOM: You can go.

SAM: Oh, okay. I was just waiting. In case.

TOM: In case of what?

SAM: Well, some people might offer a tip. At this point. A little extra cash for our troubles? "In these uncertain times…" You know. "Essential workers are all heroes." Right?

TOM: We paid with our credit card.

SAM: Right.

TOM: So, we're done, right?

SAM: Oh, I see.

TOM: I mean, there was a delivery charge.

SAM: Right. And also a "tip" field.

TOM: Right.

SAM: You left that blank. I saw the receipt.

TOM: Yeah, because we paid the delivery charge.

SAM: Some people might, at this point, also give the delivery person money in cash. You know, given that we're currently risking our health to deliver you dinner so that you can stay at home.

TOM: Whatever. What do you want, a medal?

SAM: I'm just saying that, while you're keeping safe and socially distanced in your house there, I'm going to dozens of houses a night just hoping I don't catch the 'rona.

TOM: You get paid for this, right? You're not a volunteer, right?

SAM: Yeah. You want to know what they pay delivery people?

TOM: I just want to get my food.

SAM: So what's stopping you?

TOM: You're on my doorstep.

SAM: I'm keeping my mandated distance. I'm socially distant. Look at me. I'm sooo socially distanced.

TOM: Are you going to let me get my food or not?

SAM: You're really not going to tip me? You're going to let me risk my neck so you can eat Moo Goo Gai Pan from the safety of your little bubble and not tip?

TOM: Jesus Christ. Here.

(Tom digs out his wallet and grabs a few bills. Tom only sticks his hand out the door and tosses it vaguely in the direction of Sam.)

TOM: Here! You need money? Here. Thank you for your service, you brave Corona-warrior! Thank you for your service!

(Sam picks up the money while Tom glares at him. Sam turns to leave.)

SAM: Enjoy your dinner!

TOM: Yeah, enjoy your five bucks. Now go and take the virus back home where it came from.

SAM: What did you say?

TOM: You heard me.

SAM: I've been in this town all my life. The virus got nothing to do with me.

TOM: Where do you think it came from? Some lab in Wuhan. The... The wet markets, some shit like that.

SAM: And what does that have to do with me, exactly? Have you ever been to China, man?

TOM: Nope.

SAM: Great. Well, we're even then. I've never set foot there. I know like five words of Chinese and they're all about what to order at a dim sum.

TOM: But you are Chinese, though.

SAM: No, I'm American. At least, I think I'm American until someone reminds me that I'm not.

(Pause.)

TOM: This is not the level of service I'm used to from The Golden Dragon. Whatever, man. You came here, when I just wanted to order some food. Because I'm scared shitless to step foot outside the house because one day they say this and one day they say the exact opposite. And you give me attitude because I didn't know I'm expected to tip on top of the delivery fee? I might be a little short, right now, you know what I'm saying? Turns out, I'm not one of the essential people who can still work from home, you know? But I still gotta eat, you know?

SAM: I'm sorry. I'm sorry to hear that.

TOM: Yeah, sure. You're sorry. But you got to lay on a guilt trip on me, so I hope that makes you feel better. Are we done here? Can you go so I can eat?

(Sam looks at Tom. Sam leaves the dollar bills back by the door.)

SAM: Here.

TOM: What?

SAM: You keep that. I don't want it.

TOM: No, no. That's yours. You take it.

(Tom sticks his hands out of the door and tosses it back towards Sam, who tosses them back at Tom.)

SAM: No, I didn't know that you had—

TOM: No, you were right. You take it.

SAM: No, really—

TOM: For fuck's sake, take it you son of a bitch! Take it before I ram it down your throat!

(Pause. Sam picks up the dollar bills. Sam begins to leave.)

TOM: I don't want it to be like this.

SAM: Like what?

TOM: Like this. Everyone scared. Everyone at each other's throats.

SAM: You think I do?

TOM: In 2016…When I voted…I didn't think it would turn out like this.

SAM: I did.

TOM: You did?

SAM: Well, if not exactly this, but something like this. It was always going to be something.

TOM: It's gotta get better, right?

SAM: I don't know if it's gotta be anything. What evidence do you see that things are going to be better?

TOM: We can't live like this forever, right? They gotta let us out. We gotta go and…meet friends. Go shopping. Get haircuts. Look at me. We gotta get out, we gotta start living again. I'm going nuts in here.

SAM: I am out. I'm seeing people now. I don't recommend it. Scary.

TOM: It's gotta be better than this.

SAM: You'd think.

TOM: I'm sorry about what I said before. The China stuff. I didn't mean anything by it.

SAM: C'mon, man. You meant all of it.

TOM: I'm not the type of guy to say something like that.

SAM: But you did. So, you are.

(Pause. Sam shakes his head.)

SAM: There are so many of you.

TOM: So many of who?

SAM: You! You…you listen to what that orange guy says and you actually believe it! You watch Fox News. You believe every single conspiracy theory. And you'll order Chinese food on a Thursday night.

TOM: Well, maybe not from The Golden Dragon next time.

SAM: I just don't understand you guys. Any of you. I've lived beside you all my life, but I've never understood you at all. All the stuff we learned in school. The "rah rah" America stuff. The flag waving, "Land of the Free" stuff. It all goes away real quick when push comes to shove. We're dying out here.

TOM: Delivery guys?

SAM: What?

TOM: When you say you're dying—

SAM: Us. The "essential" workers who can't quit or else everyone starves or runs out of toilet paper. We can't squirrel ourselves away in a house like you. The checkout clerks and the pizza delivery guys, they're the ones who you have to keep running out there while you hide.

TOM: I don't want to hide. But they say you gotta. All the experts. Part of me thinks this really is a conspiracy. A hoax! It's just some weird hallucination of so-called experts and…the media. Is this really worse than the flu? For God's sake. They just want to cut off our balls. That's all this is really about. And for what? The flu?

SAM: You're not gonna call this fake news. C'mon.

TOM: I mean…It might be.

SAM: You think so? You really think so? When are you all going to stop being so stupid?

TOM: Will you stop calling me stupid, you little slant-eyed fuck? All you guys do is talk down to us. I'm not stupid. I'm just not buying the garbage they're trying to sell me. This "Kung Flu" is nothing.

(Sam looks at the bag of food and considers. After a moment, Sam opens the bag of food and takes out a Chinese container box of food and opens it.)

SAM: You really think this is nothing?

(Sam lowers his face mask and deliberately breathes on the food.)

TOM: What the hell are you doing?

SAM: Nothing. Like you said.

(Sam closes the box and returns it to the bag.)

TOM: You put your filthy germs on my food, that I paid for!

SAM: But it's just the flu, right? You're not scared of the flu, right? Go on, dig in! Mmm…mmm…

TOM: I'm calling the fucking restaurant—

SAM: The restaurant is dead anyway. The restaurant is dead, this town is dead, this fucking country is dead. It just doesn't know it, yet. We're a zombie state!

TOM: You know, I could have you arrested for what you did. Breathing on my food. You're mad at me for not tipping you, whatever. But I didn't ask for any of this.

SAM: And I didn't ask for a president who doesn't believe in science. But here we are.

TOM: I recognize you, you know? My little brother, Corey. He was in your class. Your parents own Golden Dragon, am I right?

SAM: Yeah, so?

TOM: It's a small town. Word gets around.

SAM: So, what? Let the word spread. "This little slant-eyed fuck" says, enjoy your delivery, and good night!

(Sam exits. Tom looks at the bag of contaminated food through his storm door.)

CLASP
by Toby Malone

for TJ Young

CHARACTERS

JOE
ROB

SETTING

A park. Or a parking lot. Somewhere public, and indistinct. It doesn't really matter where it is, but it's definitely outside.

(At Rise, it's nighttime, and we hear the distant buzz of traffic. There's not a lot of it. There's a flickering light, as though the public streetlight is guttering. Kind of a seedy spot. Finally, a man enters, looking around. Clearly waiting for someone. This is Rob. Rob is wearing a face mask, like the kind we all know now, to ward off COVID-19. He's also wearing a ballcap with a plastic face guard on it. On top of this, he is also wearing blue surgical gloves. This guy's taking no risks. He stands, and waits, nervously. As he stands, his face guard starts to fog up a little. He looks around cautiously and takes off his hat and tries to buff it a little, but his gloves make it tough. As he's preoccupied, another man enters from the other side. He's not wearing as much PPE as Rob but he's still pretty well masked, with a bandana pulled over his lower face. This is Joe. He's looking expectantly towards Rob, thinking that this is the guy he's here to meet. As he nears, he waves awkwardly, but not being seen, he steps closer.)

JOE: Hey, man…

(Rob is completely startled, jumping back and scrambling to get his headgear back on, trying to maintain his six-feet social distance.)

ROB: Whoa!

(Joe, in turn, is startled by this reaction. He nervously gestures to make up for it.)

JOE: Sorry, dude, I…
ROB: No! It's just…You…
JOE: Sorry, man. My bad.
ROB: I'm just…not used to…
JOE: I know, sorry. I shoulda said somethin'.

(They look at each other. They're both cagey.)

ROB: Sorry, I…
JOE: Is it Rob?
ROB: Rob?
JOE: Are you Rob?
ROB: Joe?
JOE: Yeah! I'm Joe.
ROB: From Craigslist?
JOE: You got more than one of these tonight?
ROB: No, I…
JOE: A Grindr Joe, too?
ROB: No! No, I would never…
JOE: It's cool, man. I'm just teasin'. You doing okay?
ROB: Yes. Yeah. Yes. I…Yes.
JOE: Changin' your mind?
ROB: No. No! It's not that. I just…
JOE: It's weird, right?
ROB: *(Relieved for common ground)* SO weird. Six months by myself, all cooped up, I thought I was gonna go crazy.

JOE: We don't have to…

ROB: No. We do. I need to.

JOE: I wasn't sure when I…

ROB: Me either.

JOE: It was kind of just an impulse and I…

ROB: Me too.

JOE: So, you haven't done this before?

ROB: Like this? No. You?

JOE: Back before, this was never a big deal, ya know? But now…

ROB: Yeah. I know.

(Awkward beat.)

JOE: But I think I need this.

ROB: *(Hurriedly)* I do too.

JOE: Did you bring the stuff?

ROB: Yes. I'm always really careful and I…

JOE: Yeah, you look really careful.

ROB: I went in this morning.

JOE: St. Mike's?

ROB: Mount Sinai.

JOE: Okay, cool.

ROB: You?

JOE: St. Mike's, couple hours ago.

ROB: And you're good?

JOE: I wouldn'ta come if I wasn't.

ROB: Right, right. I'm just…

JOE: No, I get it.

ROB: My mom is pretty old, and I gotta be sure…

JOE: Yeah, cool man.

ROB: Can I…see it?

JOE: Like, now?

ROB: I wanna see it before anything happens.

JOE: Yeah, cool. What about yours?

ROB: Yes. Of course. Uh…mine's on my phone.

JOE: *(Embarrassingly uncool)* Oh, nice. Mount Sinai got it sorted out.

ROB: It's a text. Here.

(Rob pulls out his cell phone and holds it up to Joe. As he does, Joe pulls a piece of paper out of his back pocket and holds it up to Rob. They both take a second to figure out what they're seeing, read carefully. Finally, they're satisfied. They put their things away.)

JOE: Hey, congrats man.

ROB: Thanks. You, too.

JOE: You worried?

ROB: Clearly.

JOE: So why you doin' this then? Why not get in a bunker and wait?

ROB: Because when I read your post, I knew that's what I needed. In my heart and soul. Right now. After all of this. I need it.

JOE: *(Tearing up a little)* It's weird, right? Back before, I didn't really like people that much, but now…

ROB: Now it's different.

JOE: So, you're negative as of when?

ROB: Eleven-thirty I got the test. I didn't see anyone else as I left. Straight home, three showers. Lysol and gloves, double mask and face shield.

JOE: Damn. Makin' me look like a chump.

ROB: I…go overboard sometimes.

JOE: It's all good. We'll keep the masks on, okay?

ROB: Yes, of course.

JOE: I just don't…

ROB: I get it, I was kind of worried I'd get here and you'd tell me you wanted masks off.

JOE: Like I lured you down here to…

ROB: No! Just that you might think…

JOE: No, trust me, I'm taking this seriously. I just need something, you know? To get me through.

ROB: I get it. I hear you.

JOE: So, should we do this thing?

ROB: Right here?

JOE: Why not?

ROB: You don't mind if we're seen?

JOE: As far as anyone knows, we're in each others' bubble. Right after this we go home, disinfect, new test tomorrow, and hopefully we…

ROB: Feel better.

JOE: Right.

ROB: Okay, so how do you want to do it?

JOE: Nothing fancy, just normal style.

ROB: Okay. Here I come.

(Rob hesitatingly moves towards Joe, who also moves forward. They come close to each other, and tenderly, gently, trepidatiously, they clasp one another in a giant bear hug. And they just stand there, hugging, feeling human contact. They stand, and clasp, and breathe. This is not sexual. This is human contact.)

JOE: Oh my God.

ROB: This is…

JOE: I…

(They hang on to each other. A giant sob escapes Joe. Six months of pent-up frustration and lack of contact with the outside world bubbles out of him.)

ROB: *(Starting to pull out)* Are you…

JOE: *(Desperate not to lose contact)* I'm okay, I just…

ROB: It's okay, buddy. Let it out.

JOE: You have no idea how much I needed this.

ROB: I know, buddy, I know.

(They stand and hug for a long time. Uncomfortably long for the audience, in fact. But these two men hold each other and sway, feeling the touch of another person for the first time in six months. And just for a moment, the world is a better place. Joe gets himself under control and seems to change a little. And so, slowly, reluctantly, they disengage.)

JOE: That was…

ROB: Yeah. Wow.

JOE: I…I'm sorry. I…

ROB: I get it, man. No need to apologize.

JOE: I never do stuff like this.

ROB: You shouldn't be ashamed of who you are.

JOE: I'm not, I just…

ROB: I get it.

JOE: Anyway, I have to go.

ROB: Yeah, totally. Do you want any…

JOE: Actually, that would be great.

(Rob pulls out his Lysol and squirts some on Joe's outstretched hand. They both disinfect.)

ROB: Go get tested tomorrow, okay?

JOE: You too.

ROB: And if you want to do this again…

JOE: I don't wanna make a habit of this. It's not right.

ROB: I get it.

JOE: Sometimes you just need something different, you know?

ROB: I know. It's okay.

JOE: *(Panicking)* Don't tell anyone about this, okay?

ROB: Why would I…

JOE: Sorry. Sorry. I know.

ROB: I'm not going to tell anyone.

JOE: It's the fines, you know?

ROB: Sure.

JOE: Well, anyway. See you.

ROB: Bye, Joe.

(Joe gives Rob a long look and turns to leave. He stops short and turns around, unable to say what is on his mind.)

JOE: I…

ROB: What time's your test tomorrow?

JOE: It'll have to be after my shift. I haven't booked it yet, but maybe… three?

ROB: See you back here at four.

(Before Joe can reply, Rob smiles and walks away. Joe pulls his mask down, his lip trembling. Emotion overwhelms him as the lights go down.)

THE PEOPLE WHO CALL THE PEOPLE SHEEPLE

by David Don Miller

CHARACTERS

CAMERON	20s-50s, not exactly a conspiracy theorist, but believes in enough conspiracy theories that it really doesn't matter
TERRY	20s-50s, moderate, generally sick of polarized, radicalized thinking
MORGAN	20s-50s, vulnerable, malleable, maybe gullible, maybe cunning

SETTING

Early 2021. A lunch lounge at just about any American workplace.

(At Rise, coworkers Cameron and Terry are at a table in their employee lounge at the end of lunch. Terry wears a cloth mask. Cameron has one too, but it's lowered to chin level. Cameron has just completed some kind of rant.)

CAMERON: Hey, I'm just telling it like it is!

TERRY: But…you do realize it sounds crazy, right?

CAMERON: What's crazy about it? The guy was in federal prison. In Manhattan. On suicide watch. It's well known he had videos of the liberal elite on his private plane doing all kinds of shady stuff! You don't think they had him put to death to cover their tracks!?

TERRY: No, no. Not that part. That seems plausible. Even though the names on that fly list were a far cry from just the liberal elite.

CAMERON: So, what's your problem?

TERRY: My problem starts when you say they are trafficking children through a network of pizza places! And that there is a cabal of Satan-worshipping pedophiles running the country who are murdering babies and taking extract from their adrenaline glands because it gets them high!

(Beat.)

CAMERON: I'm just telling it like it is.

TERRY: Like it is?! That is completely outer limits! Tinfoil hat time!

CAMERON: You trust the government? You trust the media? Gah, I feel sorry for you.

TERRY: Listen. I've always thought that a healthy skepticism of media and government is a good idea, but to dismiss everything they say out of hand is…is madness! You've been taken in by the tactics of a fascist!

CAMERON: Here we go! Comparing everyone to Hitler! And you say I sound crazy!

TERRY: Did I call anyone a fascist?! I said the tactics of a fascist.

CAMERON: You mean like taking away our guns? Don't get me started!

TERRY: No! Get started! You already started! Nobody's taking away your damn guns!

CAMERON: Then why are bullets so expensive all of a sudden?

TERRY: Oh, I don't know, maybe because all the gun nuts think their guns are going to be taken away? So they buy up all the ammo? Deplete the supply, raise the demand? Gee, I know it sounds crazy. It's called Capitalism!

CAMERON: Soon to be communism. Don't even get me started.

TERRY: Oh, okay.

CAMERON: Don't think so?

TERRY: Do you even know what communism is?!

CAMERON: You think I'm stupid?

TERRY: I didn't say that. I asked you what communism is.

(Beat.)

CAMERON: It's what they got in Russia!

TERRY: Really?

(Beat.)

CAMERON: China. And they're trying to pull the same mind control crap right here. You think I got this mask on by choice?

TERRY: Yeah, no, I get it. Only two million people are dead. Why kick up a fuss?

CAMERON: You believe that? I feel sorry for you.

TERRY: What the hell do you mean?! They're dead! You're saying they're not?

CAMERON: Maybe they are, maybe they aren't, but they're sure not all dead from the PLANdemic.

TERRY: Plandemic.

CAMERON: Do you even doubt it?

TERRY: Doubt what exactly?

CAMERON: I can show you…all kinds of stuff on YouTube. Guy goes into the hospital with cancer and dies. They say it's the Corona. Woman falls down with a broken hip and dies. They say it's the Corona. Somebody's in a frickin' car accident. Corona.

TERRY: And what would they stand to gain by that?

CAMERON: Follow the white rabbit!

TERRY: What white rabbit?

CAMERON: The white rabbit'll lead you to the money! Follow the money!

TERRY: What money?

CAMERON: The money the government gives them.

TERRY: For?

CAMERON: For saying people died of the Corona! And now they're trying to push out these vaccines? Don't get me started.

TERRY: Stop saying that! *(Beat)* So, you're not gonna take it?

CAMERON: What? The vaccine? Hell no! Are you?

TERRY: I don't know yet.

CAMERON: You're thinkina puttin' that crap in your body? You don't know what that does!

TERRY: Well, presumably it's going to stop me from getting sick.

CAMERON: Stop you from getting sick? It's gonna make you sick, and that's what they want! And that's just the beginning! Who knows what they're giving you?! It's all part of the plandemic!

(Beat.)

TERRY: Morgan's gettin' it.

CAMERON: What?!

TERRY: *(Consulting his phone)* In fact, he's probably on his way back here right now.

CAMERON: Oh my god, no!

TERRY: Why don't we see what he has to say about it before we jump to conclusions?

CAMERON: Because I'm already past that! I've heard the call to action.

TERRY: On YouTube?

CAMERON: And Facebook. And I suggest you wake up before you wind up like the rest of these sheeple!

TERRY: Sheeple, huh?

CAMERON: Yeah, sheeple!

TERRY: You know, every time I hear someone say that word, or read it on the internet, all I have to do is dig a thought or two deeper, and you know what I find?

CAMERON: What?

TERRY: The people calling the people sheeple are the sheeple.

CAMERON: The people…what!? Listen, I don't wanna get in a thing with you. You do you, that's your business, but I've seen through all this already. The Media, the Left, the String Pullers, the Puppet Masters—the Communists…they're all in it together. And you can bury your head in the sand and call me names, but I'm gonna be patient because I care about you. God cares about you. But he also needs you to wake up to the evil before you can understand the evil.

TERRY: The EVIL!?!

CAMERON: Wakey, wakey. Eggs and bakey.

(Enter Morgan, stiffly. He looks affected. Hard wired in some odd, electric way. He quivers as he quietly sits. Cameron and Terry watch him with grave concern. With a shaky hand, Morgan pulls down his mask to have a sip of water from a plastic bottle, but the shaking is so severe he can barely get the bottle to his mouth.)

CAMERON: Hey. You okay?

MORGAN: I…I don't know. I…think so. *(He quivers a bit more)* M-maybe not, I don't know.

CAMERON: What happened?

MORGAN: Th—th—the—they…the place was run like…a well-oiled machine. There were lines of patients…And they had these stations with medical people, masked people, but people also wearing face shields and they…they were so friendly…almost too friendly. I moved right through—boom boom boom. And then…I got to one woman…And I answered a bunch of questions…and filled out some papers…and I was taken to a room…and another woman asked me the same questions all over again…including my name and date of birth…and then? She stuck the shot in my arm!

CAMERON: *(To Terry)* Ya see?

TERRY: See what?

CAMERON: When's the last time any medical facility you been in worked that efficiently?

TERRY: When's the last time they needed to roll out a vaccine for a friggin' pandemic?

CAMERON: You're really buying into this! I feel sorry for you.

TERRY: Buying into what!?

CAMERON: The Democrats' plot to bankrupt our citizens and sell us to the Communists!

TERRY: Oh, my f—…Will you listen to yourself? You're out of your mind!

MORGAN: AND EVERYTHING WENT BLACK AFTER THAT!!!

(Terry and Cameron freeze.)

MORGAN: Everything went black and…I could feel some kind of… anesthesia-type substance coursing through my veins…

(Terry and Cameron are riveted.)

MORGAN: BUT IT WAS DIFFERENT…!

(Terry and Cameron jump, startled but still riveted.)

MORGAN: Because even in the darkness…my brain still worked. I could hear…I could feel them lift me onto a gurney…and wheel me down a hall…and…must've made a mistake because…I don't think I was supposed to hear or feel what happened next.

(Terry and Cameron are utterly galvanized, hanging on Morgan's every word, who is beginning to quiver more vigorously, this time edging up on an emotional breakdown.)

MORGAN: I…could hear them talking about ch-ch-ch-ch-chip placement…whether I was going to be a better candidate for the one that we swallow or…the microscopic version that g-g-gets injected into the blood. And I hear them get on a call…a Zoom call to some…Communistical enclave…and…I don't know what the guy said on the other end because…it was all some kind of Communese!…and then…whoever was in the room with me, he started speaking it back! Then the nurse… then someone else…I guess he must've been the anesthesiologist because as soon as he said something, he hits me with another needle and…*(Crying)* I came to for just a second…and I could see all their faces! Their masked, terrible faces! Why was there a whole team of medical personnel around me!? For what was supposed to be a vaccine shot!? And the people in the room! They weren't even Communistic!…They were…Americans! Just like you and me…SPEAKING Communese! They've…they've…BOUGHT! RETRAINED! REPROGRAMMED…THIS PANDEMIC!… THIS VACCINE! It's…AN INSIDE JOB!!!

(He shakes more vigorously. Cameron pulls out his phone and starts recording.)

CAMERON: Can you back up and say like all of that all over again?
TERRY: What the hell's the matter with you? He needs our help!

(Terry comes to Morgan and puts his hands on his back to steady

the quivering.)

TERRY: Morgan! Morgan, you alright? *(It's not working)* I think I better call 911.

(As Terry pulls out his phone, Morgan suddenly acts like he is hearing a voice.)

MORGAN: What?!...Yes!...I will! I can do that...I will do what you say...I will wear a mask. For all the rest of my days! *(He pulls his mask from his chin back to his face)* I will spread your fear. I will spread your lies. I will spread the dogma of the Deep State. I will bankrupt my comrades...I will sell them into servitude...I will vote blue...I will falsify other votes for blue...I will support the anti-gun lobbies...I will support my local sex trafficker-slash-adrenochrome dealer-slash-pizza place...I WILL CHAMPION THE WORDS OF AOC!!! I will...I will...I will...

(He faints and collapses on the floor. Terry rushes to help him.)

TERRY: Morgan!!!

CAMERON: Holy crap, this is gonna go viral.

TERRY: WHAT IN GOD'S NAME IS THE MATTER WITH YOU!?! HE NEEDS OUR HELP!

CAMERON: It's too late for him. But not for you. Or me. I'm gonna post this, sit back, and watch the storm from the shelter of my home.

TERRY: But there won't be any shelter from this!

CAMERON: Tell that to my shot gun, my AR-15, and my many, many glocks. People are gonna wake up. Finally.

TERRY: Don't do it! No, Cameron, don't go! Okay, I believe you!

(Cameron stops) You were right all along, okay? Please don't go.

(Cameron leaves. Terry watches him go. A count of five seconds. Morgan slowly, calmly gets up and sits. Terry scoffs and shakes his head as he walks to his chair and sits. They face off. Morgan chuckles.)

MORGAN: Told you.
TERRY: Unfriggin' believable.

(Terry pulls out a wad of cash and slaps it down in front of Morgan.)

MORGAN: Double or nothing his video really does goes viral.

THE VARIANT
by Robert Paul Moreira

CHARACTERS

FATHER	Late 40s
DAUGHTER	Eighth-grade Student
FRIEND 1	Female, same age as Daughter
FRIEND 2	Female; same age as Daughter

SETTING

Fall, 2020. A bright morning in South Texas. In the car outside Daughter's junior high on the first day of school.

(At Rise, Father and Daughter sit side-by-side in the car, waiting for the line to move up to the front gate. Friend 1 and 2 stand stage right and left, both wearing masks and typing into their iPhones. As the Friends type away and deliver their messages with rising intensity, Daughter scrolls through her iPhone in growing discomfort.)

FRIEND 1: u BITCH!
FRIEND 2: SLUT!
FRIEND 1: HO!
FRIEND 2: STUPID!
FRIEND 1: LOSER!
FRIEND 2: FREAK!
FRIEND 1: RETARD!
FRIEND 2: THOUGHT WE FORGOT?
FRIEND 1: IDIOT!
FRIEND 2: WORTHLESS!
FRIEND 1: TRANNY!
FRIEND 2: LESBO!
FRIEND 1: WTF R U?

FRIEND 2: USELESS!

FRIEND 1: TOTAL ZERO!

FRIEND 2: PILE OF SHIT!

FRIEND 1: go CUT urself again!

FRIEND 2: go PUNCH urself!

FRIEND 1: go STAB urself!

FRIEND 2: go HANG urself!

FRIEND 1: u should DIE!

FRIEND 2: KILL urself!

FRIEND 1: no one cares HAHA!

FRIEND 2: no one cares HAHAHA!!!

FRIEND 1: ur UGLY face!

FRIEND 2: HIDEOUS!

FRIEND 1: HORRIFIC!

FRIEND 2: MONSTER!

FRIEND 1: yeah MONSTER!!!

FRIEND 2: ur parents shouldve ABORTED!

FRIEND 1: ur parents DIVORCED because of u!

FRIEND 2: ANIME sux!

FRIEND 1: MITSKI sux!

FRIEND 2: POPPY sux!

FRIEND 1: MELANIE M sux!

FRIEND 2: ZHEANI 2!

FRIEND 1: ALL UR MUSIC SUKS!!

FRIEND 2: BIG BALLS SUKS HAHA !!

FRIEND 1: whats the point HAHA?

FRIEND 2: of BEING U HAHA???

FRIEND 1: of LIVING HAHA?

FRIEND 2: of EXISTING haha?

FRIEND 1 AND 2: *(Top of their lungs)* WHATS THE POINT HAHA???
WHATS THE POINT HAHA???
WHATS THE POINT HAHA???

HAHAHAHA!!!!!!!

(Daughter drops her phone frantically. Pause. Lights fade on Friends.)

FATHER: *(In good spirits, to Daughter)* Hey, hey, are we that nervous? Don't worry, we're almost up front, Miss Eighth Grader! I want you to have a fantastic first day, okay? Oh, and don't forget that today is also momentous. Thanks to our great Texas governor, you don't have to wear this anymore. *(He dangles a face mask from his forefinger)* Isn't that wonderful?

(Beat. She rips the mask from him and puts it on. They both sigh and stare deep into the Audience.)

ONE KIND OF FEAR
by Laura Neill

CHARACTERS

CJ	New Nurse
ALEX	Experienced Nurse

SETTING

An empty hospital room.

(At Rise, CJ enters and sees Alex.)

CJ: Miss Alex?

CJ: What are you doing in here? Sorry. I mean. I think Dr. A is looking for you.

ALEX: I'll be there in a minute.

CJ: Is there anything I can help you with?

ALEX: No.

CJ: If you're doing an equipment check, I can do it for you. I know things are busy.

ALEX: Things are busy? Is that what we're calling it?

CJ: I guess.

ALEX: I don't have to do an equipment check. I know what the status is.

CJ: Yeah.

ALEX: You can go back to whatever you're doing, you don't have to babysit me.

CJ: Right. I wasn't trying to…

ALEX: I just meant, I'm fine.

CJ: I didn't think you weren't fine.

ALEX: Oh.

CJ: Are you not fine?

ALEX: No, no. I just told you, I'm fine.

CJ: Okay, good.

ALEX: Okay, good.

CJ: Then I think Dr. A…

ALEX: In a minute.

(A moment.)

CJ: Are you going to do hospital corners?

ALEX: What?

CJ: My mom was a nurse too, and sometimes when my dad got home and they had a fight, she'd come upstairs to my and my sister's room and make our bed with hospital corners. Even though it was already perfect. It made her feel better, I guess.

ALEX: Hospital corners.

CJ: Yeah.

ALEX: I'm not upset.

CJ: Got it.

ALEX: Is your mom all right?

CJ: What?

ALEX: She must be older. Is she doing all right now?

CJ: Oh, I—well. She's on her own in Jersey. She won't let anyone come visit her, now.

ALEX: Right.

CJ: I mean, we can't.

ALEX: I know.

CJ: But my mom isn't that old. I mean, how old do you think I am? So I keep telling myself she's going to be okay.

ALEX: Right.

CJ: Are you worried about your mom?

ALEX: Is that your way of reminding me that, unlike you, I'm old as dirt?

CJ: No, I just—

ALEX: I'm not worried about my mom. Or I am, but I'm not in here because I'm worried about my mom.

CJ: I know, you're not upset.

ALEX: *(Suddenly)* I'm worried about me. For the first time in my life, I'm worried about me. And I don't know what to do with it.

(A moment.)

CJ: You're always telling trainees that it's okay to be scared.

ALEX: That's something I say.

CJ: All right.

ALEX: It's okay to be scared at the beginning, when everything is new, when you get blood on your shirt for the first time, all right? It's okay to be scared then.

CJ: And it goes away?

ALEX: No, of course not. I mean, you'll always care a little when someone codes.

CJ: A little.

ALEX: There isn't enough room. With everything we do, there isn't enough room to care about everything. There isn't enough room for all this fear.

CJ: It's okay to be scared now.

ALEX: NO. Because when I am scared, when I am scared for myself instead of being scared for them, I end up hiding in our one empty room and hoping no one will find me even though Dr. A is looking for me and 413 needs dinner and 417 needs meds.

CJ: I'll cover 413 and 417 and Dr. A.

ALEX: And you'll get infected for me, and you'll take it home to someone you love.

CJ: I have a mask.

ALEX: For now. For now you have a mask.

CJ: Plus, I only have roommates. Craigslist, you know.

ALEX: You think this is funny?

CJ: I think you can't think about it! Because if you think about it, you end up here and you stay here, and you can't stay in this empty room right now.

ALEX: I know.

CJ: There are people who need our help.

ALEX: I KNOW. My whole life there have been people who need my help and I have given it to them. I have given every inch of myself to this hospital and the people who walk or roll through its doors, and I have not been afraid. I have been caring and giving and sarcastic when they need it, and more than that, I have been Precise and On Point and Done My Job Well. I have seen broken bones and broken lungs and bloody brains and sure, I have been scared, but never, not once before today, have I been scared for myself. And now my hands are shaking. *(She holds them up)* My hands are shaking.

(A moment.)

CJ: Watch.

(CJ loops one of her own hands into the other.)

ALEX: What are you doing?

CJ: My hands shake all the time. Try it.

ALEX: I don't have time for newbie games—

CJ: Looks like you do.

(CJ demonstrates holding her own hands again. After a moment, Alex does it, reluctantly.)

CJ: Now your forearms.

ALEX: This is silly.

CJ: It's not. (*And Alex grips her own forearms*) Now…

(And CJ wraps her arms around her own torso. Alex looks reluctant, but she does it. They are standing there, giving themselves hugs.)

CJ: Squeeze. *(They do)* There are things we can't fix, Miss Alex, and there are times we're gonna be scared. Because there are gonna be times when we have to rely on other people to get their act together and help us. To get us what we need to do our jobs. And that freaks me out, too. Because we're nurses. We're the people who never rely on anyone else, because we're the ones everyone turns to. Right? *(She hugs herself, Alex nods.)* And, Miss Alex, that's beautiful. That's beautiful that we've been that for everyone, that we were able to do that for so long. Well, so long in your case, not so long in mine. But it's gonna be beautiful when other people get their act together, too. It's gonna be beautiful when some feds walk in that door with those N95s. It's going to be perfect. Until then, all we can do is hold our own hands and give ourselves a hug. That much, we can always do. Miss Alex? You can always hold on to yourself.

(A moment.)

ALEX: And how did you get so smart, newbie?

CJ: Well, I've been absolutely terrified every day I've walked in here, so for me, this isn't that much of a shift.

ALEX: *(Laughing)* You were already peeing yourself.

CJ: And crying in the bathroom every day. Yes, ma'am.

ALEX: But it's a different kind of fear, CJ.

CJ: No, it isn't, Miss Alex. There's only one kind of fear. The kind we don't let stop us.

(Alex nods.)

ALEX: Dr. A was looking for me, right?

CJ: Yes, Miss Alex.

ALEX: Just Alex is fine.

(They share a smile, a deep breath. Alex leaves for work.)

THE CULLING WORLD

by Joyce Newman Scott

CHARACTERS

ANNIE	50s, a housewife, paranoid and going insane
BRUCE	50s, her husband, living in an apartment closing in on him

SETTING

The kitchen. The present, or the not too far future.

(At Rise, Annie washes dishes. She glares disapprovingly at Bruce as he unwraps a food container and tosses it in the trash.)

ANNIE: What are you doing?

BRUCE: What? It all goes in the same place.

ANNIE: It's recyclable.

BRUCE: One tiny plastic container? Who's gonna notice?

ANNIE: *(Overtly emotional)* That's right. Who will notice with all the other headlines, and political fighting…not to mention a deadly virus.

BRUCE: Okay, what's really bothering you?

ANNIE: Have you seen what happened with the minks recently?

BRUCE: The minks…the minks…again. Tell me why you're obsessed with the minks.

ANNIE: Because they brutally killed 17,000,000 tiny animals. Men dressed in hazmat suits chased and picked up the feral ones by their tails…tossed them into a wood pulper. I couldn't hear over the roar of the engines, but I imagined them screaming as they went in.

BRUCE: *(Trying to calm her)* Fake news. You know, people trying to foist more fear on us. Irresponsible journalism. That's what the president's been saying, right?

(Annie shoots him a dirty look. They've had this argument before. Beat.)

ANNIE: I saw the pictures on the BBC. Then read about it in *The Wall Street Journal* and *Financial Times*.

BRUCE: Okay. What if it's true?

ANNIE: So, you admit that it's true? I'm not exaggerating this?

BRUCE: They gassed the ones designed to breed, right? I mean…what about all the farmers who lost generations of their livelihood? Their economy is now crumbling.

ANNIE: That's what this boils down to. Greed. Money. Failed economy? *(Beat)*…they showed videos of the caged ones, being gassed then loaded onto trucks. Tiny little innocent lifeless bodies loaded onto shelves. It was horrible…where is the compassion for life?

(She starts to cry, and Bruce puts an arm around her to comfort her.)

BRUCE: The word is CULLED. And at least they gassed the caged ones. And buried them. That was humane. And it was necessary to kill them all to stop the virus. Every war has its sacrificial lambs.

ANNIE: *(Fighting her building anger)* But it didn't stop the virus, did it?

BRUCE: What do you mean?

ANNIE: This morning they showed pictures of the dead bodies surfacing from one large mass grave…the gasses they used to kill the poor little creatures…made them rise out of the ground. The decaying bodies are now polluting the water and air. *(Beat)* One COVID virus mutates into another virus. It mutates, Bruce. Doesn't that scare you?

BRUCE: It's happening in Denmark, that's a long way from here. And that article isn't even a main headline here in the states.

ANNIE: Where does this all stop? We're not hearing a big deal about it. And the COVID virus started in Wuhan, and we didn't hear anything about it until it was too late. Now, hundreds of millions of people are dead. And there are people still who believe this is all a stunt to gain sensationalism.

BRUCE: For Christ's sake. Annie stop! I can't do this anymore. We used to travel. San Francisco. London. Paris. We laughed. We sang. Now, it's isolation. We haven't left this apartment in a…I feel like the walls are closing in on me. I want my old life back.

ANNIE: It's too late.

BRUCE: So, what's the latest on this strain?

ANNIE: The hospitals in the UK are separating the new class of virus. It's not responding to the inoculations. We haven't even found a cure, and Mother Nature is figuring out a way to screw us. *(Beat)* Shh…listen. You can hear them.

BRUCE: *(Staring, concerned about her mental state)* Honey…stop. Did you call the doctor, like I asked you to?

ANNIE: I'm not crazy, Bruce. Mother Nature is trying to CULL us. *(Beat)* I think climate change and all the issues we're facing are totally related and linked together. The identical thing.

(Bruce opens a cabinet door, looks for something, then slams it closed. Like a tiger trapped in a cage)

BRUCE: Stop. I'm begging you. I just can't take it.

ANNIE: We're locked down…and nature explodes someplace else.

Maybe the earth is an organism that has its own biology. What if WE are the virus? If we don't change our behavior, the Earth will find a way to get rid of us…so it can live.

BRUCE: Please, stop. Shh. Breathe. Just breathe.

ANNIE: What if we start to become those bodies? Little minks. What if before you know it, the trucks are coming for us?

BRUCE: Honey, that's irrational.

ANNIE: Is it?

(She dries her eyes. And wipes her hands on a towel. Outside, the sound of a large truck grinding its motor grows louder, fiercer, more menacing. They stare at each other in a palpable alarm, as panic sets in.)

BRUCE: What do you think that was?

ANNIE: It's either the recyclable pickup truck… or…

BRUCE: *(With building terror)* A wood pulping truck to come for the human bodies?

ANNIE: Bruce…Are we…are we the minks?

(Outside, we hear the piercing sound of a woman. She screams. A painful, agonizing cry. There's a knock on the door; Bruce answers. As he opens it, he sees a man in full hazmat gear.)

MAN IN HAZMAT SUIT: *(As solemn as a funeral director)* Come with me, please. It's your turn.

(Bruce clutches Annie in his arms, protectively, just as the light fades.)

ZOOM LIKE NO ONE IS WATCHING

by Serena Norr

CHARACTERS

DAVID	35, Teacher
HILLY	37, a Mother of five

SETTING

A Zoom Meeting; March, 2020, 5:40pm.

(At Rise, David enters a Zoom chat. He adjusts his bow-tie and sits up. Hilly enters the chat. She is wearing an oversized t-shirt, and her hair is placed in a messy bun. Her video isn't on.)

HILLY: *(Confused)* Helloooo? Is this thing on? Freakin' technology!

DAVID: Hi, there, Hilly! It's me, David! I'm here, but I can't see your face.

HILLY: I hate this shit.

(The clicking of the keys is heard for a few beats. Her face finally appears on the screen.)

DAVID: It's working now!

HILLY: I'm such a boob when it comes to technology. None of this stuff comes naturally to me.

DAVID: It's not for everyone. So, um…is this your first time?

HILLY: Clearly! So, what do we do now?

DAVID: Oh, I don't know. Talk…get to know each other.

HILLY: Sounds thrilling. You look like your profile picture, you know.

DAVID: Thank you!

HILLY: That's not a good thing.

DAVID: Oh. Okay. So, umm…tell me more about yourself.

HILLY: It was pretty much summed up in my bio. Did you even read the damn thing?

DAVID: Yeah, but those things don't really paint the picture of who we really are.

HILLY: Not like the two lonely losers we actually are.

DAVID: Speak for yourself! I'm not a loser, at least, I don't think I am.

HILLY: But lonely?

DAVID: Yeah, well, life isn't easy right now. I actually did one of these things last week. But it didn't go so well.

HILLY: Why not?

DAVID: We didn't click, as they say.

HILLY: So, you're a freak?

DAVID: No. No. Well, maybe I am. Maybe we all are.

HILLY: Speak for yourself, buddy. I'm as normal as they come. So…you're a teacher or something?

DAVID: Yeah. I teach seventh grade science.

HILLY: Damn, that's a rough age.

DAVID: It's not as bad as people make it out to be. I mean, they are awkward and weird. Kind of like me. I like it enough. What about you? I think that part was blank on your profile.

HILLY: I'm in between stuff. I was waitressing at a BBQ place before everything shutdown.

DAVID: That's cool.

HILLY: *(Laughs)* No, it's not. It was just a job. I needed something to get me by…for now.

DAVID: I hear ya. *(Takes a swig of his beer)* Cheers!

(Hilly takes a drink of her Mountain Dew.)

DAVID: What you got there?

HILLY: Mountain Dew. There's nothing else like it. I don't drink alcohol.

DAVID: Okay. That's cool.

HILLY: Yeah—I got rabid a few too many times. Gotta stick to things I can control now.

DAVID: Like a wild beast?

HILLY: Like a fucking train wreck, man. You have so many jokes.

DAVID: Yeah—I'm full of them. So, ummm…have you done anything fun…while you've been at home?

HILLY: Don't have time for fun with five kids to homeschool.

DAVID: Kids?

HILLY: Yeah, kids. Is that a problem?

DAVID: No. No. I just didn't know. So, ummm…how old are they?

HILLY: Nineteen, seventeen, sixteen, nine, and four.

DAVID: Shit. That's a lot of kids. How old are you?

HILLY: You're rude. You should never ask a grown woman how old she is.

DAVID: Sorry. It's just…some of those kids are like old…like they're almost adults.

HILLY: Now, you get what I mean when I say I'm in-between things. I've spent most of my life having children.

DAVID: You must have your hands full.

HILLY: I hate that phrase. People who have no idea what the hell to say, say stupid shit like that.

DAVID: Sorry. It just sounds…exhausting. I can barely get myself together and you have four people to deal with.

HILLY: Six people. I'm tired. Every single day. I feel it in my bones. Which is why this is nice…to see other people who don't want something from me. Who aren't constantly demanding of me.

DAVID: You must have been young when you started having them.

HILLY: I was 16, or was it 17? Whatever, it's all in the past—I don't live there anymore. Life's a bitch.

DAVID: Or some might say a beach.

HILLY: What?

DAVID: Nothing. Now, I'm the idiot.

HILLY: We are all dumbasses. Some of us are better at hiding it. So, do you go first or should I?

DAVID: Go first?

HILLY: Take off your shirt.

DAVID: I think you're confused.

HILLY: Oh, man, c'mon! We've gone through the pleasantries, now it's time to get down to business.

DAVID: I think you've gotten this wrong. The date is just like a talk…a "get to know you" sorta thing.

HILLY: So, you've never messed around on a first date?

DAVID: Well, I guess…but this is Zoom, and I don't think you do that here. I don't even know you.

HILLY: You're really boring.

DAVID: So, I've been told. But we could talk…get to know each other or whatever.

HILLY: I was able to escape for 15 minutes. Any more than that and they will start looking for me. So, if you want to waste our time talking, so be it.

(David loosens his tie and takes a swig of his beer.)

DAVID: So…ummm…how long have you been divorced?

HILLY: You are a fucking idiot.

DAVID: What? I'm just curious.

HILLY: *(Takes a sip of her drink)* I'm not divorced.

DAVID: What? So, why are you on this call?

HILLY: I'm getting divorced. I just have to break it to Dave. It's a process…

DAVID: Your husband's name is Dave? Okay—that's a little weird.

HILLY: Things are only as weird as you make them out to be. Stop making such a big deal out of nothing.

DAVID: I guess I'm a "live by the rules" sorta guy.

HILLY: Yeah, how's that working out for you?

DAVID: *(Thinks)* It's not.

HILLY: I feel bad for you.

DAVID: I could say the same for you.

HILLY: You could, but you really don't know shit about my life. About my struggles.

DAVID: And you don't know shit about mine! I was actually looking for someone real. Someone real to talk to…to maybe date.

HILLY: Like the girl from last week.

DAVID: Yeah.

HILLY: I could be that girl.

DAVID: I don't think so.

HILLY: What's it like to follow the rules until you are just a shell of a person? Hasn't this quarantine taught you anything about life?

DAVID: It's taught me a lot, actually. My Dad died from it.

HILLY: Shit.

DAVID: So, I don't appreciate you telling me I'm a loser or a weirdo or something. I've been through a lot. I don't know how I'm supposed to live without him.

HILLY: Damn, I'm so sorry. I don't know how to stop sometimes.

DAVID: And you know the worst part? I didn't believe in any of this shit when it first started happening. I was still going out and living my life, or whatever you want to call it, until he got it. And even then, it didn't seem real.

HILLY: None of this seems real.

DAVID: What if your husband finds out?

HILLY: He's barely my husband anymore. He hasn't been for years. He's a shell of who he was, and I was too, but I don't want to live like that anymore. I still need to be touched, to be kissed, to feel someone's love.

DAVID: Maybe we can chat again.

HILLY: Yeah, maybe.

DAVID: I loosened my tie for you.

HILLY: Look at you! Living on the edge.

DAVID: For me, it is.

HILLY: Good. I'm proud of you. *(She removes her shirt; she is in a bra)* Can you see what I did for you?

DAVID: Oh, yes. I do.

HILLY: Dance for me.

DAVID: What?

HILLY: Dance! Or is that something you don't do on Zoom.

DAVID: I don't dance.

HILLY: Everyone can dance. Just move your body and don't overthink it.

(Hilly gets up and starts to move. She doesn't adjust her camera, so you only see the lower half of her body dancing.)

HILLY: Dance with me.

(David gets up and adjusts his camera so he can still be seen. He dances.)

DAVID: This is kind of fun.

(They dance together; get lost in the moment.)

DAVID: Hilly, you have to adjust the camera. I can't see your face.

(Hilly is deep in the dance and doesn't hear David. He brushes it off and continues to dance.)

HILLY: There you go. Feel free! You are alive.

DAVID: I feel amazing!

(There is a knock at Hilly's door. It continues to get louder.)

VOICE: MOM! I need to use the computer! MOM! C'mon! What are you doing in there?

HILLY: *(Sits back down, puts her shirt back on)* Shit, party's over.

DAVID: Oh, no! I'm having so much fun with you. Hilly, I don't know…I was thinking…Can we do this tomorrow?

(Hilly's Zoom square goes black; she's left the meeting.)

DAVID: Hilly? Hilly?

(David gets up and continues to dance. He realizes his Zoom meeting is still on and leaves the meeting.)

THAT'S WHAT 911 IS FOR

by Ayvaunn Penn

CHARACTERS

SOMALIA FLINT	20s, Female, any Race; abused woman seeking help
ALEX FLINT	20s, Male, any Race, and her abusive husband; also in Chorus
CHORUS	Any race, all other characters

SETTING

2020; USA; Any Busy City Street, Grocery Store Interior/Exterior

(At Rise, a single person in a mask is walking briskly. Then a second person. Then a third, then fourth, then fifth. The trickle of people becomes a sea of people in masks. Heads bob up and down as they walk. It is fluid motion. This fluid motion becomes dancing—dancing that tells the story of city hustle and bustle. It feels like the crowded sidewalks of New York, except everyone is six feet apart. Every now and then, someone breeches social distancing, causing a brief fallout before fluid motion and rhythm is regained. All of the masks are white except for one that is red. It is on a woman. Her name is Somalia Flint. The aforementioned action continues throughout the following lines until otherwise noted.)

CHORUS: These are the times we relax
These are the times we spend time with family
In these times we make bread instead of buying it
It's a trend
These are the times we binge-watch TV
These are the times we eat through worn pocket books
These are the times we make countless trips to the pantry and

refrigerator
These are the times we gain weight then watch positive body image videos on YouTube
We use this time to better ourselves
We use this time to become our best selves
We use these times to mourn loss
In this newly limited time, we try to live before we die
These are the times of COVID

SOMALIA FLINT: These are the times I fear
There is no relaxation for me
These are the times I wish I was near extended family
In these times, he kneads my face for his bread of power
For yeast he uses my tears
This has been a trend for years
These are the times I binge watch the joy of others just out of my reach
These are the times I eat through worn sorrows
These are the times I make countless trips to the grocery store
Buy nothing
Window shop for safety
These are the times I lose weight but wish I could gain it
I wish he'd use this time to better himself
I want to use this time to better myself
I use this time to mourn loss
The COVID shut down gave you time to pursue your passions and work from home
The COVID shut down took my job and locked me up with the devil
But for now I'm out
Notice how I walk briskly
Notice how I notice the wind on my face
Notice how I notice this mask is perfect for hiding my bruised lips

I notice that you notice I'm wearing sunglasses even though it's cloudy
Don't worry about that
Just keep walking
If only social distancing could be enforced at home, too
Six feet between me and you

CHORUS: Six feet between me and you

SOMALIA FLINT: I never thought I'd need a stranger near, but I do.

CHORUS: Six feet between me and you
Six feet between me and you

(Continuous flux of movement. The masked crowd dissipates briefly leaving Somalia alone on stage before they reenter. This time, the Chorus members form the aisles and shelves of a grocery store. Others reenter with shopping baskets and carts. Chorus members acting as shelves hold grocery goods. When shoppers need something from a shelf, "the shelf" places the item(s) into the shoppers' carts and/or baskets. This new world builds around Somalia. She stands in the midst. The shoppers navigate the aisles like ants marching through an ant farm. There is a synchronized rhythm to their movement. They all move in a single direction; all aisles are one way.)

SOMALIA FLINT: *(Pursuing after a shopper)* Excuse me
Excuse me, miss
Ex…excuse me
May I um
I know this is an unusual request, but…
May I please borrow your…?
May I please borrow your cell phone?

SHOPPER 1: I'm sure the store has a phone you can use.

(Shopper 1 continues on her way.)

SOMALIA FLINT: Excuse me
    Excuse me, sir

(Shopper 2 rushes past.)

SOMALIA FLINT: Excuse me
    May I
    Do you
    Do you have a moment?
    It's an emergency
SHOPPER 3: That's what 911 is for

(Shopper 3 hurries off.)

SOMALIA FLINT: Someone please
    This is my moment
    Someone please
    This is my chance
    I don't often get away from my husband
    It's now or never
    (Removes her mask to reveal her busted lip) I can't be gone too much longer or he'll be suspicious
CHORUS: We're suspicious of you
    Reaffix your mask
    6 feet
STORE MANAGER: Miss
    What seems to be the problem?
SOMALIA FLINT: Do you have a phone I could use?
STORE MANAGER: We have a phone, but it's not for public use
SOMALIA FLINT: An exception
    Please?

STORE MANAGER: I'm sorry
Not for public use
SOMALIA FLINT: My matter is urgent
STORE MANAGER: Store policy
I'm sorry
CHORUS: We're sorry
There's shopping to be done
Shopping to be done
6 feet
6 feet
Keep your distance
STORE MANAGER: But customer service is what I do
SOMALIA FLINT: Oh, thank you
STORE MANAGER: At the coffee shop at the front of the store is a charging station for your phone
SOMALIA FLINT: But I don't
STORE MANAGER: I'm more than happy to charge your phone for you while you shop
SOMALIA FLINT: I don't have a phone, that's why
STORE MANAGER: Oh
Well I'm sorry
That's what I can do
CHORUS: That's what s/he can do
STORE MANAGER: You might try the pay phone outside
SOMALIA FLINT: But…
STORE MANAGER: Let us know if you need anything else
CHORUS: 6 feet
STORE MANAGER: It's our pleasure to serve you

(Store Manager scurries off.)

CHORUS: 6 feet

(The flux of shoppers continues in their rhythmic flow through the aisles.)

SOMALIA FLINT: Spare change anyone?

(The Chorus of shoppers break rhythm and scatter. The shelf Chorus members immediately follow. Some go off stage while others remain and reconfigure into passersby on the street and a pay phone. This all transpires in fluid continuous movement. Somalia stands in the midst. She checks her old watch. She squints to read through the cracked face.)

SOMALIA FLINT: Gotta hurry
Gotta hurry
Gotta hurry
(To the passerby) Excuse me
Excuse me please
Do you have spare change?
Do any of you have spare change?
I need to use the pay phone
CHORUS: Who doesn't have spare change?
SOMALIA FLINT: I don't!
I don't have spare change
Nor do I have spare time

(Somalia removes her mask, revealing her busted lip; then, her sunglasses, revealing her black eye.)

SOMALIA FLINT: This is an urgent matter

(Staggered, the Chorus freezes and gasps as they stare at Somalia's

bludgeoned face. The passerby freeze one by one until finally everyone is still. Awkward silence. Beat.)

CHORUS: Urgent matters call for 911
Calling 911 is free
Reaffix your mask
6 feet

(The Chorus resumes their bustle down the street. Somalia looks at her watch, the pay phone, then back at her watch. Then, the pay phone. She picks up the receiver. Since the payphone is comprised of Chorus members, picking up the phone looks like taking one of the Chorus members by the arm and speaking into their hand. Oh, the irony. At a glance, it looks as though a hand is outstretched to stroke Somalia's cheek in comfort. But alas, that is not the case. Or, could it be that the pay phone is the only fragment of consolation that appears? To dial 911, Somalia draws the numbers on the chest of the Chorus member acting as the phone receiver. This has a rotary phone feel. With the completion of each number drawn, we hear a chime. The Phone Receiver Chorus Member creates a vocal ring tone and proceeds to voice the 911 Dispatcher on the opposite end of the phone call.)

911 DISPATCHER: 911
What's your emergency?
SOMALIA FLINT: I need to report a domestic violence incident
911 DISPATCHER: Are you the victim, or are you calling on behalf of someone else?
SOMALIA FLINT: I'm the victim
He…
My husband…
Punched me in the eye and mouth

911 DISPATCHER: Are you in immediate danger?

SOMALIA FLINT: Uhh…

No?

I left the apartment

Under the guise of making a trip to the grocery store

But my husband is still at home drunk as far as I know

Probably still in a rage

And curfew is about to kick in and…

I'm afraid to go home

911 DISPATCHER: Ma'am

If you are not in immediate danger

There is nothing I can do

SOMALIA FLINT: I don't understand

911 DISPATCHER: You can go to the police station and file a report, but I cannot dispatch an officer based on the information you provided to me

I suggest you do one or a combination of the following as you deem fit:

File a report with your local police station

Call your local domestic violence hotline for assistance

Stay at a shelter overnight or for as long as needed

SOMALIA FLINT: I don't have a car, and…

I don't have a phone

The phone I'm using now is a pay phone

It's at a grocery store I walked to from my apartment

There's no public transit out here

Even if there were…

I wouldn't have the money

911 DISPATCHER: Ma'am

SOMALIA FLINT: I don't have money

911 DISPATCHER: Ma'am

SOMALIA FLINT: To get to the police station or a shelter

I can't afford to go anywhere I can't walk to
And the shelters have been turned out due to COVID running ramped
You know that
I called 911 because I don't have money to make a paid call

911 DISPATCHER: Ma'am

SOMALIA FLINT: No one
Including the store
Has been willing to let me borrow their phone
Ma'am/Sir, please

911 DISPATCHER: Ma'am
Domestic violence lines are usually toll free
You should be able to dial the number from the pay phone you are using now

SOMALIA FLINT: Are you able to give me the number for the domestic violence hotline?

911 DISPATCHER: Unfortunately, ma'am, I do not have that information to share

SOMALIA FLINT: But I need help now!
If you could just send an officer to my home
Arrest my husband
Have him removed
I'd have enough time to...

911 DISPATCHER: Ma'am
You have confirmed that you are not in immediate danger
911 is for immediate dangers
I have provided you with what I can at this time
I advise you to visit your local police station
Do not hesitate to call back if you find yourself in immediate danger

SOMALIA FLINT: But I

911 DISPATCHER: Goodbye, ma'am

(The sound of the call disconnecting is followed by a dial tone. These sounds are generated by the Phone Receiver Chorus Member. Slowly, Somalia pulls the hand of the Phone Receiver Chorus Member away from her face. She stares at it. Beat. Somalia then stares into the face of the Phone Receiver Chorus Member. Beat. Somalia throws the Phone Receiver Chorus Member's hand, sending the arm of the receiver swinging. Beat. Somalia then catches the hand of the Phone Receiver Chorus Member and properly "hangs up" the phone. This may look like placing Phone Receiver Chorus Member's arm diagonally across their chest and latching their hand on their shoulder. Somalia takes a deep breath as she considers her options. Passersby continue walking in flux.)

SOMALIA FLINT: Maybe he left the apartment?
No
He's probably passed out from all that alcohol
If he is there…
You have no way to call for help
No more cell phone
No more house phone
If he is there…
If he is alert…
He'll be furious you've been gone this long
There's no telling what he'll do
No
You can't risk going back
(Beat) Spare change anyone?
CHORUS: A pandemic spares none
SOMALIA FLINT: Spare change, someone
CHORUS: 6 feet
SOMALIA FLINT: Can anyone point me in the direction of the

police station?

(None of the passersby pay Somalia any mind.)

SOMALIA FLINT: Please?
What does a woman have to do to get help around here?
CREEP: I got all the help you need right here, doll face
SOMALIA FLINT: 6 feet!
Stay away from me

(Creep keeps trucking. Somalia has an idea.)

SOMALIA FLINT: I can't use the phone, but…
Maybe they'll call for me
Maybe
Maybe they'll call the police station for me
Maybe the store manager can call an officer for me who will take me to the police station

(Somalia makes for the doors of the grocery store, but they are now closed and locked. These automatic sliding doors are comprised of Chorus members. Somalia sees an employee just on the other side of the door. She knocks feverishly on the "glass" to get their attention.)

SOMALIA FLINT: Excuse me!
Hey!
Excuse me!
Please!
STORE EMPLOYEE: We're closed, ma'am
SOMALIA FLINT: No wait
Please!
I have an emergency

STORE EMPLOYEE: Yeah sure

That's what 911 is for

Use the pay phone

We're closed

(Store Employee disappears from sight as s/he fades into the depths of the store.)

SOMALIA FLINT: I just tried calling 911!

Apparently I need to be in immediate danger for them to do anything!

I don't have money for the pay phone to call the local police station

Nor do I know the phone number for the local police station

Will you please call the police station for me?

Please ask an officer come take me to the police station

Please!

(Somalia gives the store glass a few more pounds with her fist.)

SOMALIA FLINT: I'm not a criminal

I'm not a robber or a thief

Please

Please let me in or at least…

Call a police officer for me

I can wait outside while you do

Please

I'm not crazy

I promise I'm not crazy

Even though…

It sounds crazy when I say I called 911 and they won't help me

They said to go to the police station but I don't have a way to get

there
That's why I need you to call an officer to the store for me
To come take me to the police station
This is an emergency!

(The lights go off in the grocery store.)

SOMALIA FLINT: Maybe one of the other stores along here will call for me

(Somalia goes from storefront to storefront. Each storefront is simulated by a different chorus member or set of chorus members. As Somalia approaches each one, the storefronts vocally chime "Closed.")

CHORUS: City curfew

(Chorus members dissipate. They gradually exit the stage, leaving Somalia standing alone.)

SOMALIA FLINT: *(Under her breath)* Curfew…
(Beat) Guess I have no choice but to go…
Home

(Somalia starts walking. After a while, she has a realization that stops her in her tracks.)

SOMALIA FLINT: Wait…
I'll just break curfew
Yeah
When the police comes through for curfew check, I'll just explain everything, and…
Hopefully they'll take me back to the station to file a report

(The barking of a dog. Somalia walks back to the grocery store and sits outside. She waits. She waits. And…she waits. The streets are desolate. Not a soul moves about. As the night progresses and the moon waxes full, a cold breeze begins to pick up. A newspaper goes tumbling by and Somalia catches it—a few pages of it, at least. The remaining pages blow into the night. She takes what's left and wraps herself in it as she sits leaning against the grocery store building. She begins to nod off to sleep—curled up in a ball. A masked Alex Flint manifests in the distance. Not making a sound but looking left and right as though searching for someone or something, he moves in the direction of the grocery store. He picks up on Somalia's presence. Stops. Stares. Beat. Alex resumes walking. Somalia, sound asleep, does not hear the approaching footsteps. Once in range, he shouts in a booming voice.)

ALEX FLINT: So, you needed space, huh? I'll give you space!

(Seven gunshots ring out. Blood pours from the holes torn into the sheets of newspaper hugging Somalia's now limp body.)

ALEX FLINT: Till death do us part

(Alex takes off running and disappears into the night. Thunder. Lightening. Winds pick up blowing city and parking lot trash such as fast food bags, paper napkins, paper cups, candy wrappers, newspapers, etc. The trash sticks to Somalia's blood-soaked body which is still curled up in a ball in front of the grocery store. What appears as a pile of debris from a distance is in actuality a bleeding heart prematurely ushering a soul into heaven. Several beats. A patrol car comprised of Chorus members slowly rolls down the street. They look left then right. Right then left. Ahead and back. Back and

ahead. Never noticing limp Somalia covered in debris and left for dead. Just as the patrol car passes the grocery store, another crack of thunder.)

ENNUI GO
by Joni Ravenna Sussman

CHARACTERS

ANN	Late 30's/Early 40's; attractive but in an effortless, natural way
MOTHER	

SCENE 1

(At Rise, Ann is onstage in the kitchen peering out the window. There is a wooden table with chairs, and a mask on the table. On the wall hangs a framed portrait of a younger Ann, with her mother and an older brother who looks like Ann. Mother enters. She says nothing for a bit, just watches Ann. She frowns, then makes her way to the stove and cracks eggs into a pan.)

MOTHER: *(Disapproving)* Why don't you come have some breakfast?

ANN: *(Still peering)* In a bit.

MOTHER: *(Angry)* This is an obsession! I'm starting to worry about you!

ANN: The wind's so bad, I'm afraid it's going to blow the nest away. She's sitting on the eggs, but I can tell she's scared! The palm frond is swaying up and down so much it looks like a green kite on a short leash, with a brown cup, clinging to its center. It's like a hurricane!

MOTHER: No such thing as hurricanes in the desert. And a spider's web is a lot stronger than you'd think. That nest isn't going anywhere! Now, get away from that window. Let the hummingbird alone.

ANN: *(Still peering)* Oh no, Oh god!... *(Then relieved, as though whatever she saw resolved itself)* Oh, thank God!

MOTHER: *(Aside)* ..."God ?" Don't let her fool you. She uses the term strictly as a figure of speech. Which is why I'm worried about her.

I think she's gone and lost her mind and God's not going to find it for her now! "God!"

ANN: *(Aside)* I use the term strictly as a figure of speech. God left me a long time ago.

MOTHER: *(Aside)*...She thinks I don't know she stopped going to Mass.

ANN: *(Aside)* My mother doesn't know. All the churches are closed because of COVID anyway.

MOTHER: *(To Ann)* Get away from there. Come have eggs! The kind you can eat!

ANN: *(Aside, reverent)* But the hummingbird nest almost makes me rethink that...the "atheist" box I check off on any form is an audacious ask. I suppose it must be human nature to want to classify people, to put them in a box. But the Holy Cross shelter?! Still...I miss volunteering there. I miss everything and everyone. Thank God for the hummingbird. Otherwise, there'd be nothing to do but watch TV.

MOTHER: I mean it, Ann! Now!

(Ann crosses to the table, sits.)

ANN: *(Aside, under her breath...)* Ugh.

MOTHER: How about a hand?

(She points to the skillet. Ann dons mitts, takes the skillet to the table, sets it down, as mother gets O.J.)

MOTHER: *(Seeing the skillet on the table)* What are you thinking? You can't put that hot skillet directly on the table!

ANN: Shoot, sorry.

(She quickly lifts the skillet, throws a towel underneath it, then rests it down again.)

MOTHER: Do you have any idea how expensive that table is? Rosewood is very rare, you know. Anyone can have a Maplewood, or an Elm or a…I had to search to find that table! You wouldn't dream of laying a hot plate on the Rosewood piano, would you!

ANN: Sorry! *(To audience)* She bought the table to match the aforementioned piano in my den. Which she passed down to me after my brother died. And though it obviously doesn't sound the same as it did when Johnny played, it retains his essence, or at least the essence of his artistry, which was considerable!

MOTHER: *(Attempting a more upbeat tone)* So, what's on the agenda for today?

ANN: If you want me to go to the store again, just say so, Mother.

MOTHER: *(To audience)* She's obviously forgotten tomorrow's my birthday. Do you see a cake anywhere?

ANN: *(To audience)* Oh, Shit. Tomorrow's her birthday! It's hard to remember what day it is these days…I won't question orders that rain down from on-high, though. Along with giving up prayer, I've learned to stop questioning anything—a blessing, ironically!

(The two sit, eating, silently.)

ANN: *(To Mother)* They're yummy.

MOTHER: (*To Ann)* You used to hate them when you were younger. Said my sunny-side-up eggs had snot on them. But this was the only thing Johnny would eat after he got sick, remember?

ANN: Of course. *(To audience)* That's when God left me…when Johnny died. I was young, but I can remember him transforming almost overnight from a handsome twenty-five-year-old into a confused, frightened stranger, ravaged by a strange new virus called HIV. 'Course, back then, no amount of prayers sent, ears bent, or dollars spent could help. It was a death sentence in the 80's…

just like COVID-19 is now…well, for people my mom's age… *(Frowns)* Which is why she's been living with me for the last five months. Oh, and did you know that Dr. Fauci was also the AIDS expert back then, like he is now for COVID? Those Italians just don't age! Anyway, he said older people have to be really careful…at least until there's a vaccine…The fact that there's *still* not a vaccine for HIV is something I try not to think about. *(To Mother)* So do you want Chocolate or a Lemon Chiffon Birthday Cake?

MOTHER: Whichever costs less. I'm just glad you remembered! The way you're waiting on those hummingbird eggs to hatch, I thought they'd be the only births we'd celebrate this month!

ANN: *(To Mother) Never! (To audience) Almost*!…At least it's something to do. God, how my brother would have hated being cooped-up like this! Johnny was a free spirit…But, he might have also appreciated the upside: The observation of small things that had gone overlooked, when social life distracted us from real life, both its horrors and its little treasures, like hummingbird nests.

MOTHER: Well, the wind's finally died down.

ANN: Then I'll fill up the hummingbird feeder!

MOTHER: But the sugar water's attracting gnats!

ANN: Exactly!

MOTHER: Gnats and bees! And there are already so many gnats everywhere! It's been so wet these last few months. I thought it never rained in the desert! Gnats everywhere! And now your hummingbird feeder is bringing them right up to the door!

ANN: If the gnats are closer to the nest, it makes her hunt easier.

MOTHER: Hummingbirds live on pollen.

ANN: They live on gnats and pollen! *(To audience)* She doesn't know everything!…I fell in love with hummingbirds after Johnny died because I positively, absolutely knew he'd been reborn in the form of a hummingbird in my backyard. It would come right up to me when I went outside. Sometimes it even followed me! That's when I knew the hummingbird was Johnny, so I decided to study all about them. I learned that the Native Americans believe they're harbingers of good news. And that their tongues, which are twice the length of their beaks, can dart in and out 15 times per second, slurping nectar and spreading pollen from flower to flower, thousands of times a day! Yep…I was certain the hummingbird was Johnny…Until I realized its real target was the gnats which were following me. I must sweat a lot. But hummingbirds still remind me of my brother just the same…God, he would have loved this nest and the two jellybean-sized white eggs inside.

MOTHER: When are you going to the market, Ann? We also need milk. Oh, and toilet paper! Be sure and get toilet paper! You never know when there's going to be another run on toilet paper.

ANN: …Look! The momma's back, squatting. *(To audience) At least that squatter-mater constructed her home. She didn't commandeer her daughter's…*Oh, I don't mean that. My poor Mother…She's been through so much. But couldn't she try to help with grocery shopping? As long as she wears a mask, it'd be good for her to get out. Good for both of us.

MOTHER: *You didn't answer me!* When are you going?

ANN: Now, Mom. I'm going for the cake *NOW*!

MOTHER: Don't be petulant! It's not my fault I can't go to the market!

ANN: I didn't say anything!

MOTHER: No, but you were thinking it.

ANN: *(To audience)* …And as usual, she was right.

<u>SCENE 2</u>

(At Rise, Lights change to show the passage of three days. We hear a faint buzzing noise coming from outside. Ann's tone has changed. She sounds fairly ominous now.)

ANN: *(To audience)* You'd have thought that the portion of the pink icing on the cake which had said "Mother" three days ago, but now says "Moth," might have been a warning. But it wasn't. It should have signaled to me that the universe had unleashed more than just a virus in my backyard. But it didn't. Oh God... *(To Mother)* Mom, look! Are those the deadly Asian Giant Hornets they showed on the news last week? The ones in Seattle?

MOTHER: Just because COVID came from Seattle, doesn't mean those killer hornets will too.

ANN: But, if they are the Giant Murder Hornets, then the hatchlings don't stand a chance!

MOTHER: You're obsessing again! I'm calling Dr. Monaco.

ANN: I only count four, but each one is like two-inches long, with a three-inch wingspan!

MOTHER: I told you not to hang that feeder so close to the nest. They're after the bees. *(To audience)* I'm worried about her.

ANN: *(To audience)* The news said they're nicknamed "Murder Hornets" because they use their long, spiked mandibles to tear the heads off bees and carry the bees' thoraxes back to their nests to feed their young. They're found in the tropics of East Asia, where the climate is humid. But recently, they'd spread to British Columbia and then on to Washington State where this kid watched one kill a mouse in under a minute! I saw the video he uploaded to YouTube. It was gross. It showed the hornet's crab-like pincers digging into to the mouse's back. And then it plunged its supersized stinger into the neck. The poor mouse struggled...but not for long. *(To Mother)* Why'd it have to rain so much this season? Why'd I have to hang the bird feeder, which I know the bees love, so close to the nest?! Why did the mother hummingbird have to choose a pygmy palm frond only six feet off the ground for her nest, making it possible for me to interfere in the first place!?! I'm such an idiot!

MOTHER: Stop it!

(Mother picks up cell, dials.)

ANN: *(To audience)* Of course, she's right. They're after the bees, not the hatchlings. But the mother hummingbird doesn't know that. *(Calling out, gently to the bird)* There-there…No!…Don't!…Stop! *(To Mother)* Mom, she's dive-bombing them now! The mother hummingbird! She's just pissing them off. I only see one chick. There's just one chick in the nest now. Mother, come look!

MOTHER: *(Into phone)* She'd been doing so well, for so long. But now she's in her head all the time, and she's obsessed with this humming—

ANN: *(Crying)* Oh God no!

MOTHER: *(Putting cell down, crossing to Ann, looking out the window)* Oh dear!

ANN: What are we going to do? They'll kill the other chick, too.

(Seeing her daughter distraught, Mother makes an unlikely decision.)

MOTHER: I'll get the tennis racket…I'll bust the feeder open. The bees will leave and the hornets will follow them.

(Mother exits.)

ANN: *(Calling offstage)* Mother, no! *(To audience)* But it was too late. The next thing I knew, she was swinging at the bird feeder. *(Calling offstage)* Mother, stop it! *(To audience)* The news said the hornets inject a neurotoxin, which can cause cardiac arrest. If she got stung, we'd have to go to the hospital. And as you know, if markets are dangerous, the hospitals are practically COVID-19 breeding grounds! *(Calling offstage)* MOTHER GET IN HERE!

(Ann helps the old woman inside, then slams the sliding glass door shut. Mother lays the tennis racket on the wood table.)

MOTHER: I'm fine. I'm fine.

(After a moment, we hear buzzing. Ann turns in the direction of the sound and notices that one of the hornets is inside.)

ANN: Go to your room, Mother!

MOTHER: But—

ANN: Now—*(To audience)* You can see how irrationally she's behaving. I'm worried about her.

MOTHER: *(To audience)* You can see how irrationally she's behaving. I'm worried about her. She's been so well, for so many years, but now—

ANN: *(To Mother)* Do you want to get stung? Do you want to go to the hospital? To die? Because I'll be fine…But you'll die. One way or the other, it's not safe for you. Now go to your room!

(Mother exits. We hear more buzzing. Ann looks around. The buzzing stops.)

ANN: *(To the hornet, as though she sees it, gently)* That' right. You just stay where you are while I find something to trap you.

(Ann picks up the face mask which is on the wooden kitchen table. Then she picks up the apron and the hand mitts, donning both. Finally, she pulls out a large pot. We hear the buzzing again. Ann raises the pot, comes down onto the wood table with a thud. She smiles, believing herself victorious.)

ANN: Aha! Sequestered at last!

MOTHER: *(Offstage)* What's going on, Ann? Are you okay?

ANN: *(With her hands on the overturned pot on table)* I'm fine! Stay in your room! *(To audience)* Damn flying monster! You tell me how this thing is any different from the Chinese bat that unleashed the stupid pandemic in the first place?! Which led to me living with a well-meaning, but totally INSANE mother who wields tennis rackets that piss off murder hornets? *(Beat)* Of course, who knows if the bat story's true. Because lately, what's been unleashed into the atmosphere even faster than pandemics, hornets and bats, is a shit-load of misinformation! Thank God I have you to talk to. Helps me make sense of it all.

(We see Ann scrape upside-down pot along wooden table. But then she hears the buzzing again. It's NOT coming from underneath the pot. This hornet is buzzing toward her. She grabs the tennis racket and flails at the hornet, accidentally striking the wooden table with the racquet.)

MOTHER: *(Offstage)* What in God's name is going on in there?

ANN: *(Calling Offstage)* I'm trying to kill it without getting stung, Okay!? *(To audience)* Wait until she sees these dents in the table. But I think I got it.

(The buzzing is coming from near the door. The buzzing stops.)

ANN: *(To audience)* Damn! *(To hornet)* Score 0-0. No sting, no pest control. But I see you. *(To audience, whispering)* See it? *(She motions toward the "door")* It's inserting itself right between the door and the hinges. *(Stealthily)* If I open the door quickly, I can squish it!

(She grabs the door handle, pulls.)

ANN: *Oh no!*

MOTHER: *(Offstage)* Are you okay?

ANN: I'm fine. Stay in your room!

MOTHER: *(Offstage)* But it doesn't sound like you're in the kitchen anymore?!

ANN: *(To audience)* And again, she was right. I'd opened the door; but instead of killing the hornet, I'd given him a tour of my home. There we both were, in the den, the hornet perched on the lid of the revered Rosewood Steinway; And Me…six-feet away…wondering what to do next. And just then, as you might expect…

MOTHER: *(Offstage, frantic)* The piano! Ann, don't hurt the piano!

ANN: Mom, don't! *(To audience)* But sensing that the Rosewood piano—Johnny's piano which now graced my den—might be in jeopardy; she stormed in. I had to make a quick decision…and like all important decisions, no room could be left for second-guessing. Down went the racket onto the hornet with a blow and a crack that rendered the upper right quadrant of the Steinway's rosewood lid irreparably damaged, and the tennis racket ruined…But so was the Murder Hornet. It was on the floor, dazed. I smashed it with my shoe…An espadrille, then came back in here.

(Mother enters into the kitchen.)

MOTHER: *(Her voice quivering, about to cry)* Johnny's piano!

ANN: But if you'd been stung…

MOTHER: *(Softly)* How could you?

ANN: If you'd been stung, you could've died.

(Mother exits.)

ANN: *(To audience, as she demonstrates)* I scraped the dead insect off my shoe—using the most minimal amount of toilet paper possible—

and threw it away. Then I looked out the window, over at the hummingbird nest…But it was empty. *(As though through a window, talking to the universe, talking to the hummingbird mother)* "…I know it hurts to lose someone you love. It hurts something awful…But On We Go, mama hummingbird. For this too shall pass." *(Beat, to the audience)* Then I closed my eyes, and for the first time in a very long time…I prayed to God that was true.

DAY ONE – VIEW FROM ABOVE
by Robin Rice

CHARACTERS

EMILY A house sparrow
DAVE A house sparrow

SETTING

Mid-March, 2020. In a tree above a sidewalk in a city.

(At Rise, two sparrows are in a tree beside a city sidewalk. Dave has a twig in his beak. Emily is worried.)

EMILY: Spit it out.
DAVE: Mmmfupf.
EMILY: I can't understand you.
DAVE: Mmmmfupffffumm.
EMILY: Spit out the damn twig.
DAVE: Mmmfu—
EMILY: DAVID!

(He finally spits out the twig.)

DAVE: Goshdarnit, Emily, our new nest won't get built by itself.
EMILY: Something's different.
DAVE: You keep saying that.
EMILY: For a reason.
DAVE: Egg-laying time is coming on fast.
EMILY: Well, I know that.
DAVE: All right. I'll play. Make it quick.
EMILY: It's not a game.
DAVE: What's different?

EMILY: Humans.

DAVE: Oh, them.

EMILY: Something's happening.

DAVE: Too hot. Too cold. Too much rain. Not enough rain. It's always something with them.

EMILY: I need you to take this seriously.

DAVE: The nest is nowhere near done.

EMILY: Look at them.

DAVE: Who?

EMILY: The humans.

DAVE: Do I have to?

EMILY: Yes!

DAVE: Where?

EMILY: On the sidewalk. Coming and going.

DAVE: Ho-hum.

EMILY: They're different I tell you.

DAVE: Different how?

EMILY: Significantly.

DAVE: Like?

EMILY: Here comes one.

DAVE: Hat Woman?

EMILY: Remember her?

DAVE: Every morning, same time, walking east to west.

EMILY: Hurrying.

DAVE: Yeah.

EMILY: Look.

DAVE: Same old same old.

EMILY: She's not hurrying.

DAVE: She always hurries.

EMILY: Exactly.

DAVE: Maybe her office is opening late. Maybe she's sick of her job and wants to get there late so they'll fire her. Maybe she's thinking about buying a new spring hat. Maybe she drank too much alcohol last night and she's tired.

EMILY: Has any of that ever happened before?

DAVE: I guess not.

EMILY: How many mornings have we seen her? How many afternoons when she goes west to east?

DAVE: *(Shrugs)* A hundred?

EMILY: Five days she comes back and forth, then two days off, then five days on. All of last spring, last summer, last autumn and last winter. Now it's spring number two and for the first time Hat Woman is walking at half speed as if she's dragging a big, invisible rock.

DAVE: Here comes Big Boots. Clomp. Clomp. I could do without that dude.

EMILY: Is he the same as always?

DAVE: I'm not going down to get a close look. One time he kicked me with a big boot like I was a dead leaf in his way.

EMILY: What's over his nose and mouth?

DAVE: A paper thing. Like a Halloween thing.

EMILY: Like a mask.

DAVE: Half a mask.

EMILY: It's not Halloween, Dave.

DAVE: You never know what humans will come up with next. Remember leopard-print leggings?

EMILY: What about her across the street?

DAVE: You gotta learn to accept change, Emily.

EMILY: I'm telling you something is wrong, David!

DAVE: Yesterday her hair was pink. Today it's purple. So?

EMILY: Her head is drooping like a sad dog. She's worried sick about something and now I am too.

DAVE: Turn around. I'll rub your tail.

EMILY: DAVE.

DAVE: Want me to get you a seed?

EMILY: Something is gravely wrong.

DAVE: You not helping to build our nest is what.

EMILY: Listen to me!

DAVE: You know very well listening is not a skill we male sparrows excel at.

EMILY: *(Seeing something upsetting)* Oh!

DAVE: Down at the corner?

EMILY: The lady with the baby carriage.

DAVE: *(Calls)* Hey, lady, the light's green!

EMILY: *(Calls)* Don't cross!

DAVE: Lady!

EMILY: Lady!

DAVE: No!

EMILY: Stop!

DAVE: *(To Emily)* Swoop!

(Emily and Dave swoop down on the woman.)

EMILY: Swoop!

DAVE: Left!

EMILY: Swoop!

DAVE: Right!

EMILY & DAVE: SWOOP!!!

(The woman stops and waits for traffic before crossing. They return to the branch and breathe a sigh of relief.)

DAVE: That scared the shit out of me!

(Emily nods soberly.)

DAVE: *(Trying to make her laugh)* Literally.

(Emily looks like she's about to cry.)

DAVE: You always laugh when I…When I say…When I let one loose and then I say…

(Emily is very sad and upset.)

DAVE: Don't cry, Em! You're right. This is no laughing matter. That woman has been taking care of that baby, walking that baby carriage across this street since before winter. She has always, always, always stopped and waited for the "walk" sign.

EMILY: What would make her cross into traffic with her baby?

DAVE: Something's filling their heads. Something not about birds.

EMILY: Nothing to do with us.

DAVE: They're usually so careful not to hurt their bodies.

EMILY: They usually overdo it.

DAVE: Like how they're afraid they'll starve, so they eat more than they need.

EMILY: They're afraid they'll freeze, so they pile clothes on.

DAVE: They pave over fields so they can walk easy and not trip.

EMILY: Cut down trees so branches don't fall and bonk them on the head.

DAVE: Shine lights at night so they don't bump into things.

EMILY: How're we gonna build the nest with this going on? How many humans are going to need us to swoop down and keep them from stepping in front of moving cars? What kind of parents are we going to be with no nest and shattered nerves?!

(Dave puts a wing around Emily to comfort her.)

EMILY: I feel like when those boys threw rocks at us.

DAVE: Like when we were learning to fly and there was that big wind?

EMILY: Like when I was sitting on our eggs last spring and a cat was climbing the tree.

DAVE: I pecked him!

EMILY: You did, didn't you?

DAVE: Right in the butt!

EMILY: My hero. *(She puts a wing around Dave)* But what can we do about this? Keep watch from our nest? We don't even have a nest.

DAVE: We will. We'll finish building it. You'll lay the eggs. We'll sit on them till they hatch. Then we'll feed our babies. We'll hold up our end of the way things should be.

EMILY: Keep on as if nothing's different?

DAVE: I believe that's important. That's what we need to do.

(A moment.)

EMILY: That patch of dry grass over there—it would make a nice, soft nest liner.

DAVE: There's more good sticks by the stoop.

EMILY: Dave?

DAVE: Yes, my love?

EMILY: I'm feeling hopeful.

DAVE: Four eggs?

EMILY: It feels like a five-egg year.

A RELUCTANT NARCISSUS DROWNS HERSELF

by Rachel Rios

(At Rise, an empty space. A woman sits alone on the floor in front of a large mirror. She touches hands with her reflection. She leans in close, looking at her face. She wrinkles her nose and covers her reflection with her hand.)

WOMAN: I built my life on the touch of others. I was the person who would wrap their loved ones in long, warm hugs, reach out and grab someone's hand when they were down. People liked that about me. Now, it makes me a pariah. *(Aside)* This isn't an easy time to be alive for someone whose feelings of love come from someone else's touch. *(Looks at her hands)* I feel like a creature. *(Addressing her reflection)* And you're certainly a creature. Uncanny monster. *(Aside)* Don't talk to her. She's horrible. *(Touches her reflection)* Frigid. I've read people saying that this time has changed them. That it's robbed them of so many things. Or it's given them so many things. I haven't changed at all. But if I had, I don't think I would have minded. How can you mourn your sense of playfulness withering, your longing and throbbing for adventure fizzling, your fire being extinguished? That is survival. That's how you adapt. I am in a terrible stasis. I am less evolved, and should probably die out.

(She puts her forehead against the mirror. She turns.)

(Aside) I don't know what I did to deserve being stuck in isolation with someone I hate so thoroughly. *(Turns back to the mirror)* Cold cold cold, why are you so cold. *(Aside)* I never touch myself. Sexually or otherwise.

(She puts her feet up on the mirror and looks at her crotch.)

Never.

(She puts her feet down and poses.)

I am a consumable. Market value, entirely dependent on demand. I've gone the way of the pet rock. *(To the mirror)* Don't look at me like that! You're just a lump, too! A misshapen lump, *(Leans in and makes big eyes)* With googley eyes. *(Aside)* She's a terrible bitch, isn't she? I wish I could chalk it up to some childhood trauma or something, but no, she's just like that.

(She tries to arrange the hair of her reflection.)

We've tried all sorts of things to make this cohabitation tolerable. *(Aside)* None have worked. *(Wiping a smudge off her reflection)* There's simply not much one can do when faced with a fate as grotesque as mine. *(A blueness crosses her face)* I suppose it is fate. Isn't it? None of my friends were very physical. Touch was something they learned, in spite of their nature, to love me. *(Puts her legs around the mirror, lays her head on it)* We used to lay together, legs braided, for no reason. A pile of people, pieced together like broken dolls. Even when we got sweaty, no one would move. Because this was simply what was done. My friends also had large pillowy breasts. And before a particularly important event, we would press our breasts together like this.

(She gets in front of the mirror and presses her chest against it.)

(Aside) With clothes on. *(Looks down at her chest)* And it was silly. But it was ours. That's love... What I mean by fate is, can you ever really learn to love someone in any permanent way? Or will the time always come when people return to their nature, and the conditions they constructed to make you happy fall away. And you stand alone in the rubble. This is the rubble.

(She catches a glimpse of herself in the mirror and is startled.)

God! What a specter. *(Aside)* Haunted by my own ghost. *(Looks to the mirror)* She and I are caught in a sport where there are no players, only spectators, and we'll watch each other, forever, waiting for someone—Anyone—to enter the court. They have a stare off. *(Aside)* Sartre was a lying sack of shit. *(To the reflection)* Please give me some space, I'm trying to breathe. You awful, brutal thing. Yes, you! *(Aside)* What I mean by fate is, is that everyone has a spirit. And along the way, you make a series of betrayals to that spirit. Your choices are metaphysical Judas's that twist your spirit up into something...unrecognizable. And at some point, you confront yourself, you see you must honor your spirit, and untwist it. What I mean is. I'm worried that I am everyone's betrayal. *(She looks at herself)* Perhaps I am a great trickster. A con artist of love. Entangled people's spirits in the pursuit of it. And now I am wrung from the fabric of their existence. Perhaps I am the rubble. *(To the reflection)* And now we are just two Things in tandem loneliness. *(Considers the reflection)* I say "Things" because we are creatures alike but strangers to each other. That is a Thing that I do not recognize. Terrible wretch. No wonder we're alone. *(Aside)* That's my greatest Earthly fear, you know. Being alone. I would rather be dead. *(Considers the reflection)* Though, judging by the look of her, it is entirely possible I am already dead. If this is life eternal, I would rather cease to exist. Evaporate. *(Breathes hot air onto the glass, watches it fade)* If only this body went that quickly. I imagine death is a much nastier thing. Though, perhaps the decay is just the spirit clinging to the body, reluctant to part from the thing that housed it for so many decades. I wouldn't cling to my body. Frankly, I wouldn't mind sluffing it off like a heavy coat on a hot day. *(Aside)* Grim thoughts for grim times. *(Looks to the mirror)* I heard about a man who died in the shower with the water running. It was days before he was found. And when they got to his naked, waterlogged body, they picked him up, and his skin just slid off him. Like the skin off a rotisserie chicken. I wish you could do that living. Shed layers of yourself, like a reptile. But keep going until there's nothing left. *(Aside)* She hates when I talk like that. *(To the mirror)* What do you care, you horrific thing! This is what happens when we're alone! *(Aside)* Apologies for her, *(To the mirror)* Yes, there is fault! It's your fault! *(Aside)* Please don't listen, *(To the mirror)* You cannot say that! This is a prison you built and now I'm shackled to you, you foul beast! I'm saddled with you for all eternity in this black hole, devoid of all warmth. What do you have to say for yourself, you useless wretch? *(Hitting the mirror; a hollow, clanging sound rings out)* Can't even hurt you because you're nothing. *(Hits the mirror again)* Do you hear that? You're empty. You're empty, you're empty, you're empty! We'll die alone here because of you! You are the lowest of all entities, you are the definition of unlovable. *(Tears welling in her eyes)* I hate you, I hate you, I hate you!

(She cries. She watches the tears roll down her reflection's cheek.)

Oh no. No no no, don't cry, *(trying to wipe the tear from her reflection's cheek)* I'm sorry, don't cry…

(She tries again and again. She turns away from the mirror. She reaches her hand, slowly and shakily to her face, and wipes the tear away. The

touch dissolves her further, though these tears are gentle and warm. She caresses her own face. She wraps her arms around her body and holds herself.)

MELTED IDOLS
by Lavinia Roberts

CHARACTERS

BRIDGETT	Female; computer scientist
VOICE 1	Female; her unconscious mind
BARDON	Male; a poet and a dreamer
VOICE 2	Male; his unconscious mind

(At Rise, Bardon is waiting on Zoom. He is clearly checking himself out in his camera, fidgeting. Bridgett shows up. She is dressed professionally.)

BRIDGETT: Hey.

BARDON: Hi.

VOICE 1: A shirt. A t-shirt.

VOICE 2: Like a seedling
Leaves outstretched
My gaze is drawn
To the life-giving warmth Of your eyes.

VOICE 1: This is an interview for the great privilege of potentially being my boyfriend, and you are wearing that?

VOICE 2: I have sculpted idols, forms
But in your presence they are melted down And replaced
With the divine.

BARDON: Hey.

BRIDGETT: Sorry, I'm late.

VOICE 1: I was passive aggressively deliberating whether or not I was going to actually Zoom with you or cancel at the last minute.

BRIDGETT: Tech issues. I haven't done many of these Zoom date things.

VOICE 1: Except for that one last week. And the one yesterday. And the one scheduled tomorrow.

BARDON: Yeah. Me either.

VOICE 2: There are no past regrets
Future fears
Only the present
Firmly ground
When light spreads
Beneath your eyes
A smile
That separates light from darkness.
That births the universe.

VOICE 1: Why did I agree to this? I could be streaming that new documentary on orchestrated objective reduction.

BARDON: So, you have any plans for the weekend?

VOICE 1: Postulating about whether or not consciousness stems from the quantum level inside neurons or is a product of connections between neurons.

BRIDGETT: Laundry. Just like, cleaning. Maybe streaming, binge-watching something.

BARDON: Cool. Yeah, I mean, I'm reading mostly. I noticed you liked reading. On your profile.

VOICE 1: Everyone says they like reading on their profiles. And traveling. And spending time with their family and friends.

BRIDGETT: Yeah. I read. I mean, I read things.

BARDON: So, what are you reading?

BRIDGETT: *Programming the Universe: A Quantum Computer Scientist Takes On the Cosmos*. Seth Lloyd. It's, you know, kinda old, but a classic.

VOICE 1: Whoa, look at his bookshelf?

BARDON: Sounds cool.

VOICE 2: Every quark.
Is alive.
In the flames

Sacred fire
Your breath
Makes my flesh living
A golem
I require
a life-giving kiss.

VOICE 1: There are no women or people of color on his bookshelf. None. Zero.

BARDON: Yeah, you have a PhD, right? In Computer Science?

VOICE 1: His books. All white guys. White poets. Whoa. What?

BRIDGETT: Yeah. Computer Programming. But programming that works more like consciousness. Instead of multiprocessing or multi-threading.

VOICE 1: Run. Run now. Abort date.

BRIDGETT: Hey. That's some book collection you have there. You know, I really need to start making dinner.

VOICE 1: He's buying it.

BRIDGETT: I'm really hungry.

BARDON: Oh, right. Yeah. Sure. I need to finish up an anthology of poetry by Nayyirah Waheed.

BRIDGETT: "You
not wanting me
was
the beginning of me
wanting myself
thank you"
She's great. You're into poetry?

BARDON: Yeah, I mean, I took classes. In undergrad. Double major in Botany, Plant Science, and English Lit. Hence all the white male poet books that I had to read.

VOICE 1: Oh.

BRIDGETT: Oh.

BARDON: But I'm really into Zora Neale Hurston, Gwendolyn Brooks. Some hip hop feminists like Porsha O. But mostly mystical poets. Like Rumi. Like Hafiz.

VOICE 1: Don't Surrender
Your loneliness so quickly.
Let it cut more
Deep.

VOICE 2: Let it ferment and season you
As few human
Or even divine ingredients can.

BRIDGETT: Yeah, me too. I like Hafiz, too. And Rumi.

BARDON: Sorry, I run a greenhouse, and I didn't have time to change before this. A succulent emergency. The newbie overwatered the Aloe plants. I had to re-pot them. Last minute.

VOICE 1: He nurtures plants. Kinda cute.

BRIDGETT: No, it's fine.

BARDON: And you said this was the best time for you, so I came straight home…

BRIDGETT: No, you look great. Fine. I mean, you look fine. It's fine.

BARDON: You look…

VOICE 2: Like sunlight
On a frozen lake
A sight that warms
And freezes the heart
Still, breathless

BARDON: Amazing!

BRIDGETT: Thanks.

BARDON: So, dinner.

BRIDGETT: Yeah.

BARDON: Don't let me stop you.

BRIDGETT: We could chat over the phone while I cook maybe? If you wanted to?

BARDON: Oh, yeah. Sure. I'll message you my number. In chat. Now.

BRIDGETT: So, I'll see you soon. Or hear you soon. Over the phone.

BARDON: Yeah. Okay.

VOICE 1: The beauty of the heart
    is the lasting beauty:

VOICE 2: That sees beyond seeing itself.

(Bardon and Bridgett leave Zoom.)

COVID'S HERE, BUT SO ARE WE
by Rich Rubin

They say William Shakespeare wrote *King Lear* during the time of the plague.
Well, if I've learned one thing during COVID, it's this:
I'm not William Shakespeare.
I'm joking.
I kind of knew that already.
Actually, I've learned *more* than one thing.
I've learned that people can be amazingly resilient.
Also, amazingly stupid.
Honestly, just wear a mask, people!
It's "liberty *or* death," remember?
Not "liberty *and* death."
But I digress.
Let's get back to resilient.
And Shakespeare.
Well, not Shakespeare, exactly.
Me.
And writers like me.
Writers today.
We're just like writers yesterday.
And hopefully tomorrow.
We write.
That's what we do.
That's what we *have* to do.
Why?
Well, because—

(Beat.)

It's not all that easy to explain.
It's kind of hard, actually.
Even for a writer.
Think of it this way:
When you're happy, you smile, right?
And when you're sad, you frown.
And when you're angry, you probably raise your voice.
At least just a little.
You do.
You can't *help* doing it.
And we're no different.
Writers, I mean.
Except for this:
Our happiness, our sadness, our anger—
All those feelings and more—
Well, somehow, as if by magic, they turn into—
Well, words.
Not just for us to speak.
For *actors* to speak.
And those words turn into Scenes.
And those Scenes turn into Acts.
And then—if we're lucky, very lucky—
And sweat blood just a little—
In the end, there's a play.
That's how we raise our voice.
By writing plays.
When times are good, when times are bad—either way, we write.
And who can say?
Maybe that's when writing is most important.
When times are bad. Like now.
So, what's the message here?
What's the bottom line?

Well, the bottom line is this:

COVID's here, but so are we.

Writers.

And the plays we're writing now. The stories we're telling now.

Stories about you.

And us.

All of us.

What we're all going through. So many stories to tell.

For us.

Our children.

Our children's children.

King Lear?

Maybe not.

But check back with us in a week. In a month.

In a year.

We're just getting started.

MOVIE REEL
by Jack Rushton

(Any couple, any age, any gender. At Rise, they stand at opposite ends of the stage. Each person speaks the alternating line.)

When will we…
Do…
The things we used to…
Do.
And feel the same way…
Again.
When will we dream…
Our dreams from before…
And dream like we used to…
Again.
What will we do…
When the past slips away…
And we've forgotten our touch…
Our feel.
So soft…
So real.
How can we remember the feelings…
We had…
And feel like…
We used to.

(Beat.)

I see you, standing there.
I hear you, standing there.
If I could touch you…

I could heal you…
Standing there.
Standing there.
I hear you.
I see you.
I need to feel you…standing there.
Alone.
Why can't we…
We can't.
Why don't we…
We won't.
Let's live the same way…
As before.
Maybe tomorrow…
Maybe someday.
Maybe forever…
Standing here, alone.

(Beat.)

When will we do the things we used to do?
And feel the same way again?
When will we dream our dreams from before
And live as we used to, again?
What will we do as time passes by…
And we are still in this time of today?
Our touch, our feel…
Our past, so surreal…
I haven't forgotten, have you?
I'm beginning to.
Movie reel. The images will find their way.

(Beat.)

I can't.

Try. Harder.

I want to.

Close your eyes.

It's…gone.

Come closer, closer still…

(The couple moves towards each other.)

Even closer, now stop.

And now…

(Cautiously, hesitantly, they reach out to each other.)

And now…

(They interlace their fingers.)

And now…

(They slowly withdraw their hands and then softly touch their hands to their own faces.)

Don't breathe.

Just listen.

(Beat.)

Do you hear it?

(We hear the click-click-click-whirl of an old-time movie projector.)

I do.

(The lights begin to flicker.)

Do you see me?
I feel you.
I see you.
I see you.
I feel you.
One touch…
Is all it takes.
Standing here.
One touch.
Is all it takes.
Standing here.
Movie reel.
Our movie reel.

(They embrace as the lights keep flickering and the projector click-click-clicks away.)

Let it play.

WHERE ARE YOU?

by Alvaro Saar Rios

CHARACTERS

MOM	50's or 60's
DAUGHTER	40's

SETTING

In the thick of the COVID pandemic; Somewhere in the cyber-ether on FaceTime or Zoom or something similar.

(At Rise, a black screen. A phone rings. Moments later, Daughter and Mom appear. Mom is surrounded by smoke. We also hear some really loud bumpin' music.)

DAUGHTER: Where are you?

(Black screen. Daughter and Mom disappear. Moments later, phone rings again. Daughter and Mom appear. The music is gone and the smoke has thinned. From time-to-time, Mom will speak to someone else, but we don't see or hear them.)

MOM: Hello, my beautiful daughter.

DAUGHTER: I think you hung up on me.

MOM: Pressed the wrong button. *(To other person)* Don't call me that. I did.

DAUGHTER: Who is that?

(No response.)

DAUGHTER: Mom. Who is that? Who are you with?

MOM: I would prefer not to tell you.

DAUGHTER: Is it a she? You can at least tell me that.

(No response.)

DAUGHTER: Okay. Then, where are you? Mom, where are you? Why aren't you at home?

MOM: You're at my house?

DAUGHTER: Yes. Where are you?

MOM: Why are you at my house?

DAUGHTER: Well, I saw you turned off the tracking on your phone. I thought something was wrong, so I texted, but you never responded. Then, I called, but you weren't answering. So, I dropped by your house. Are you with Celia? Did she do that? Turn off your tracking? Because I know you don't know how to do that.

MOM: I am not with Celia. Her kids won't let her come out.

DAUGHTER: Good. Ya'll don't need to be out and about. Mom, I need you to do something.

MOM: What?

DAUGHTER: On your phone. Go to Settings. *(Beat)* Mom. Do you hear me?

MOM: Yes.

DAUGHTER: Go to Settings on your phone.

MOM: Why?

DAUGHTER: Because I want you to turn the tracking back on.

MOM: Why?

DAUGHTER: Because I want know where you're at.

MOM: *(To someone else)* Where are we? *(Beat)* We...are on the freeway. Now you know where I'm at, so stop asking.

DAUGHTER: What freeway? Where are you going? Can you at least tell me that? Where you're going. You're not supposed to be going outside. You're supposed to stay home.

MOM: I'm grown. I can do whatever I want.

DAUGHTER: Mom, it's dangerous.

MOM: Nothing wrong with a little danger. Remember when you said that to me?

DAUGHTER: No.

MOM: You were still in high school.

DAUGHTER: Mom. That's like twenty-five years ago.

MOM: You called me to tell me you were going out with your friends. And you wouldn't tell me who you were with even though I asked. And before you hung up, I told you, "Don't do anything dangerous." And you said—

DAUGHTER: Nothing wrong with a little danger.

MOM: See! You do remember.

DAUGHTER: Mom. This is different.

MOM: How?

DAUGHTER: It just is.

MOM: You could have ended up in a coffin. You just got lucky, that's all. If that truck wouldn't have stopped, it would have killed you. Yes or no? Yes or no, mi'ja? You're not the only one who can ask questions.

DAUGHTER: Yes. Okay. Yes. I could have died. But I didn't.

MOM: Oh shit!

DAUGHTER: What? What "oh shit?"

MOM: Nothing. I wasn't talking to you.

DAUGHTER: Don't tell me nothing. Mom, who are you with? Mom? Mom?

MOM: I'm not telling you, so stop askin'.

DAUGHTER: Will you at least tell me what just happened? Please.

MOM: The person I'm with has a daughter. Probably, about your age. And the daughter just sent a text. Said she is coming looking for us because…my friend forgot to turn off the tracking on her phone like a tonta.

DAUGHTER: You said "her?" Who are you with? Laura? I told you that you weren't supposed to go out with her.

MOM: It's not Laura.

DAUGHTER: Last night, when I came over, you promised you would stay home. I said, "Just a few more months. That's it, and everything will be back to normal." You don't remember me saying that? And now…now you're out…wherever you are.

MOM: Can you say that again? I wasn't paying attention.

DAUGHTER: Mom!

MOM: I was doing something. Now, you have my complete attention.

DAUGHTER: What were you doing?

MOM: Turning the tracking off on my friend's phone. *(To other person)* Yeah. I got it.

DAUGHTER: You told me you didn't know how to do things like that.

MOM: I know what I told you.

DAUGHTER: You lied to me? What else have you been lying to me about?

MOM: *(To other person)* Slow down! No. That's not her. It's not. Now what did you say?

DAUGHTER: What's going on, now?

MOM: My friend. She thinks she saw her daughter's car. No. She's not following us. It's not her.

DAUGHTER: Where are you, Mom? Please, tell me. Why? Why won't you tell me?

MOM: I'm done with staying at home. Done.

DAUGHTER: So, you'd rather die? Is that it? Rather be out on the streets than at home safe?

MOM: You do realize that everything you are saying to me is exactly what I would say to you when you were 16. And did you listen to me? I begged you. Pleaded with you. StayhomeStayhomeStayhome. But your ears were filled with cement. Nothing I said was going in. Now it's my turn, and you want me to listen to you.

DAUGHTER: Is that why you left? Because of something I did when I was sixteen?

MOM: No. That's stupid. *(To other person)* What? Let me see. Yeah. That car is flashing its lights.

DAUGHTER: Are you being pulled over? Mom, where are you?

MOM: It's not the police. It's just a car behind us flashing its lights at us. *(To other person)* Do you know your daughter's license plate?

DAUGHTER: Did the daughter find you?

MOM: Hold on, let me put my seatbelt on.

DAUGHTER: You're on the freeway, and you're not wearing a seatbelt? Mom!

MOM: Don't worry. I got it on. *(To other person)* Go ahead. Step on it. Watch out for that—Okay. GoGoGo!

DAUGHTER: What's going on?

MOM: I'm gonna have to call you back.

DAUGHTER: Why? Why do you have to hang up?

MOM: We think her daughter found us and we're trying to lose her, so I'm going to need to help navigate.

DAUGHTER: Mom, where are you? Where are you Where are you Where are you?

MOM: Don't slow down. You're losing her. Woooohooooo!!!

DAUGHTER: Mom. Please.

MOM: What?

DAUGHTER: Please, tell me where you're at? Please.

MOM: You sound like you're going to cry.

DAUGHTER: I am going to cry. I'm scared, Mom. I don't want you to die. I know you are tired of staying at home. Day after day. But I don't want to lose you. Did you at least take—

MOM: Protection? Yes. Yes, I did.

DAUGHTER: Can I see it?

MOM: You don't trust me?

DAUGHTER: Please.

(Mom shows a face mask.)

MOM: Happy?

DAUGHTER: I'd be happier if you were here. In your house. Safe. It's only a few more months. That's it. Then, things can start going back to normal.

MOM: And what if I don't want normal?

DAUGHTER: What are you talking about? Why would you say that?

MOM: I don't. I don't want normal.

DAUGHTER: Everybody wants normal.

MOM: Not me. *(To other person)* You want me to drive? I can drive. Just pull over.

DAUGHTER: Mom, you're not supposed to be driving. You don't even have your glasses with you.

MOM: How do you know?

DAUGHTER: Because they are right here on the counter. Where you always leave them.

MOM: We'll be all right.

DAUGHTER: Will you at least tell me why you don't want normal?

MOM: *(To other person)* Give me a sec. What was that?

DAUGHTER: Why don't you want normal? You can go outside. Be with your friends. You can do whatever it is you're doing now, but you'll be safe. That's what normal is.

MOM: To you. To me, normal is you not calling every day. Not even once a week sometimes.

DAUGHTER: Ma—

MOM: You asked me. I'm speaking. Let me finish.

DAUGHTER: Okay.

MOM: Normal is you not having dinner on the porch with me anymore. It's you not calling me up to help me figure out what I should order for groceries. Normal means riding in a car with a stranger to my appointments or wherever else I need to go because you can't take me. I know it makes it easier for you when I just use an app and someone else can take me. But I don't like riding in a stranger's car. I never even liked riding in taxis. But I did it because then I wouldn't have to bother you to take me somewhere. And it always seemed like I was bothering you. Ever since not normal happened, you insisted on taking me where I needed to go. "It's safer, Mom. We don't know where those Uber drivers have been?" 'Member saying that? Normal means not hearing you tell me what happened while you were at work even if it's the same thing that happened the day before and the day before that. Normal is you not texting an emoji or those pictures with words on them. Normal is you not calling me back. Sometimes for days. Normal is slowly disappearing while not being noticed. Meme! That's what I meant. Those dumb pictures with words on them. The ones you send from time to time.

DAUGHTER: I knew what you were talking about. I'm sorry, Mom. I—

MOM: Remember when you were sixteen and you promised you would call, but you never did? Don't make me promises. I've had enough of those. I'm going to let you go. I'm not going to drive. I just want to be present with my friend who doesn't live close like you do. My friend who lives in another town, who came and picked me up because she is also not excited about normal coming back.

DAUGHTER: Will you call me when you get home?

MOM: I will. I promise. But I mean it.

DAUGHTER: I love you, Mom.

MOM: Love you too, mi'ja.

(Mom disappears. Kind of.)

MOM: *(To other person)* Okay. You can turn the music back up.

DAUGHTER: Mom. Your phone is still on. You didn't hang up.

(Loud bumpin' music kicks in. Moments later, Daughter disappears. Black screen.)

YOU CAN NEVER BE TOO SAFE

by Martin Settle

CHARACTERS

LEFT

RIGHT

SETTING

A plain stage.

At Rise, the characters Left and Right enter the stage from left and right. Both have face masks. They are looking at their phones as they walk, not paying attention to one another. They bump into one another and end up touching each other in an attempt to avoid falling. In the process, they drop their cell phones.

Suddenly, they realize their proximity and back off six feet, leaving their phones in the middle. They simultaneously take out their hand sanitizers and wipe themselves down, then simultaneously go into their pockets and take out surgical gloves to retrieve their phones. When they go to retrieve their phones, they approach the phones together and then realize they'll be in proximity again and back off.

Left holds up one finger; he has an idea. He takes out a tape measure and measures off six feet to the phones. Then he reels it in, wiping the tip of the tape measure with a sanitary wipe. When he's through, he places the tape measure on the ground as a marker. Then, he signals he'll go first, and Right will go second. He runs to his phone, picks it up and returns to his six-foot spot. Right does the same.

They clean off their phones with sanitary wipes, then take off their gloves, turning them inside out. They look at their phones next. It takes a moment, but they realize they have the wrong phones. They slap their heads and then signal to each other that they have the wrong phones. They put down their phones, take out their hand sanitizers, and wipe their hands.

They put on surgical gloves again. Right signals he'll go first in replacing the phone, while Left will go second. Right leaves the phone; Left does the same, then picks up his original phone. As Right goes to retrieve his phone, we see Left searching himself to find sanitary wipes. He begins to panic and texts Right (he knows his phone number now from when he recovered the wrong phone), who is wiping down his phone and taking off his gloves. Right looks at his text message, then looks across to Left. Left shows him he's out of wipes. Right shows Left that he has a hefty package of wipes and shakes his head "no," then follows that up with a little taunting dance. Left takes out his wallet and holds up a one-dollar bill and one finger. Right shakes his head and holds up ten fingers. You can see that Left is angry. But he takes another bill from his wallet and crumples it up. Left runs to the middle ground and places the "ten" on the ground. Right then proceeds to take the "ten" and leave a wipe. Left cleans his phone while Right uncrumples the bill and realizes it's a one.

Right quickly texts Left. Left receives the text, starts to laugh, and gives Right the finger. They approach each other aggressively. They throw their phones at each other, then start wrestling each other to the ground, each trying to strangle the other. As they're fighting, they smear hand sanitizer on each other. Pretty soon they wear out and lie on their backs exhausted. As they sit up, they both take off their masks and look at each other. Then they put their arms around each other and decide to die with laughter.

CRB THERAPY
by Joseph Sexton

CHARACTERS

AMY	20s, Female
MEGAN	20s, Female
PETER	20s, Male

(At Rise, two women are at an outdoor café chatting. They are doing the pull down mask, sip coffee, replace mask routine. As they chat, Peter approaches.)

AMY: This is the first time I have been out in, like, six weeks.

MEGAN: I know what you mean. What a year it has been. I sit in the house and have conversations with my dog. My whole day is organized around providing optimal canine care.

PETER: Excuse me.

MEGAN: Yes?

PETER: I couldn't help overhearing. It sounds like you are suffering from CRB. COVID Restrictions Burnout. If you don't mind my interrupting, I have discovered a helpful therapy, and I would like to share it with you.

AMY: That's okay. We are getting along fine.

PETER: It's easy, and I swear it helps.

MEGAN: Are you selling something?

PETER: Oh, no. I'm just trying to lift the boat by helping others.

MEGAN: Okay, what is it?

PETER: It is called fuck therapy.

AMY: Stop right there.

MEGAN: We are not interested.

AMY: Pervert. Go, go, go.

PETER: No, no it is not like that. Here let me show you.

MEGAN: I think we have heard enough.

PETER: It will just take a second.

AMY: And then you will leave us alone.

MEGAN: And we don't have to do anything.

AMY: And this has nothing to do with your pants.

PETER: Not at all, but I suggest you try it. Here let me show you. FFFFFFUUUUUUUUCK! Ahh.

(As he says this, he raises his arms and slowly makes fists and tenses his muscles and on the last K sound he releases the tension like he is throwing something heavy on the ground. Peter smiles and looks relieved.)

MEGAN: That's it?

PETER: It is so easy, and it really works. Try it.

MEGAN: No, that's al…

AMY: I will. What do I do?

PETER: You stand up, and as you say "fuck" you slowly tense and raise your arms, and when you get to the K, you drop that weight.

AMY: Can I use a different word? I don't like to swear.

PETER: Trust me, it works best with "fuck."

AMY: Well…fuck it, then. I will give it a shot.

(She raises her arms and says "Fuck"—but more like she has just hit her thumb with a hammer.)

AMY: I don't feel anything.

PETER: Try again. It's more of a build and release. FFFFFFUUUUCK! Ahh. See?

AMY: FFFFFFUUUUUUUUCK! Umm!

PETER: That's better.

MEGAN: This is ridiculous, and I am sure the other people here don't want to listen to a bunch of swearing.

PETER: They should all try it.

AMY: C'mon, Megan, it really works. You should give it a try.

MEGAN: But I am fine. What bothers me is people getting into my business and telling me to relax. I just need to get out of my neighborhood. Go to a real restaurant. Have a drink without worrying about what I am breathing in.

PETER: I have an idea. Try first thinking about something that is really bothering you, and then do the therapy.

MEGAN: Like, uh…I miss traveling?

PETER: Yes. Now say it slowly…

MEGAN: I—miss—traveling.

PETER: And build…

MEGAN: FFFFFFUUUUUUUUCK! Ohhh!

AMY: Did it work?

MEGAN: I think…I feel less tense. That was very specific. I do feel less tense.

PETER: See, a little fuck therapy is good for everyone. Sure this has nothing to do with sex? I feel so relaxed. I am going to do it again.

PETER, MEGAN & AMY: *(All together)* FFFFFFUUUUUUUUCK! Ahh. Ohh. Umm.

MEGAN: I do feel better.

AMY: What a great way to release tension. *(To Peter)* Hey, what is your story?

MEGAN: Do you live around here?

PETER: Actually, I am embarrassed to say it, but I have been traveling lately. Sharing the therapy with anyone who will listen. Before that, I spent most of the last year working in uh, politics. But then one day a few weeks ago, I suddenly realized I was on the wrong side of history. But the good news is I discovered this therapy for the stress of living through these times.

AMY: *(Surprised)* Fuck!

PETER: I let myself believe that, with times as they are, we Americans just needed to hunker down and pull up the bridge. I was wrong. We all really need to work together. FFFFFFUUUUUUCK! Ah, that's better.

MEGAN: I am a little concerned that this therapy might actually be addictive. Do you find yourself compulsively doing it?

PETER: You are right, the therapy does need to be used responsibly. I was at the grocery the other day and…I couldn't control myself.

MEGAN: Oh my god. Was that the only time?

PETER: No. FFFFFFUUUUUUCK! Ah, that's better.

MEGAN: Amy, I think we have been exposed!

AMY: I am already unable to leave my house without a mask on my face.

MEGAN: FFFFFFUUUUUUCK! Ohh. I don't think I can stop.

AMY: FFFFFFUUUUUUCK! Umm. How dare you expose us!

PETER: Don't worry. You are only reacting to a very real anxiety caused by the pandemic. As it subsides, so will your anxiety, and eventually they'll both disappear. You only do it because you need it.

MEGAN: Do you promise it's going to go away?

PETER: Well, there are variants and mutations and about eight billion people to vaccinate…

PETER, MEGAN & AMY: *(All together)* FFFFFFUUUUUUUUCK! Ahh. Ohh. Umm.

AMY: Do you think you can do it too much?

PETER: The truth is, you can only do it as much as you need to.

MEGAN: I feel like the more I do it, the less effect it has.

AMY: I am getting anxious.

PETER: We could try a three-way?

AMY: A three-way?

MEGAN: I thought you said this wasn't about sex.

PETER: We are so past sex.

AMY: C'mon, Megan. Live in the moment. Let's do a three-way.

PETER, MEGAN & AMY: *(All together, three times now, with some variation)* FFFFFFUUUUUUUUCK! Ahh. Ohh. Umm.

MEGAN: Ah! I feel better.

AMY: We just needed to up the dose.

PETER: With this therapy we will get through this.

MEGAN: Hey, let's all go back to my place. We can social distance around the fire pit and do more therapy.

AMY: I could use some more therapy.

PETER: I thought you would never ask.

OUT OF AN ABUNDANCE OF CAUTION

by Leda Siskind

CHARACTERS

JERRY	30s-60s
DEE DEE	30s-60s

(At Rise, a blindingly white medical operating room. The overhead florescent lights buzz annoyingly and one of them flickers occasionally. There are two doors, one stage left and one stage right. All the surgical equipment—the operating table, stainless steel tables, IV drip stands, medical instruments, etc.—are covered in protective plastic. After about ten seconds, the stage right door is opened. We see a white, puffy, parka-covered arm that reaches in, with a white gloved hand holding a spray can that is aimed at the knob. The knob is sprayed. Satisfied, Jerry walks in. At first glance, Jerry appears to be dressed in one of those medical containment suits that professional personnel wear when working with highly infectious patients. But upon closer inspection he is wearing an upside-down fishbowl over his head, and his puffy parka is stuffed underneath white painter's overalls. He is wearing one white rain boot, perhaps with a clown face on it, and one white high-top sneaker. In other words, he looks ridiculous. He puts down the spray can and pulls out a checklist. The stage left door opens. A long, fuchsia-gloved hand turns the knob, then sprays the knob with a disinfectant can. Dee Dee enters. Dee Dee's neck and turbaned head can be seen through a square, clear, soft plastic box, perhaps the kind that would store sweaters. She is wearing a plastic Roman gladiator breastplate over a mirrored disco dress, with army fatigue pants underneath the dress and very high black patent leather boots. The opera gloves run past her elbows. In other words, she looks ridiculous, as well. They both

spray the air between them. Dee Dee puts down her spray can and pulls out a checklist.)

JERRY: Are you Dee Dee?

DEE DEE: Are you Jerry?

JERRY: I have to verify you're Dee Dee before I can answer that.

DEE DEE: Why would I even ask if you're Jerry if I wasn't Dee Dee.

JERRY: Just being cautious. The dating app said I should verify.

DEE DEE: What are the chances of another Dee Dee showing up at precisely nine o'clock at night at the MidCentury Hospital's Operating Room Number #3 for a first date?

JERRY: Oh-kaaay, but we can't be too careful. That's why we're meeting here to begin with. You have your checklist?

DEE DEE: Yeah, but—

JERRY: Then let's do that before anything else.

DEE DEE: Can't we say "hello" first?

JERRY: Hello?

DEE DEE: Remember that? I'm not going to shake your hand or—

JERRY: *(Recoiling)* What?!

DEE DEE: I'm not! Just…"Hello, I'm Dee Dee."

JERRY: Jerry. Checklist.

(They both look at their checklists.)

JERRY: "One: I have been sprayed with disinfectant after entering the operating room." Yes.

DEE DEE: Yes.

JERRY: "Two: I have washed my hands for at least twenty seconds twenty times in the last two hours." Yes.

DEE DEE: Yes.

JERRY: "Three: If I have sneezed, I have used a tissue—and then destroyed the tissue and threw it in a trashcan—and then destroyed the trashcan." Yes.

DEE DEE: Yes.

JERRY: "Four: I have disinfected tables, doorknobs, light switches, handles, desks, computers, phones, keyboards, sinks, toilets, countertops and my collection of glass cats—"

DEE DEE: Excuse me?

JERRY: "I have disinfected tables, doorknobs, light—"

DEE DEE: You have a collection of glass cats?

JERRY: Oh, sorry, that…just…snuck in there. It's…it's not a huge collection—they're miniatures, really, it's silly—

DEE DEE: How many?

JERRY: About…three hundred.

DEE DEE: Me, too.

JERRY: You too what?

DEE DEE: I have a collection of miniature glass cats. Well, tigers, actually.

JERRY: How many?

DEE DEE: Four hundred and two.

JERRY: *(Back into the checklist)* "Five: I have socially distanced myself from other people by at least seven feet for the last ninety days." Yes.

DEE DEE: Yes! And the distancing is driving me crazy!

JERRY: "Six: I have worn a facemask—"

DEE DEE: Aren't you?

JERRY: Aren't I what?

DEE DEE: Going crazy? I mean, I haven't talked to another human being face to face in over three months! I may not look it, but I'm losing my mind!

JERRY: You do actually—

DEE DEE: The phone, the Internet, the Skyping, the texting—it's not the same! *(Beat)* What do you mean: "I do, actually?"

JERRY: I mean, sorry, but what you're wearing…

DEE DEE: Didn't you read my profile? I'm a fashion designer! Cloth is my medium! And I'm fully protected from germ contact! *(Beat)*

Besides…have you looked in a mirror?

JERRY: Not without disinfecting it first. *(Beat. Back to the checklist)* "Six: I have worn a facemask—"

DEE DEE: They're almost impossible to find now. *(Beat)* What is that, anyway, on your head? A fishbowl?

JERRY: *(Puts down the checklist)* Yeah.

DEE DEE: You…you didn't destroy any fish to—

JERRY: No, no. *(Beat)* I found it lying around at my last gig. Before the virus.

DEE DEE: Your profile said you're a painter, right? Would I have seen any of your work?

JERRY: Yeah…on Broadway and Fifth. *(Beat)* I'm a house painter.

DEE DEE: Oh! I didn't catch that reading your—*(Trying to reframe)* And you have a collection of glass cats!

JERRY: Yeah. I inherited them from my grandmother and kind of kept going. *(Beat)* They cheer me up.

DEE DEE: Were you close to her?

JERRY: Yeah. She was very smart and funny and…my family sort of ignored her. But I loved her.

DEE DEE: I had a grandmother who was special like that. She told me I should be strong and quick…like a tiger.

(Four beats as Dee Dee and Jerry stare at each other.)

JERRY: That's…Wow.

DEE DEE: Wow what?

JERRY: *(Not knowing how to proceed, he goes back to his checklist)* "Seven: I have avoided touching—"

DEE DEE: Did that touch you?

JERRY: What?

DEE DEE: What I said about my grandmother. Did that touch you?

JERRY: *NOTHING'S SUPPOSED TO TOUCH ME!*

DEE DEE: No, I meant metaphorically, what I said about my grandmother.

JERRY: Yeah…it did.

(Beat.)

DEE DEE: Sooo….We both adored our wonderful grandmothers, we both collect glass cats, and we both are, um…fashionably creative.

JERRY: Your profile said you like saltwater taffy.

DEE DEE: *Yes*! Especially fresh! Where you can see them pulling it—

JERRY: Yeah! Like at Little Jimmie's on the Boardwalk—

DEE DEE AND JERRY: Atlantic City!

(They stare at each other, surprised and pleased. Four beats.)

DEE DEE: I didn't think I'd say this, but…did…you bring your heart?

JERRY: I was afraid to, you know, in case I'd be disappointed. *(Beat)* But I'm not. I brought it.

DEE DEE: It's up to you. I don't want to pressure you or—

JERRY: No, no. *(Beat)* I like brave and quick. *(Beat)* And pretty.

DEE DEE: Thank you, Jerry. That's really sweet. *(Beat)* You sure you want to?

JERRY: Yeah, I think I do. I have a good feeling about this.

DEE DEE: Who goes first?

JERRY: Both at the same time.

DEE DEE: Ooh! You're brave and quick ,too!

(They both slide a gloved hand inside their respective chest covers—Jerry inside his overalls and Dee Dee inside her gladiator breast-plate—and each of them pull out a small clear plastic box in which a mechanical heart beats. They place the boxes facing each other about a

foot apart on the operating table. Jerry's is larger than Dee Dee's; Dee Dee's has embroidered gold thread sewn on it. Four beats as they take in what they've done.)

DEE DEE: I…I didn't sanitize it or—

JERRY: It's okay. *(Beat)* I didn't either.

DEE DEE: I just thought…a heart—

JERRY: Yeah. They're messy things, anyway.

DEE DEE: Yours is so big.

JERRY: Yours is a heart of gold.

DEE DEE: Embroidered! Can I…would it be okay with you if we moved them closer together?

JERRY: Let's go for it!

(They each move their respective hearts closer so that the boxes almost touch. Four beats as they take in what they've done.)

DEE DEE: Maybe this is too brave and quick, but…out of the box?

JERRY: Yeah, we're really thinking out of the box here.

DEE DEE: No, not meant metaphorically this time. I mean really out of the box.

JERRY: Wait. You mean, touching?

DEE DEE: That's what hearts do. They touch. They are touched. They're not socially distant from joy or pain or…or…

JERRY: Or?

DEE DEE: Or…whatever comes before you give your heart away.

JERRY: Wow, Dee Dee. *(Beat)* I've never given my heart away. Always scared it would be broken.

DEE DEE: I understand. *(Beat)* Me, too. *(Beat)* I guess the question is… how long do you maintain an abundance of caution? When do you step around and go outside of it?

JERRY: I don't know. *(Beat)* Maybe now.

(They both gingerly lift up the plastic cases of their hearts so that the hearts touch.)

DEE DEE: Ohhhh!

JERRY: I feel…different.

DEE DEE: How?

JERRY: Sort of…raw. *(Beat)* But in a good way.

DEE DEE: Me, too. *(Beat)* Tingly.

JERRY: So…now what? Should I text you? Zoom?

DEE DEE: No! Let's meet here! Operating Room #3! Nine o'clock, next Wednesday night!

JERRY: Whoa!

DEE DEE: Feel okay?

JERRY: Yeah! You?

DEE DEE: Yes. Feels *right.*

JERRY: Same here! Till next week, then, Miss Dee Dee!

(He blows a kiss at her; she blows one back. They both go to their respective doors, pick up their sprays, spray the air in front of them, spray the knobs, and leave. The hearts remain beating together.)

A LIGHT IN THE DARK
by Kyle Smith

CHARACTERS

JESUS

PETER

(At Rise, an empty church. A single light glows from the stage of the church. Jesus (pronounced "hey-zuice") walks through the pews sweeping the floors, bopping along to his smartphone's music. He gets into it, walks up on stage and sings into his broom. The sound of glass breaking from offstage. Jesus doesn't notice and keeps on jamming until he sees Peter enter.)

JESUS: Fuck.

(Jesus hides. Peter scans the church. He doesn't see anyone. Peter walks through the church, pilfering whatever he can. Jesus is conflicted. He decides to stand up.)

JESUS: Um. Excuse me?

PETER: Jesus Christ!

JESUS: What are you doing here?

PETER: *(Pulling out his wallet)* I'm sorry, uh, Father, the stores are fucked—uh—empty. I figured you might have something useful.

JESUS: I'm not a—

PETER: *(Pulling out a hundred, offering it to Jesus)* I just need supplies.

JESUS: *(Pocketing the hundred)* Welcome, child, we're happy to have you.

PETER: Thank you, uh, Father. I'm sorry for breaking in, I didn't think anybody would be here.

JESUS: We always have someone in the building. It's um, the Lord's will.

PETER: You got any toilet paper?

JESUS: Uh, yes, my child, let me grab you a pack.

(Jesus walks to his janitorial station and pulls out a pack of toilet paper.)

PETER: Thanks, Father…uh…?
JESUS: Borges. Jesus Borges. And you?
PETER: Peter. Any food?
JESUS: Yeah, totally, uh let me…

(Jesus searches the space for Communion wafers.)

PETER: I mean, if you don't need it.
JESUS: Not a lot of visitors. You know, gatherings of more than ten people, and all…
PETER: Right.
JESUS: Here we go.

(He pulls out a Tupperware full of wafers.)

PETER: Are you sure you don't need them?
JESUS: It's just going to waste here. And we can make more when things die down. It's basically just flour and water. We've got a kitchen downstairs. They make them in batches, the…body of…Christ.
PETER: What about the Tupperware?
JESUS: Take it.
PETER: Here, I'll just…

(Peter pulls out a roll of toilet paper and wraps the wafers in toilet paper.)

PETER: I don't want you to be totally fucked—uh, screwed—if I—

JESUS: I understand. Well, if there's nothing else... *(Beat)* Is there anything else?

PETER: You got any of the, uh, blood of Jesus?

JESUS: I'll grab you a bottle.

PETER: I don't drink a lot, it's just. Every store nearby has nothing.

JESUS: Of course, my child.

PETER: And it's been hard.

JESUS: I know.

PETER: It's been so hard...

JESUS: *(Sighing)* ...Do you want to talk about it?

PETER: It's this whole thing. I'm so scared, Father. I'm scared day in, day out, and I'm losing hair and, my boss couldn't keep the restaurant open, and I got laid off, so I can't afford to pay rent. I can't afford...

(Jesus looks at Peter. He pulls out the hundred-dollar bill.)

JESUS: Take this back.

PETER: No, I couldn't.

JESUS: I still have a job. Take it back.

(Peter grabs the bill.)

JESUS: Well, if that's all—

PETER: It's not. Everything's cleaned out, wherever I go. Honestly, I don't even believe in God. I just needed stuff and nowhere else had any. This is awful, I broke into a house of God—

JESUS: Probably would've been worse if you did believe in Him.

PETER: I mean, I'm open to the idea, but I think He'd probably be pretty upset with me.

JESUS: He forgives people. He'd probably forgive you.

PETER: There's a thing, right, a Mass? Can you do it for me?

JESUS: Oh, no…

PETER: Please, Father. I'm so scared.

JESUS: You need to make confession, and there's other…uh…stuff.

PETER: Yes! Let me confess!

JESUS: You know, it might be better if you come back tomorrow.

PETER: Forgive me, Father, for I have sinned.

JESUS: Uh…What…What have you done, my child?

PETER: I broke into this church.

JESUS: …Is that all?

PETER: I'm trying to think of it all. Uh. Okay, it started when I was four years old, my sister had one of those dandelion flower seed things and she wanted to blow it, but I grabbed it and blew the seed things, and she started crying. And then a few months later—

JESUS: How about we keep it to things done in the last couple of months.

PETER: Don't you need to hear them all?

JESUS: Just give me the highlights.

PETER: Oh. Okay. Um. I had sex with my best friend's ex-girlfriend. I, Uh. Oh, I've definitely said things like "Jesus Christ" in the bad way. That's a sin, right? I'm pretty sure that's…I, um, I convinced my fiancée to use plan B. We weren't—we weren't really ready for a baby and…She broke up with me a few months later. I didn't cry when my mom died. There's one, uh, respect your elders right? That's one of the deadly ones? I felt like I wanted to, but nothing came.

JESUS: Is that all, my child?

PETER: I think so, at least of the big ones. Wait! No! I lived with that fiancée for a few months. And we. Uh. We had sex. Like a lot of sex. Premaritally.

JESUS: You're done?

PETER: Yeah, I think that's it.

JESUS: Okay, great. You're absolved.

PETER: What about the…Hail Marys?

JESUS: Right. Say five Hail Marys.

PETER: You're gonna have to help. I don't really know the…

JESUS: Oh, okay, let's see. Uh…Hail Mary full of grace, the Lord is with thee…Blessed are thou amongst women and blessed is the fruit of thy womb…Holy Mary, Mother of God, pray for us sinners, now and at the hour of our death…Amen.

PETER: I've got to say all that five times?

JESUS: Just say "Hail Mary" five times. I think He'll get the point.

PETER: Right. Hail Mary. Hail Mary. Hail Mary. Hail Mary. I feel like it's working. Hail Mary.

JESUS: You are absolved of your sin.

PETER: Thanks, Father. Should we do the wine and cracker thing?

JESUS: …Sure. Can you pass me the—

(Peter passes the wine and the communion crackers.)

JESUS: Right. Um. Lord, watch over this man. Make sure he doesn't do anything…uh. Bad.

(Jesus unscrews the wine bottle and offers it to Peter. Peter takes a swig. Jesus grabs a cracker from the toilet paper bundle and puts it in Peter's mouth.)

JESUS: Amen.

(They both hesitate for a second.)

JESUS: Shit!

(Jesus pulls out a bottle of hand sanitizer, he squirts some into his hands, then passes it to Peter. Peter squirts some into his hands, wipes

them down, and then squirts some into his mouth, swishes it around and spits it out.)

PETER: Oh, that tastes bad.

JESUS: Go with God, my son.

PETER: Can we do a hymn?

JESUS: You don't know any hymns?

PETER: Do a simple one, I'll catch on.

JESUS: Uh… *(Singing)* Jesus loves… *(Speaking)* Um. *(Singing)* Jesus… Jesus… *(Takes a breath, then sings)* Sometimes I feel like a motherless child.
Sometimes I feel like a motherless child.
Sometimes I feel like a motherless child.
A long way from home.
A long way from home.

PETER: Yeah, I can do that.

PETER AND JESUS: *(Singing)* Sometimes I feel like a motherless child.
Sometimes I feel like a motherless child.
Sometimes I feel like a motherless child.
A long way from home.
A long way from home.

(Jesus is moved. Peter is smiling.)

PETER: Thank you, Father. My first Mass. Moving, even with the panic over the cracker. Won't be my last.

JESUS: Go with God.

PETER: I will. And I know you said to keep the… *(Reaches into his wallet)* But I gotta give you something. Here's $20. Thank you, Jesus.

JESUS: *(Grabbing the cash)* No problem.

(And Peter's gone. Jesus watches him go. He pulls out his headphones and plugs them in. He grabs his broom and starts sweeping.)

JESUS: *(Singing)* Sometimes I feel like a motherless child.
A long way from home.
A long way from home.

CONTACT TRACING
by Amy Tofte

CHARACTERS

GINA KRUSS	40s, Female; a public health RN; motherly
KATHY ROHN	50s, Female; conspiracy theorist; aggressive

SETTING

Two different households in 2020 America.

(At Rise, a video screen snaps on to Gina in a fleece with an official state seal. Her screen background is a home workspace that looks cleaned up. She organizes files. There's a water bottle with a straw and hand sanitizer. She checks her image on the screen and adjusts the angle on the camera and lighting, then gives up. Her hair has been better; she's mostly abandoned makeup, and she's tired. Whatever. Gina types, working from a document. Pretty soon a ping. She uses her mouse to click something on her screen and is joined by Kathy on another screen who is visible but muted. Kathy's television is on in the background of a well-loved house.)

GINA: Hi, Ms. Rohn? Oh. Hello? I think you're on mute. *YOU'RE ON MUTE. What the hell, Gina…she can't hear you. (Waving and pointing)* MUTE…

(Gina types in the chat. Kathy accidentally screen shares photos of grandchildren and some guns.)

GINA: Oh. No. That's not—Please, please don't be crazy, lady…You're *on MUTE!*

(Kathy figures it out. She's loud at first.)

KATHY: ...with what the Sam Hill is going on anymore! Are you there? Hello?

GINA: Hi! I'm here. All good. Can you please turn the TV down?

KATHY: *(Adjusting the television)* Hate this thing—Ugh—Hate you stupid computer—

(Kathy smacks her computer, shaking the camera.)

GINA: It's all good! Hello, Ms. Rohn. How are you feeling today?

KATHY: ...What?

GINA: Am I saying that correct? Kathy Rohn?

KATHY: Yeah. What's this about? Are you from the Governor's campaign?

GINA: I'm calling because you had a positive test for the virus—

KATHY: Who. Are. You?

GINA: I sent the link to this call in my email. I'm Gina with the Department of Public Health. Can I get some information to verify you're the Kathy Rohn on my contact list?

KATHY: Like what information?

GINA: Well, is your birth date...March 10th?

KATHY: Yes...

GINA: Great. And I have an address here for 2938 Crest View Drive—Correct?

KATHY: Holy—What the—How do you know that...?

GINA: You completed a form at the test site. They should have mentioned someone would be contacting you. Please know this call is on a secure network and our talk is completely confidential. Kathy? I work for the State. That's why the Governor's name is on the—

KATHY: DEEP STATE—Oh, my lord...Deep State!

GINA: No, no, ma'am. The State Department of Public Health. I report to the Governor's office—

KATHY: How on earth did you get to me? Back up. Who are you again?

(Kathy starts writing down notes.)

GINA: My name is Gina. I'm a Registered Nurse with the Health Department.

KATHY: I thought you worked for the State?

GINA: Yes. The STATE Health Department. I'm a government employee.

KATHY: You're a government nurse?

GINA: Yes. I guess I am. If you check the signature of my email, there's contact information for my supervisor, if you'd like to call her and—

KATHY: You're not a doctor?

GINA: No, ma'am. I'm a nurse—just like in a hospital—but I'm conducting contact tracing so we can track the community spread of the virus and help those infected get well—

KATHY: WHOA STOP. It's happening—They said it would happen—Ho, my word…MARVIN! *(Shouting off camera)* MARVIN, THEY'RE IN THE COMPUTER! YOU WERE RIGHT!

GINA: Ma'am—

KATHY: MARVIN! THEY BEEN LISTENING ALL ALONG!

GINA: Could I go over some information with you? And ask you a few questions?

KATHY: And I gotta few questions for YOU. You people are destroying the COUNTRY.

GINA: …I only need to find out who you've been in contact with since your positive test on Tuesday because they might now be at risk—It also helps us understand—

KATHY: You're not even real. You could be a—animated or something—Avatar!

GINA: Okay…Are you feeling well today? You think you might be running a fever?

KATHY: *(With a small cough)* HA!

GINA: A low grade fever can sneak up on you. Other symptoms like fatigue and aching joints—

KATHY: BULL!

GINA: Ma'am—

KATHY: It's a DAGUM HOAX! There is no virus! There is no virus! There is no DANG virus!

GINA: Ma'am—I'm sure you've seen the local news. It's putting people in the hospital. Our local hospital. We're experiencing a surge in cases across the state and we're hoping—

KATHY: HOAX! FAKE NEWS AND NOT REAL. You know it, I know it, EVERYONE knows it!

GINA: I don't know that. But if you can maybe help me understand who—

KATHY: HOOOOOOOOOAX!

GINA: —else you've been in close contact with. That would be very helpful. And, again, this is confidential. No one will know you gave me this information.

KATHY: OMG. MARVIN!

GINA: Is Marvin your husband? Do you have others in the house that you could have exposed?

KATHY: I'M NOT TELLING YOU A THING! Right to MY privacy! Wait a second…Gina…? Gina…I know you…I know I know you.

GINA: I don't think we've met. I always pass on names I recognize—

KATHY: I recognize you…I don't think I liked you then either…

GINA: I'm so sorry. But if you could help me understand who you've been in close—

KATHY: Can't find me in your human tracker, huh? Wanna know why? 'Cause we don't do flu shots. EVER. We don't let the government put things inside us! EVER. I didn't even birth my babies in a hospital. Whadya think of that?

GINA: Well, I think a flu shot helps prevent flu and has no means to track you. Now, your phone company, on the other hand, might be tracking you through its GPS function, but—

KATHY: Like you're not in cahoots with the phone people. I'm president of our Facebook Group and we are UNCOVERING things. Deep things. It's all lies! Lies and bait!

GINA: Ms. Rohn—

KATHY: Your politeness doesn't fool me. WHAT-HAVE-YOU-DONE-TO-THE-CHILDREN?

GINA: …Facebook Group, huh?

(Gina is using her mouse and typing, looking at something on the screen that we don't see.)

KATHY: And I'll be a knuckle's uncle if I'm givin' you information. I have RIGHTS!

GINA: WHOA. Huh…I think you're right…

KATHY: I'm gonna report you—got your name here, your email—and I'm telling everyone about this. How you got into my home with a camera and all—Wait…right about what?

GINA: I think we have met. You and Marvin are members at First United…

(Kathy stops. Gina types and scrolls.)

KATHY: I knew you had trackers!

GINA: Nope…We're Facebook friends, Kathy. I'm never on this—I'm on your Facebook page right now…Oh, and here's your Anti-Vax Group—

KATHY: WHAT? You can't do that! How are we friends? You liar—

GINA: We were both on the church fundraising committee. Remember? Back when I did church.

KATHY: Gina…Gina K?

GINA: *(Clicking through Kathy's online profile)* Gina Kruss. Yes. And… it looks like you were at a church picnic Wednesday. Oh, Kathy. So much close contact. AFTER your test? When you thought you might be sick? Three-legged race…really? No masks. OH…here's some kind of dinner party last night…

KATHY: Get off my Facebook! You can't do that—

GINA: I kinda can. If we need to investigate, we sometimes do so online. Are you on Instagram? Oh! Yes, you are. A hot tub party? Really, Kathy? During a pandemic? And look…no masks. And maybe… no swimsuits? Kathy. Who's this guy Billy you're tagged with…that's very close contact. I thought Marvin was your—

KATHY: Stop it right now—I really remember you now. I REALLY NEVER liked you!

GINA: You can always change your privacy settings. And you really… really…should…

KATHY: How do I do that? *(Coughs a bit)* Can you show me?

GINA: I look at all these photos and there are places here I go. Where I might take my kids. They asked you to self-isolate when you got tested, right?

KATHY: *(Coughing)* …but…it's a hoax…

GINA: Oh, wait. Ah. I see. The dinner party—These are friends from your work, right? The hot tub party are the same people tagged at… Homegrown Insurance. Where you are…the Office Manager. You guys have a great website. I can just call everyone at your work—

(Gina takes notes as she reads off the screen.)

KATHY: NO! Are you gonna tell them I gave them something?

GINA: I can't reveal that. They will never know who gave it to them if they test positive. But I will suggest they all get tested and quarantine if you've been near them like this—

KATHY: Right. Like they won't figure it out.

GINA: Anyone can carry the virus and not even feel sick. What if they visit an elderly parent? And you could have stopped them? I think you know this is real.

KATHY: But if they fire me…I'd lose my insurance. I can't lose my job—

GINA: Quarantine is only a little more than a week—

KATHY: But you can't shut down the world! That kills even more people! The Governor says it's not so bad. That's your boss, right? RIGHT—you said that?

GINA: Yes. The Governor is ultimately my boss.

KATHY: Well, the Governor has rallies all the time and never wears a mask. Why's your boss saying one thing and you come telling me hide in my house when I can't afford to?

GINA: …I wish I knew what, if anything, is going through the Governor's head. The CDC clearly discourages large gatherings. They recommend social distancing—

KATHY: I. WILL. NOT. You can't make me do anything.

(A dirty scowl from Kathy.)

GINA: Correct. I cannot. Would you say you're feeling irritable, Kathy?

KATHY: Maybe 'cause there's a member of the Deep State in my computer.

(She coughs.)

GINA: Irritability is a symptom. So is persistent cough. Do you have a thermometer? Would you take your temp while we're on this call? Where's Marvin? May I speak to him? The hot tub party? Was he there? I don't see him in your photos—

KATHY: He's gone to the store. Stay outta my photos!

GINA: Why aren't you at work today? Did you call in sick? *(She goes back online…)* Oh, look…"Feeling horrible this morning…burning up. Must have overdone it at last night's hot, hot, hot tub…" That was you this morning…

KATHY: Was not—

GINA: It's on your Twitter…timestamp…8:44 a.m.

KATHY: …I've only got two personal days left. I'll have to go back.

GINA: Okay, smart alibi for work. But it's been a few hours. I'd like to get a temperature from you. Do you have a thermometer? Do you feel warm?

(Kathy stares at Gina, vulnerable and stifling her cough. She's looking a little scared and not well.)

GINA: You can take anything over the counter for fever reducer, okay? But if your fever persists, I'd like you to call me back. In fact, do you have a regular doctor…?

(Gina clicks and scrolls around online.)

KATHY: You…deep state Troll! *(Coughs a bit)* SCIENCE FREAK!

GINA: Oh, look, Dr. Lamuda. That's a great office. I suggest letting him know. Looks like you had…back surgery last year? How'd that go?

KATHY: You're gaslighting me…Marvin says everyone is gaslighting us—

GINA: I'm asking you about your back surgery. I know sometimes surgery doesn't stop the pain. Did they give you opioids after your surgery?

KATHY: My back is pretty good. Good. *(Coughs a little)* Better. I threw out the pills. I know what you're getting at—I threw 'em out cold turkey. There was gonna be a problem there.

GINA: Good. And good for you. I don't care about church or politics or the Governor or Facebook groups. All I care about right now is your health. I want to help you be well and stay well. I don't wanna call you back and find out you're not here anymore because you ignored symptoms. Or because Marvin or someone at work told you it's not real. Your body knows what's real and what's not. What's your body telling you about this virus?

KATHY: You sound honest. I'll give you that. Sorry I said I never liked you. I am a little irritable.

GINA: We need you to self-quarantine and take care of yourself. Okay?

KATHY: *(Thinking a bit, digesting it all)* But you got no right to tell me how to live my life. *(Cough)* It's my life and no one's business. *(Cough)* No one ASKED YOU to help me.

GINA: *(Pretty spent, and yet…)* Yes. No one specifically asked me to help you. But aren't you glad I am?

(Kathy is glad, but can't say it out loud.)

GINA: I'll check back soon. And before I forget, according to Facebook… Happy Anniversary!

(Kathy lights up, ready to start a new tirade. Gina ends the call before she can speak. A moment with Gina, recovering. She takes an aspirin then types a bit. The familiar ping…she takes a deep breath, and clicks to find a black screen.)

GINA: Mr. Peterson? I'm Gina with the State Department of Public Health. How are you—I think maybe your camera is not on…Or your mic…Hello? Hello…

LIFE ON A HAMSTER WHEEL
by Rosemary Frisino Toohey

CHARACTERS

MARNI	20s-50s, Female, any race; an actor
PETER	20s-50s, Male, any race; an actor

SETTING

The present. Marni and Peter's apartment.

(At Rise, Marni and Peter are pacing.)

MARNI: Okay. It's a difficult time. We can agree on that.

PETER: A seriously difficult time. Right?

MARNI: Absolutely. Stuck here all day. No auditions, no callbacks, no messages, the phone never rings…

PETER: Your film's postponed. My soap opera's airing reruns…

MARNI: Still and all. Are you telling me that we've now got seventy rolls? Really? Seventy?

PETER: Yeah. Give or take a dozen.

MARNI: That's, that's just…you're hoarding. You realize that, don't you?

PETER: I don't want us to run out.

MARNI: What about the rest of the civilized world? Do you care whether or not they run out?

PETER: The rest of the world does not concern me particularly. Haven't you heard? We're in a crisis.

MARNI: It's all in how you look at it.

PETER: Exactly! So, look at it, for crying out loud. Look at the empty shelves, the pictures of lines of people waiting to get into the—

MARNI: We are two people. Two people only and we don't need seventy rolls of—

PETER: How do you know? How do you know how long this will go on?

How can you be so sure there won't be a worldwide shortage of—

MARNI: Alright, I'm trying to get you to see. Now I'm asking you to hear. To listen.

PETER: Listen to what?

MARNI: The sound of trees, hundreds of thousands of millions of trees being felled in forests right now to fill our linen closet, our spare room, our who-knows-what with toilet paper that we don't need!

PETER: First. We definitely do need it. You cannot say in all truth that we don't need it, because we do. And second, even if we don't need it right now, we will need it and use it someday in the future. Therefore, it makes sense to buy it, keep it, and have it for years to come in order to—

MARNI: Years to come? How crazy is that?

PETER: You're calling me crazy? Well, guess what, Marni, I'm not alone. Half the world is crazy right now, including somebody who sings multiple rounds of Ode To Joy just because she's washing her hands!

MARNI: Which, might I add, you don't do often enough! Washing one's hands is the one sure way to get rid of the germs. That's proven science.

PETER: Well, if it's proven, and if everybody's doing it, then why isn't this thing going away?

MARNI: Science has some of the answers, not all of the answers. It's going to take time.

PETER: Aha! Time during which we're going to need multiple rolls of—

MARNI: Stop it! I don't want to hear it. Let's just chill.

(Pause.)

MARNI: It's all so amazing. The shift from where things were to where they are now.

PETER: What in particular?

MARNI: Well, your show, for one thing. It seems like an eternity ago, but the ratings for *The Proud and the Passionate* were sooo good at the start of the season. Your Doctor Bledsoe was coming into his own. With each episode I could see it, I could feel it.

PETER: Yeah, things were good. And then you got that role in the Dan Craig movie.

MARNI: Which I was waiting to hear about since forever. And now…

PETER: But, Marni, come on. You've got the role. As soon as this is over, they'll shoot it and then…

MARNI: And when will that be?

PETER: When things get back to normal.

MARNI: Yeah. The twelfth of never. Answer me this, Peter. When things actually return to some semblance of normalcy, what will I be?

PETER: What do you mean?

MARNI: By the time the world gets back to this wonderful Nirvana, what… will…I…be?

(Peter shrugs.)

MARNI: Older! I'll be older! That's what I'll be.

PETER: Easy, honey.

MARNI: And they'll want younger! Fresher! Cuter! You know I'm right, Peter. And I'll lose the damn role to some breathless, no-talent newbie who won't have a clue how to jump on a motorcycle in an evening gown. All those hours kickboxing, the money I invested in Zumba classes, what a waste! A total, absolute waste!

PETER: Hey, you don't know that. They love you. In all probability, they'll—

MARNI: Drop me in a heartbeat.

PETER: At least with a Dan Craig flick you've got a chance. Sure and certain, someday the cameras will roll. As for me…another month of reruns and the soap could go under. We've already lost two writers.

MARNI: The sad fact is, without our work, without the concrete reality of acting, what do we have? It's like we're a couple of hamsters on a wheel. Day after day after day, the same thing.

PETER: Hamsters on a wheel?

MARNI: That's what it feels like, this running in place.

PETER: I had a hamster once, you know that? Leopold, I called him. Cute little guy. Fat little cheeks. He was such fun to watch on his little wheel.

MARNI: Round and round and round…

PETER: He used his wheel so much he broke it. Had to buy another one. He took a flying leap once, nearly crashed through the window. That was something to see.

MARNI: Over and over and over…

PETER: Poor little Leopold. The guy had a hell of a heart.

MARNI: When will it end? When will it ever end?

(Pause.)

PETER: Wait a minute. Wait…a minute. What if we looked at this whole thing as…

MARNI: What whole thing?

PETER: What we're going through, the shutdown. What if we looked at it as…rehearsing a part, a role? What if we saw ourselves as working through a script?

MARNI: A script for what?

PETER: A film, a TV show, whatever…what if we saw this whole thing as prepping for an opening?

MARNI: When do we open?

PETER: I don't know. But if we could think of it as…

MARNI: I see what you mean, the opening of a show! Next spring.

PETER: Exactly! Starring you and me!

MARNI: And that would help us to…?

PETER: Well, we know what we have to do, then. It's all in the script.

MARNI: So, your hoarding toilet paper…

PETER: It's all part of the play. See?

MARNI: Right. And that means…you're not crazy. There's nothing wrong with you…

PETER: Well, I know that.

MARNI: Just like there's nothing wrong with me singing endless songs while I endlessly wash my hands. It's all part of the scene…

PETER: Which we are constantly rehearsing!

MARNI: All we need is our motivation. Which would be…survival, I guess.

PETER: And what's more critical than that?

MARNI: Kind of like Groundhog Day.

PETER: Groundhog Day On The Beach.

MARNI: On the beach?

PETER: Fifties post-apocalyptic doomsday drama.

MARNI: You're not saying this is doomsday?

PETER: No, no, honey. It's a play, remember? We're just in a play.

MARNI: A boring, repetitive play. But…it's a play

PETER: That's it. Feel it, believe it, see it.

MARNI: By God, we're going to get really good at this.

PETER: Couple of more months and we'll have this thing nailed.

MARNI: Hamsters on a wheel will have nothing on us.

(Lights down.)

THE LAST NIGHT
by Molly Wagner

CHARACTERS

VIOLET	Early 20s, Female
JACK	Early 20s, Male

SETTING

A closed concert venue with a bar.

(At Rise, lights up on a dark and abandoned concert venue. We hear a lock being jimmied and Violet enters, using the light on her phone to see. She shines it around the area and just stands in the space for a moment, her eyes closed. She hums softly to herself. Absently, she pulls her hair free from her hair tie but sends it skittering across the floor. She takes a deep breath and then gets down on her hands and knees, looking for the hair tie.)

VIOLET: Ew. Ew. Ew.

(She rests the phone on her shoulder, reaches into her pocket and pulls out her hand sanitizer—vigorously rubbing her hands together. She goes back to the floor, shining the light, bending down. Suddenly the light turns on as Jack enters. He practically trips over Violet, who screams, and they jump apart—moving far away from each other.)

JACK: Jesus Christ! What the hell?
VIOLET: You're not supposed to be here.
JACK: You're not supposed to be here.

(Violet takes her phone and points it at Jack.)

VIOLET: I could report you.

(Jack takes his phone and points it at Violet.)

JACK: Then do it. What are you waiting for?

VIOLET: You can't just break into places.

JACK: Hold up. I'm the one with the keys here.

VIOLET: You're not supposed to be out of your house.

JACK: Look are we just going to run around and keep accusing each other of the same shit because I'd like to know how long we're supposed to keep doing that for. I've got things to do.

(Jack walks towards Violet she moves back, but soon her back is against the wall and she has nowhere else to go. She screams.)

VIOLET: Don't! Don't come any closer. Please.

JACK: Do you have it?

VIOLET: I don't know. Do you?

JACK: I don't know. I don't think I do, if that makes you feel any better. But like, I haven't been tested or anything so, like

VIOLET: There's like, no way to really know.

JACK: Yeah.

(Jack's phone vibrates—the incessant vibration of a phone call. He ignores it. Jack and Violet listen to it buzz until silence. Jack walks closer, Violet flinches.)

JACK: Relax. It's more than 6 feet.

VIOLET: No, it's not.

JACK: Yes, it is. We're fine.

VIOLET: How do you know that's six feet?

JACK: Because—it. It looks like it's more than six feet. I think.

VIOLET: But you don't know. Not really.

JACK: I don't have it. I haven't been exposed or anything so

VIOLET: You don't know that either!

JACK: Okay, wait. Fine. Stay there. Jesus.

(Jack leaves. Violet looks around, trying to figure out what to do. After a few moments, Jack returns with a cable.)

JACK: Eight-foot cable. Okay?

VIOLET: Okay.

(He uncoils it and throws it towards Violet. She takes out her hand sanitizer, wipes her hands, and then takes the cable. Jack notices.)

JACK: What is that?

VIOLET: Nothing.

JACK: How'd you get a hold of that stuff?

VIOLET: I didn't steal it.

JACK: You hoard it?

VIOLET: No.

JACK: Stuff's been impossible to get a hold of for months.

VIOLET: Yeah, I know.

JACK: So, how'd you get it.

VIOLET: I just got lucky.

JACK: Sure.

(Violet quickly puts the sanitizer away. Jack picks up his end of the cable.)

JACK: I'm just going behind the bar.

(They negotiate the space, adjusting their stance until Jack makes it

behind the bar. He drops his end of the cable.)

JACK: Got a preference? Whiskey? Tequila? Gin?

VIOLET: I'm good.

JACK: Don't drink?

VIOLET: No, I just…

JACK: Dude. It's fine. You've got your precious sanitizer and nobody's been here since the Falling Flowers concert so if there were any droplets or whatever—I'm just saying, stuff's probably safe by now.

VIOLET: You broke into this place for booze? You know liquor stores are still open, right?

JACK: Kind of ironic, isn't it? It's the twenties and liquor stores are now considered essential business. Can't get a tooth pulled, but no one's gonna deny you a bottle of tequila.

(Jack grabs a bottle of whiskey, works the cable, and makes it back from behind the bar. He sits on the floor. His phone vibrates—phone call. He and Violet wait in silence for the buzzing of the phone to stop.)

VIOLET: Are you going to answer that?

JACK: Nope.

VIOLET: What if it's important?

JACK: I know who it's from.

VIOLET: Who?

JACK: My mom.

VIOLET: So, what if it's important.

JACK: It is.

VIOLET: You're seriously not going to answer it?

JACK: Want me to tell you how it's going to go? I can tell you exactly how it will go: "Hi Mom." "Hi Jack. You're Grandpa is dying." "Yes, I know. He has been for the past several months." "No, I mean he is dying dying. Right now. Dying." "Well can I come see him? Can I come say goodbye?" "No, no you can't. There are no visitors. It's too risky." "Too risky for what?" "He might get sick if he has visitors." "Oh. Right, right. Wouldn't want him to die. Oh, wait." That's how that conversation is going to go. And since there isn't really much I can do about it, then no, no I don't think I will answer the phone.

(Beat.)

VIOLET: I'm sorry.
JACK: You pried.
VIOLET: Well, I'm sorry.
JACK: Well. Yeah. I am too.

(Jack places his hand on the cap of the Whiskey bottle to unscrew it.)

VIOLET: Wait! Don't. Stop. Wait.

(Violet pulls out her hand sanitizer. She contemplates it for a moment before rolling it across the floor to Jack.)

VIOLET: Just. Be safe. Just to be safe.
JACK: You sure you want to share with me? This stuff is liquid gold. Gotta be worth what, twenty bucks a drop?
VIOLET: I'll bill you for it later.
JACK: When the stimulus check comes through?
VIOLET: Right.
JACK: Deal.

(Jack uses the hand sanitizer. He rolls it back over to Violet, opens the whiskey and takes a swig.)

VIOLET: This is weird.

JACK: No shit.

VIOLET: I don't think I've physically been in the same room with a stranger, since…I don't know.

JACK: Yeah.

VIOLET: It's not supposed to be like this.

JACK: Maybe it is. Maybe it's—

VIOLET: Our punishment? The world trying to heal itself?

JACK: Maybe.

VIOLET: You believe that?

JACK: Why not? Could be. We've fucked things up for way too long. Consequences got to happen sooner or later, right?

VIOLET: That's so morbid.

JACK: None of us are promised tomorrow.

VIOLET: Wow.

JACK: What? I'm just being a pragmatist

VIOLET: An asshole.

(Beat. Jack smiles and takes another drink.)

VIOLET: The summer before my freshman year of college I volunteered at the hospital to be a baby cuddler.

JACK: A what?

VIOLET: A baby cuddler.

JACK: That's not a thing.

VIOLET: It is! It's important, too. You know, a baby needs physical contact in order to develop and mature. Without it, they could have developmental road blocks. Human touch, human contact is vital to our existence. Humans need physical contact. We weren't designed to function without it.

JACK: Die immediately with touch, die less immediately without it.

VIOLET: Great options we've left ourselves with, huh? Then again, I suppose no one is promised tomorrow.

JACK: Why did you break curfew?

VIOLET: Why did you?

JACK: Free booze, baby.

(Jack waves the bottle around unconvincingly. He takes another drink.)

JACK: Were you hoping to find someone? Someone else?

VIOLET: No. Everyone is supposed to be inside.

JACK: So why come here?

VIOLET: I was supposed to be here. That night. The last night. Before the whole world kind of just stopped.

JACK: The concert? That Falling Flowers Concert.

(Violet nods.)

JACK: Really?

VIOLET: Why is that so hard to believe?

JACK: Their sound is shit.

VIOLET: Is not.

JACK: Is too! All that fake grunge synth shit. No thank you.

VIOLET: Just because you don't have taste.

JACK: I have taste.

VIOLET: Liking obscure hipster bands and shitting on other people's choices of music does not equal taste.

JACK: Obscure hipster bands? That's who you've pegged me for.

VIOLET: Am I wrong?

JACK: So, what happened?

(Beat.)

VIOLET: I don't know. I was scared. All of my friends, we had been talking about this concert, planning it for months. Then the reports kept trickling in and everyone was encouraging us to stay home. There were talks of closures and bans and massive restrictions and I fought with myself—is it better to get ahead of it? To be a responsible human? Or should I take advantage of the things while I can because any day now those things might not be available to you ever again.

JACK: And you sacrificed your—

VIOLET: My last night out.

JACK: I could have seen my Grandpa. When he was first admitted to the hospital, we didn't know how big this thing was, how fast it could spread. We were encouraged to stay away, but it wasn't full-out prohibited.

VIOLET: You did the right thing.

JACK: By what, buying him three more months of complete and total loneliness? Isn't loneliness just as deadly?

VIOLET: We don't know who we saved with our sacrifices, but I have to believe that we saved someone. Otherwise, it will drive us both crazy—and we've already got enough of that going on around outside. We don't need to add to it.

(Beat.)

JACK: Isn't it funny how something happens, rocks your world, shakes it to the very core—even in gradual increments you can still pinpoint the last day, the last moment where everything was normal. Down to the second.

VIOLET: I went to the movies with my parents. We shared popcorn. We were excited because it was the opening weekend and we still got really good seats. We were excited about good seats.

JACK: I puked on the subway.

VIOLET: You puked on a subway?

JACK: I puked into my backpack it was fine. We all went out after work. After the Falling Flowers concert, actually. Passing around drinks. We took a photo—I'm terrible at taking photos, but we all took a photo.

VIOLET: Right before you puked on the Subway

JACK: Right before I puked on the Subway.

VIOLET: Puking on the Subway constitutes your last normal night?

JACK: Weird, right?

VIOLET: What was it like?

JACK: Puking on the subway?

VIOLET: No. The concert.

JACK: That was a very abrupt conversation shift.

VIOLET: Were they good?

(Jack watches Violet, trying to figure out what it is she wants him to say.)

JACK: Yeah. They were incredible. You know, for a grunge, synth pop sell-out.

(Violet smiles.)

VIOLET: And everyone there, where they—dancing? Was that the last night of dancing?

JACK: They were. Everyone was dancing.

VIOLET: Do you think they knew? That the next day the whole world would just…Stop?

JACK: Yeah. I think so. That's what made the dancing even better.

VIOLET: So that's it then, isn't it?

JACK: What?

VIOLET: Coming together. Being around others. Dancing.

JACK: This things gotta end at some point, right?

VIOLET: But something has shifted. Things won't go back.

JACK: You think people will stop dancing?

VIOLET: I don't know.

(Beat. Violet looks around the space. Jack gets up, he skirts around Violet—maintaining his six feet and leaves. After a moment, the music from the speakers crackles to life as a song from the concert starts playing. Jack is still gone. Violet stands and she begins to dance, freely, on her own. Jack appears and watches her from a distance. She catches his eye and they dance from opposite sides of the room. They move closer towards one another. Violet picks up her end of the cable, Jack picks up his end. They dance. They look at each other. Violet sets down her end of the cable. Jack sets down his end of the cable. Lights down.)

WAITING (IN AMERICA)
by Robert Walikis

CHARACTERS

ADLEIGH	Female, with two children and a partner in the military overseas
BENORICE	Female, single, close to parents and furloughed
CAMERON	Female, single, mother of a large family, so has to work
DEIRDRE	Female, with a husband; her grown children live far away

SETTING

A Coronavirus testing line, 6:11 a.m.

(At Rise, Lights up. Overhead spotlights like streetlamps brighten six-foot distance markers across the stage. Adleigh, standing in line, stares ahead offstage right. A beat. Ahead of her, Benorice, also masked, walks slowly onto the stage, downstage of Adleigh. They acknowledge and notice each other as they pass fully distanced. Benorice walks to the line, stands, takes out a phone from her pocket, and starts to text. Adleigh strikes up a conversation.)

ADLEIGH: Good. Someone else is here. So glad to have some company.
BENORICE: Where's the line?
ADLEIGH: You're looking at it. I am the line.
BENORICE: Thanks. I'm just surprised. Where is everyone? Yesterday, right?
ADLEIGH: I waited yesterday, for over two hours, it was way too long.
BENORICE: I drove past. Ugh, yeah.
ADLEIGH: I gave up: "Try again tomorrow." And now that's today.
BENORICE: Yeah. Today is another day.

(Benorice returns to her phone.)

ADLEIGH: Two-thirty.

BENORICE: Pardon?

ADLEIGH: Two-thirty. I got here at two-thirty this morning. I couldn't sleep.

BENORICE: I know what you mean; these days…

ADLEIGH: I woke up at two, paced around my bedroom. Then I drove over with the kids and parked. We waited in my car, and we all fell asleep.

BENORICE: Wow. Are you doing okay?

ADLEIGH: No. Not really. There was this car coming into the lot: it startled me. The headlights woke me up, around 4:37, I think it was? I grabbed my keys, locked the car doors, left the kids, ran to the line.

BENORICE: Long time to stand here alone. I thought getting here after six was a risk. But I needed sleep. I don't sleep much, either, these days.

ADLEIGH: There were cars before the one at 4:37, but you could tell they were just driving through. And I was awake then.

BENORICE: I see why you got in line. You couldn't risk it.

ADLEIGH: The car was driving so slow. It looked full. For a minute, I imagined there were even more cars behind their headlights. A caravan. A caravan of cars. Maybe I dreamed that. Seemed real.

BENORICE: Wow. That's a really bad dream: car caravan and not being in line.

ADLEIGH: Would you tell me your bad dreams? I know I shouldn't pry.

BENORICE: It's alright. I'll tell you. It's all hunger and money and sickness and housing. And death. A lot of death. And I'm not a nightmare kind of person. These are dreams about everything. And death.

ADLEIGH: That's worse than a car caravan. Wow.

BENORICE: Sorry. I'm telling the truth more these days. Seems important. I'm so sorry if what I said bothered you. I can be pretty morbid.

ADLEIGH: No, it's just…my dreams aren't that vivid. They're all surface level. The banality of overwhelming inconvenience: limited toilet paper options, online food orders that never show up on time.

BENORICE: Change is scary enough. Put all the rest on top and it's pure horror.

ADLEIGH: I had my mace, just in case. Maybe I should have gotten a tire iron from the trunk, right? My son is a black belt in Taekwondo. Now that someone else is here, I think I'm fine.

BENORICE: Do they need to be in line too? Because I don't mind if they go ahead of me. They should go ahead of me.

ADLEIGH: No. Just me. It's just me.

BENORICE: If you change your mind, I don't mind. They are welcome to go first with you. I think I would feel better if they did.

ADLEIGH: Thank you. You're kind. I don't get a lot of kindness these days.

BENORICE: I hope you get a lot more. I'm glad to help. Glad to be here.

(Cameron enters stage left, not feeling well: wheezing, coughing, catching her breath; Benorice notices first, because of her breathing. Adleigh notices her coughing.)

BENORICE: Are you okay?

CAMERON: I'm okay. Is this the line?

BENORICE: Yes. You're in the right place.

CAMERON: Where is everybody?

BENORICE: I know, right?

CAMERON: Do you think it's closed?

BENORICE: I don't think so. The tents are still up. It's just early?

CAMERON: Okay. I need to get back soon. I walked over. Doesn't it open at eight?

ADLEIGH: You don't sound so good.

CAMERON: I know. It all came on overnight. I need to get back to my kids.

ADLEIGH: Mine are in the car. Sleeping.

CAMERON: I left my oldest in charge. He's twelve: he makes breakfast. I trust him.

ADLEIGH: How many do you have?

CAMERON: There are five. Twelve, nine, seven, five, and two. It's a lot. They're good, but it's a lot. It's just me, but my oldest, he helps. More than he should.

BENORICE: Five. Wow. I don't know how you do it.

CAMERON: I don't know either. But I think he can manage while I'm gone.

BENORICE: Do you want to get ahead of me in the line?

CAMERON: No, the line is short. When it opens, will it move quickly?

BENORICE: I would feel much better if you went ahead of me. Please?

ADLEIGH: I don't know if that's wise. I think it's better if she stays back behind you. Right? We've got masks, but just to be sure.

BENORICE: Four kids is a lot for a twelve-year-old: she needs to get back home.

ADLEIGH: Look, no offense, but you've got symptoms. I'm glad you're here, you're in line, but I can't risk it. I can't get sick if I'm not already.

BENORICE: No one can. I can't. My parents have been six weeks without anyone, getting food dropped off, neighbors nice enough to help. Now I'm out of a job, and I need to know so I can help them. But the backlog is at least a week. Not one of us will know today.

CAMERON: A week? Takes a week? I don't have time. I need to know now.

ADLEIGH: I know. We all do. I just don't want to put myself at more risk. If I'm not sick, I don't want to get it. If you're sick, I want you to know. We won't know for a week, but that's why I'm here today.

CAMERON: I can't go to the emergency room. What will I do?

ADLEIGH: If you're sick, you should go.

CAMERON: I have no insurance. I can't pay. I can't go.

BENORICE: I think you should get ahead of me, turn yourself away from both of us, and that way there's no risk to you or me or anyone, right?

ADLEIGH: I don't want her near me. Can't she just stay in line? We're all in line. Just stay in line.

BENORICE: If you're not getting much kindness, maybe you should be giving it?

ADLEIGH: I need to be safe. For my kids. Amy is overseas: there's no one else to take care of my kids. I cannot get sick. I want her to stay in line.

CAMERON: I don't want to cause a fuss. It's okay. I'll be okay. I'm fine where I'm at. I'll be okay. If it takes a week, then I'm stuck. Lose my job. Five kids. I'm stuck. But I'll be okay.

BENORICE: I hope you'll be okay. Maybe it's not what you think? Maybe it's just a bad cold. Did you get your flu shot?

CAMERON: No. No. I'll be okay.

(Deirdre arrives with a purse, coffee cup. She walks past Cameron and Benorice and then in front of Adleigh. Indignant. Mask down. Looking on the ground for something.)

DEIRDRE: Where is it? Didn't you see it? What did you do?

ADLEIGH: What are you talking about? Can you please put your mask up?

DEIRDRE: There's a note. I left it here this morning.

BENORICE: We didn't see any note. What note?

DEIRDRE: I was getting coffee and I left a note. Put it right where you're standing. I know I left it there. What happened to it?

ADLEIGH: I didn't do anything. I didn't see a note. I've been here all night.

DEIRDRE: No, I was here before you. I was here just after midnight.

ADLEIGH: I have been here since two-thirty this morning. You weren't here then, and you haven't been here. I didn't see anyone in line here.

DEIRDRE: I was here just after midnight and I left a note. I went for coffee and now I'm back. Where's the note?

BENORICE: I think there's something under your shoe. There. Yes.

(Adleigh reaches down, looking around her, and finds a small pink note, folded tightly. She puts on a glove and brings it up for all to see.)

ADLEIGH: This is your note?

DEIRDRE: Yes. I said I left a note.

ADLEIGH: Why did you leave a note?

DEIRDRE: Read it.

ADLEIGH: Why a note?

DEIRDRE: Read it.

(Adleigh unfolds the note, reads it, and is angry.)

ADLEIGH: This? You think this gives you the right?

DEIRDRE: Yes. I was here after midnight. And I left a note.

ADLEIGH: "I went for coffee. I will be back. Save my spot. Signed, Deirdre." You think this gives you the right?

DEIRDRE: I was here. That note proves it.

ADLEIGH: And you left. You left. Leaving a note doesn't save your spot. You left. This isn't the Huntington Beach July Fourth Parade, where you've chalked out your space on the sidewalk like everyone else and then you leave. You don't get to leave a note to save your spot.

BENORICE: You came here after midnight to leave a note and went for coffee?

ADLEIGH: I didn't come here at two-thirty this morning and leave a note. I sat in my car and I waited, with my kids. When I got in line, I got in line and no one else was here: no one. I didn't see your note and you don't get the right. I didn't go out to get coffee after staying up all night and expect to have my spot held by a note left on the pavement.

DEIRDRE: Do you want to get some coffee? Because I can hold your spot…

ADLEIGH: NOOOO! I don't want to get coffee and you don't get my spot and you don't leave notes. And can you keep your mask up? Please.

DEIRDRE: Okay. Okay. Fine. Fine. I'll get in line. I'm going.

(Dierdre passes Cameron, whose breathing and coughing start as Dierdre approaches. She masks up immediately.)

DEIRDRE: Oh, great. Excuse me? Can you cough in another direction, please?

ADLEIGH: Leave her alone. She's in line just like everyone else.

DEIRDRE: I just don't need this. I can't get sick and then get on a plane. I leave in two weeks for vacation, and I can't get sick.

ADLEIGH: Good God, you're insufferable. Do you have any symptoms?

DEIRDRE: No. But I can't fly without a negative test. Everyone knows that.

BENORICE: There's no requirement for testing proof. They just take your temperature and ask you questions. Have you been exposed?

DEIRDRE: Are you kidding? No. I mean, probably not. Just the neighbors. We had a cookout, but that was two weeks ago, and even though one of their family is in the ICU and a few are sick, we're fine. And the girl group. We had some drinks last Friday. Tracey didn't make it to spin class, but she thinks it's a reaction to all the gin we drank. I mean, I don't think my gardeners have it. But I can't understand them without their masks off. No, no, probably not. I hope not.

ADLEIGH: Unbelievable. Do you take any of this seriously? Does anyone you know take this seriously at all? Ever?

(Cameron has been on her phone, looking online, and dejectedly reports the news back to everyone:)

CAMERON: There's no line. There's no testing today. There's no line here.

DEIRDRE: What? Well, why the hell did I leave a note, then?

CAMERON: I just looked it up online. They moved the location to the other side of town. It opened already. I don't think I will make it.

BENORICE: Do you need a ride? I could give you a ride. In the backseat.

CAMERON: Are you sure? Okay…

DEIRDRE: Good luck. Next time, I'll leave a person instead of a note.

(Deirdre leaves. Cameron leaves with Benorice. Adleigh is left where she began, realizing she is first in a line that is not happening today.)

ADLEIGH: What do I do?

LOCKDOWN
by Brian Wallace

CHARACTERS

ELLIOT	30s or 40s
VICTORIA	30s or 40s

SETTING

The living room of an apartment or condo flat. The furniture is arranged in an L-shape, with the front door just past the longest couch.

(At Rise, Elliot and Victoria sit in silence for several moments, Victoria nursing a bottle of beer. It's a Corona, ideally—but not necessarily—and the battered lime wedge has long since drowned at the base of the bottle. Victoria slowly swigs the bottle, washing back only the dregs of the beer.)

ELLIOT: Was that the last one?
VICTORIA: Yeah.

(Pause.)

ELLIOT: That's okay.
VICTORIA: There's a little left at the bottom. You want it? *(Pause)* Here. I'm good. Have it.

(Pause.)

ELLIOT: I'd better not.
VICTORIA: Why?
ELLIOT: Just. I…just want to be careful now.

VICTORIA: I get it.

ELLIOT: It's the headlines. I'm spending too much time on the Internet. It's making me paranoid about everything.

VICTORIA: Right.

ELLIOT: It's true. I'm not even using the same fork twice. My own fork. Have you seen me do that? I keep washing it, practically in between bites.

VICTORIA: Sure.

ELLIOT: Stop saying "sure." It's true.

VICTORIA: Nothing to do with the fact that I'm a whore.

ELLIOT: You're not a whore. Stop it.

VICTORIA: You said I was. Twice.

ELLIOT: That was in the heat of the moment.

VICTORIA: Which moment?

ELLIOT: Both moments. Different kinds of heat. As you know. I'm sorry.

VICTORIA: Which time are you sorry about?

(Pause.)

ELLIOT: For the time that upset you. The first time I said it, as I recall, you didn't seem to mind. You did a pretty good job of convincing me you liked it, in fact.

VICTORIA: That was in the heat of the—

ELLIOT: That's what I said.

VICTORIA: That's when I thought you were single.

(Pause.)

ELLIOT: Yeah, I know. I'm sorry. I'm sorry I put you in this position. I keep saying it. I'm sorry I lied to you, Vicky.

VICTORIA: Victoria.

ELLIOT: Okay…

(Pause.)

VICTORIA: My friends call me Vicky. Not men who lie to me. Your privilege is revoked.

ELLIOT: Ah. Well. I don't normally lie…if it helps. I do live a remarkably honest life, other than this. If you can believe that. I didn't lie to get this place. All my documents were legit. I'm qualified for my job—overqualified, in fact. You know, a few months ago I bought some chips from a vending machine? It dispensed two bags. I left the extra one on top instead of taking it for myself.

VICTORIA: *(Dryly)* You have the purest heart of any species ever subjected to evolution.

ELLIOT: I'm just telling you. This—here—doesn't define me. I can't stop you from having a poor opinion of me—and I deserve that—but it's not the sum total of who I am. If I ran for office, this would be the only skeleton in my closet.

VICTORIA: You planning to run for office?

ELLIOT: After this? Not in your district. I just…I just hope that helps you a little.

VICTORIA: Helps me? Helps me with what?

ELLIOT: You know…understand me. Understand this.

VICTORIA: My God, you are such a condescending narcissist. Please, tell me what epiphany you have ushered me upon, Mahatma. Other than don't drink alone and go home with strange guys.

ELLIOT: That's just my point. You could have gone home with anybody…

VICTORIA: Really? Just anybody—because I'm a whore, right?

ELLIOT: No. What I'm trying to say is, you're lucky you went home with me. As despicable as my actions have been, at least I'm not a murderer or a rapist…

VICTORIA: …Oh, God, please stop…

ELLIOT: Or a psycho. I'm just a liar and a cheat. At least, I've been behaving like that. My only intention was to spend more time with you. To get closer to you. Not to harm you or take any kind of advantage you weren't willing to offer anyway.

VICTORIA: You're justifying yourself. You're trying to mitigate.

ELLIOT: Yes. I am. Mitigate, not justify. I won't say this was an aberration or anything. Clearly something was lurking beneath the surface with me. But it's certainly never been a habit.

VICTORIA: If I agree with you, you get to let yourself off the hook, don't you?

ELLIOT: Maybe a little. It would make it easier when you go. When this lockdown is over. You're the one I screwed over.

VICTORIA: Not to mention your wife.

ELLIOT: I didn't mention her. I can't bear to yet. I feel terrible. If it makes a difference, I've already deleted the app from my phone.

VICTORIA: That's covering your tracks, not penitence.

(Pause.)

ELLIOT: Penance is what you're trying to say.

(Pause. She glares at him.)

ELLIOT: I apologize. I actually debated whether to correct you. I know it isn't polite. It's just that correct usage is a weird quirk with me, for some reason. I've never been able to fight it.

VICTORIA: You must be really popular on Facebook.

ELLIOT: *(Laughs)* I have less than three hundred friends on Facebook. My dentist has over a thousand. A dentist!

VICTORIA: Fewer than three hundred friends. Not less.

ELLIOT: Touché. Anyway, I've been in a state of penitence since I woke up with you.

VICTORIA: Gee, thanks.

ELLIOT: That's not how I meant it.

VICTORIA: Penance, penitence, who cares? Sorry I didn't know which word to use. I don't live the kind of life where I need to keep either one handy.

ELLIOT: Neither do I. That's what I'm trying to get across.

VICTORIA: I should just go.

ELLIOT: You can't go. If you're caught outside during the lockdown, you'll get in trouble.

VICTORIA: I'll risk it.

ELLIOT: With beer on your breath? You'll be arrested.

VICTORIA: Let me use your toothbrush then.

ELLIOT: Not my toothbrush. Even if there weren't a virus out there, I wouldn't share my toothbrush.

VICTORIA: You are married, right?

ELLIOT: For fourteen years.

VICTORIA: Okay then, so you weren't a virgin before I came home with you.

ELLIOT: After fourteen years? No, just out of practice.

VICTORIA: Fine. So when we were having sex, you recognized it as that, didn't you? As sex, or copulation, or *in flagrante delicto*, or whatever words hyper-educated guys use to convince themselves they aren't just horny.

ELLIOT: It brought back memories, yes. I take your point.

VICTORIA: No, you don't, because I haven't gotten to it yet. My point is…this thing that's going around. It's spread by close contact. Sex qualifies. So, if I have it, you have it. If you have it, I have it. So, if I borrow your toothbrush or your fork or your beer, it doesn't make any damn difference anymore. Except that would be slightly more intimate.

ELLIOT: How would that be more intimate than sex?

VICTORIA: Because we'd be sharing them honestly.

ELLIOT: Look, we used protection. I feel fine.

VICTORIA: That's because you have no soul. I feel nauseous. Physically, I'm fine. We're probably both fine. So again, it makes no difference.

ELLIOT: It does make a difference. If they arrest you for being outside during the quarantine, then I'm going to get implicated. They'll want to know where you're coming from, who you've been with. Are you going to lie to protect me? Will you lie to protect a liar? You don't want to risk that.

VICTORIA: Not to mention my own health and safety, right?

ELLIOT: Of course. That goes without saying!

VICTORIA: Why? Why does that go without saying? My wellbeing.

ELLIOT: Look, you've caught me in the middle of the most selfish, indulgent week of my life. Okay? It's taking me a little while to come down from it. To get back to normal. If it hadn't been for the lockdown, I'd be a lot closer to it by now. You'd be gone, and I'd be guilty and miserable, but a little more decent. I'd have a little more perspective.

VICTORIA: I'm sure. A regular Saint Francis. I think I see bluebirds at the window now, vying for your attention.

ELLIOTT: Why do you keep picking at me? I'm not putting up any defenses here. But you're not making things better. You've made your point. Okay? I was a creep. But suppose for a minute that I were actually single. Would we be arguing now?

VICTORIA: You only admitted the truth because I'm stuck here and your wife is coming home. You had no choice.

ELLIOT: That's true. But that wasn't the question.

VICTORIA: Maybe I have a choice. If they're keeping the airports open for her, I can probably slip out.

ELLIOT: The airport isn't open for her, she's just on a plane.

VICTORIA: You know what I mean.

ELLIOT: They're only letting it land because the plane was already in the air. Before the lockdown. Rotten luck. Timing, I mean, not luck. I'm hoping they'll sequester her. Keep her at the airport until this lifts. Then you'll have plenty of time to get out.

VICTORIA: Really? It's not enough that you cheat on her. Now you want to stick her in a dingy airport conference room for two weeks?

ELLIOT: No, I don't want to. But it's probably the safest place for her to be.

VICTORIA: Safest for you.

ELLIOT: That too. And everybody else in the building.

VICTORIA: That's not what I meant.

ELLIOT: I know what you meant. But I meant it too. I did a bad thing. But should I die for it?

VICTORIA: You're not going to die from it. From what I hear, you have to be a thousand years old and missing a lung.

ELLIOT: Okay, do I deserve to get sick then? Laid up for two weeks wishing I were dead? I don't think so. Let's keep a sense of proportion here. And anyway, you don't actually know who's at risk. If you had any medical knowledge at all, you'd be exempt from the lockdown. So please. Don't be a science denier. Not in my home.

VICTORIA: Oh. Just. Shut. Up. Do I look like a Twitter feed? Of all the people who get to virtue signal today, you are last in line. Your morals have to be at least this high to get on that ride. *(Beat)* I have to use your bathroom.

ELLIOT: What do you have to do?

VICTORIA: Excuse me? Don't worry, I won't mess with your toothbrush.

ELLIOT: No, but I have to go too.

VICTORIA: I'll just be a minute.

ELLIOT: But what I'm saying is, you're a woman.

VICTORIA: Yeah?

ELLIOT: So, there's a limited amount of toilet paper.

VICTORIA: I'm not going to hold it.

ELLIOT: But what about me?

VICTORIA: Haven't you leaned on that question enough for one life? I've only known you since the lockdown, and I'm already tired of hearing it. Everybody else you've ever met must be dead from exhaustion.

(Victoria goes into the bathroom and closes the door. Elliot stews for a bit and then notices something on a shelf. It's a framed photo of his wife. It's a social scene, not candid, but not posed. She's at a party or function. She's dressed well and looks attractive and happy. Elliot ponders this photo and exhales deeply. Suddenly he touches his chest a little nervously and starts to breathe in and out a lot. Nothing over the top, but it's clear he is monitoring his breath, more as a test than out of panic. The toilet flushes from the bathroom, water runs in the sink, and after a few moments, Victoria emerges.)

VICTORIA: You okay? What are you doing?

ELLIOT: I tried to sigh over something just now and felt like my lungs didn't fill all the way.

VICTORIA: You tried to sigh? Nobody tries to sigh, you just do it.

ELLIOT: I just tried to do it, but it came up a little short. I'm not exactly worried, but I'd like to get one full breath at least.

VICTORIA: You're just psyching yourself out. Stop thinking about it and you'll be fine.

ELLIOT: I'll stop thinking about it as soon as my lungs fill. It's one of the symptoms, you know.

VICTORIA: So is a fever. Here, let me feel you.

(She reaches out to touch his forehead, but he moves away.)

ELLIOT: Whoa.

VICTORIA: What?

ELLIOT: Twenty seconds.

VICTORIA: What?

ELLIOT: You're supposed to wash your hands for twenty seconds. You didn't spend twenty seconds washing your hands in the bathroom just now.

VICTORIA: I didn't count. You counted?

ELLIOT: It's not up to me to count. It's up to the person who belongs to the hands. Even so, I can tell when roughly twenty seconds go by. I played xylophone in the school band. There was a lot of waiting.

VICTORIA: I bet. Probably till Christmas.

ELLIOT: To me, that sounded like a normal hand wash. A hand wash for normal times.

VICTORIA: I'm not an unsanitary person, Elliot. I washed them plenty long enough for what I had to do. Even left you some toilet paper.

ELLIOT: How much?

VICTORIA: A couple squares.

ELLIOT: A couple squares?

VICTORIA: Relax, you have plenty. How's your breathing?

ELLIOT: It's actually fine now.

VICTORIA: I thought so.

ELLIOT: I don't have any hand sanitizer. If you hadn't drunk all the beer, I'd have you soak your hands in that.

VICTORIA: I didn't drink all the beer. I drank the last beer. And I offered you the last sip. My God. You're such a passive-aggressive little martyr.

ELLIOT: Hey, tell me something. What do you think of when you see this picture?

(He shows her the framed photo.)

VICTORIA: Am I supposed to think something? She looks happy.

ELLIOT: Who do you think it is?

VICTORIA: Is it your wife?

ELLIOT: Of course it's my wife. Who else would it be?

VICTORIA: Could be anybody. Your sister, your mother, a friend…

ELLIOT: My mother? This is a recent photo. You think my mother looks like this today?

VICTORIA: If she does, you come from a very good gene pool. Why are you making me look at a photo of your wife? It's a little tactless, like you want me to feel guilty or bad or something. I didn't do anything wrong, at least not knowingly.

ELLIOT: That's what I'm wondering.

VICTORIA: Excuse me? This is on you.

ELLIOT: This photo sits in a frame on that shelf. Has done for years.

VICTORIA: So?

ELLIOT: So, it's the first thing you see when you open the door.

VICTORIA: Well, I didn't see it.

ELLIOT: You must have. I'm so used to seeing it all the time that I forgot to put it away when I went out the other night. But when I came home with you, it was the first thing I noticed.

VICTORIA: I didn't.

ELLIOT: So, whenever you go someplace for the first time you never take in your surroundings? You're that one person? I could have been a serial killer for all you knew. You didn't look around for any duct tape or a cellar door?

VICTORIA: It was dark, I had been drinking. I couldn't see.

ELLIOT: You don't wear glasses or contacts. You had LASIK surgery five years ago in February. Best decision you ever made, you said.

VICTORIA: Certainly since then.

ELLIOT: See? I'm a very good listener. That's one of the reasons you came home with me, wasn't it? Because I'm a very, very good listener.

VICTORIA: It was a refreshing and attractive quality. I had no idea its side effects were naked arrogance and the third degree.

ELLIOT: So, you come home with a man my age and see that he's got a framed photo of a woman this age, and you go to bed with him anyway. Do you see where I'm going with this?

VICTORIA: I saw where you went. Into a bedroom with me. You just said you noticed it when we came in, but it didn't stop you, did it?

ELLIOT: I nearly had a heart attack. But when you didn't say anything, I figured you were cool with it and probably knew the score.

VICTORIA: I knew nothing.

ELLIOT: Pastel bedsheets? Lavender-scented candles? Pillow shams?

VICTORIA: This is not a reflection of me. I'm not going to sit here and be cross-examined, Elliot, while you try to paint me as a slut or something just so you can be at peace with yourself. I don't deserve that. I didn't see the picture. It didn't register with me. Not everybody graduated with a 4.0, you know. Some of us are just trying to live our lives as decent people.

ELLIOT: Where did you get this idea that I have an academic background or something? I never said that.

VICTORIA: There's a lot you never said. But when you do say something, you tend to speak…precisely. Like, I hear more letters than words for some reason. That's why I asked where you were from when we met. I thought you might be Dutch or something. When you weren't, I assumed you were just highly educated.

ELLIOT: I went to college, but I majored in English Lit. I'm very well read, but I'm only smart enough to know how dumb I am. I'm only Socratically intelligent.

VICTORIA: But you have a Ph.D., don't you? Or a Master's…?

ELLIOT: No. I work in a cubicle for an insurance company. And I write movie reviews on the side. For the Internet. I did go to an Ivy League school, but they never taught me how to avoid a resume like this.

VICTORIA: Oh my God. I'm an engineer.

ELLIOT: I know, you mentioned that. Petroleum.

VICTORIA: I'm probably smarter than you.

ELLIOT: There's no probably about it. You're definitely smarter than I am.

VICTORIA: I don't feel like it.

(We hear the handle of the front door turn, and see it move. Locked, the door jiggles ferociously for a few seconds.)

ELLIOT: Uh-oh…

VICTORIA: Is that…is she…?

(Victoria rushes back to the bathroom while Elliot makes his way to the peephole. He then moves to the window. He watches outside for a few moments.)

ELLIOT: It's okay. False alarm. It was just the police. Looks like they're doing a security check. Making sure everyone is locked up. Locked in. Locked down. *(Pause)* You can come out now. *(Pause)* Hello?

(Victoria creeps out of the bathroom.)

ELLIOT: You alright? What's the matter?

VICTORIA: Why did I go in?

ELLIOT: Huh?

VICTORIA: I heard the door handle, and I thought it was your wife. I scurried into a bathroom, some stranger's bathroom, to hide like I was a schoolgirl with cigarettes…or…some bad woman. Some Hester Prynne.

ELLIOT: Points for the reference.

VICTORIA: Shut up. *(Pause)* What am I hiding for? I shouldn't be afraid of your wife. That's your problem. I shouldn't be afraid of the police, or how much toilet paper is left, or anything else that's out there, if you want to know the truth about it. I didn't do anything. I didn't bring this on myself. I made the best decisions I could, based on the best information that was given to me.

ELLIOT: It's not your fault. It's not anybody's.

VICTORIA: You would love that, wouldn't you? To suffer through no fault of your own.

ELLIOT: I'm talking about the quarantine. It's out of our control.

VICTORIA: That's the problem. I can't let that happen. I need to be in control. To some degree. I need to be home.

ELLIOT: There's a virus out there, Victoria. You could get it, you could spread it. It's fifty-fifty, at best.

VICTORIA: Everything's fifty-fifty when you have no control over anything. Virus or no virus. You asked me if I'd be angry at you even if you had been single. Probably not. But I wouldn't be feeling much different than I do now. Less aggrieved, but no more interested in you. I went home with you the same night we met, Elliot. I wasn't after anything long-term.

ELLIOT: Aha. That's the point I was trying to make. You can't judge that I misled or used you if you were just going to do the same thing with me.

VICTORIA: I wasn't done. You're not exonerated here. If I had known you were married, I never would have let you talk to me in the first place. If not for the outbreak, I'd have been long gone by now, ring or no ring—which I did notice you weren't wearing, by the way, and still aren't.

ELLIOT: It's in a drawer in my office.

VICTORIA: You keep your wedding ring in a cubicle at work?

ELLIOT: No, no. We have a utility closet I've repurposed. Sometimes I work remotely. And I write my movie reviews in there, hoping something takes off. If I can come to terms with the word count. It's tough.

VICTORIA: Doesn't seem like you would have problems with a word count.

ELLIOT: That's exactly the problem. I keep going over. Way over. I'm clocking eight thousand, nine thousand words on stuff like *Avengers* and *Frozen 2*. It's silly. The #MeToo movement has really put a damper on quality films and long-form journalism.

VICTORIA: I'm actually not surprised you would say that.

ELLIOT: Don't misunderstand. I approve of #MeToo. Just not artistically. I don't know what effect it's had on petroleum engineering.

VICTORIA: Just this.

ELLIOT: Hey now, come on…

VICTORIA: No, my intentions at the time are actually irrelevant here. You lied to me so you could cheat on your wife. If you hadn't lied, you couldn't have done that. Not with me. That makes you a horrible, dreadful person. It will always be something that you did. Always. Like those people hoarding toilet paper right now. They will always have done that. When things get better, get back to normal, and all the blue skies and picnics come back, we will still know who they are. We will know what they did. For-ever. And I'm going to be one of the loudest voices out there to remind them. Starting now. If I have to take over the Shoah Foundation to do it, I'm going to hound these people until they start hiding out in Argentina. I cannot sit by and let everyone pretend that it's okay. Any more than I can sit here with you and pretend that this is okay.

ELLIOT: A crisis brings out the worst in people.

VICTORIA: No, a bad day brings out the worst in people. A crisis tells us who they really are. You need to know who you are. So do I. And I need to have control to do that.

ELLIOT: Victoria, if you leave, if you go outside right now, it will be the most irresponsible thing you've ever done.

VICTORIA: You can tag team with this virus all you want, Elliot. You don't know me, and I'm not going to stay in your little *Doll's House*.

ELLIOT: *Doll's House*? I don't quite—oh. Ibsen…?

VICTORIA: Yeah. It's not English Lit. I think it's Scandinavian. Go with it.

ELLIOT: *Ghosts* might have been slightly more apt. Especially considering we weren't planning to see each other again. There's an irony.

VICTORIA: I'll look forward to your review. I'm leaving.

ELLIOT: You're a public health risk if you go out there. Think about what you're doing. I know something about selfishness, Victoria, and this qualifies.

VICTORIA: There's only one way you can stop me.

ELLIOT: Come on now, calm down. I'm not going to get physical with you or anything.

VICTORIA: I didn't mean that. You can call the police if you want. Of course, they'll write a report. I'll have to tell them where I've been and what we've been up to. But that's a decision you can make.

ELLIOT: That's blackmail.

VICTORIA: Not if it's up to you it isn't. Hold on a minute.

(She goes into the bathroom and returns with a roll of toilet paper.)

ELLIOT: What are you doing? What about what you just said?

VICTORIA: It's one roll. I'm taking one roll. You have at least two or three others in there. Live it up. Go nuts. Overdose on Raisin Bran. I really don't care.

ELLIOT: How do you think you're going to get home? You didn't drive here. Everything's shut down. No rideshares. You'd have to walk. Carrying a roll of toilet paper, no less. Or no fewer.

VICTORIA: No less. You were right that time.

ELLIOT: If the cops don't stop you, an angry mob surely will, they see you with that.

VICTORIA: Well, you could drive me.

ELLIOT: I'm not stepping out today. I've done enough damage for one week. I won't do more. You may not believe in redemption, but I do. Think about that.

VICTORIA: If anybody hassles us, you can stop at a drugstore.

ELLIOT: And do what? Look at the empty space? Anyway, there's no way to social distance in my car, even if you sit in the back seat. It's a

Fiat.

VICTORIA: Look, your wife's plane is going to land one way or the other. You don't know that they'll keep her. If they send her home, do you really want me here?

(Pause.)

ELLIOT: We'll have to brainstorm an explanation.

VICTORIA: I know what I'm going to say. *(Pause)* I'll get my keys.

(Elliot retrieves his keys.)

VICTORIA: I'm not that far. We should be fine.

ELLIOT: Of course, if I take you home, this means that I'll know where you live. You okay with that?

(Pause.)

VICTORIA: I trust you.

ELLIOT: Thank you. That makes me feel better. And that's allowed.

(A cell phone, plugged into a wall, begins to ring.)

ELLIOT: Not me.

VICTORIA: Oh. My phone. I forgot I was charging it.

ELLIOT: I'll get it.

(Elliot retrieves her phone, still ringing, and hands it to her. Victoria looks at it and presses ignore so that it stops ringing.)

VICTORIA: Thanks.

ELLIOT: Who's Chris?

(Pause. Victoria looks at him.)

VICTORIA: Let's go.

ELLIOT: After you, Vicky.

(They exit the apartment.)

ZOOM COASTER
by Deborah Yarchun

CHARACTERS

ASH	20s, Female
CHARLIE	20s, Male

SETTING

April 2020, NYC. On Zoom. Each in their own settings.

(At Rise, Charlie's Zoom background is of a bar. Ash uses a Zoom background with a more romantic location, like a café in Europe or a park. Charlie holds a drink. Ash does not. They stare at one another.)

CHARLIE: Hi there.
ASH: Hi.
CHARLIE: Thanks for…Zooming.
ASH: Sure.

(Awkward silence.)

CHARLIE: You got the money I Venmo'd? For your drink?
ASH: Oh, yeah. I don't drink on first dates. But thanks for the money. *(A moment as Charlie lowers his glass)* Kidding! *(Pulls out a wine glass filled with red wine)* That's a cute idea…with the Venmo.
CHARLIE: I read about it in an article. On how to…
ASH: Zoom date? What else does it say?
CHARLIE: I…don't know like…lighting tricks.
ASH: Your lighting is good.
CHARLIE: Thanks. And like, questions you can ask. What's the first thing you're going to do when this quarantine is over?

ASH: Kiss somebody.

CHARLIE: So, this is an audition?

ASH: Suuuure.

CHARLIE: How bad's the competition?

ASH: How much time do you think I have?

CHARLIE: I'm sorry. This is kind of…awkward.

ASH: More awkward than it would be in person? *(Charlie nods)* Hold on. Sending you something.

(Charlie smiles. A second later he changes his Zoom background to match Ash's.)

ASH: So now we're in the same place with things. Also, I never have first dates at a bar.

CHARLIE: Gotcha.

ASH: Your dates aren't normally awkward?

CHARLIE: Oh, well, I mean—they are. It's Tinder and all.

ASH: Mine too.

(They both breathe a sigh of relief.)

CHARLIE: Writer, right?

ASH: Right. I mean, I'm studying literature. Interestingly, we'd just had a unit on love and illness. Lots of Shakespeare, Keats, and references to fleas. I guess it's a good thing COVID isn't carried by a flea.

CHARLIE: I don't know…then we'd just like kill all the fleas. They're not like bees.

ASH: Bees fleas.

CHARLIE: You're the bees knees…

ASH: What are you studying?

CHARLIE: Magic. Just kidding. Economics. Which right now feels like magic. *(Awkward pause)* Hold on…hold on…This date interrupted by a backwards roller coaster. *(He quickly changes his background to a video of a roller coaster)* WHEE!

ASH: *(After a moment, putting her arms up, playing along)* Whee!

CHARLIE: Zoooooomm!

ASH: Okay, that's making me seriously dizzy.

CHARLIE: Sorry. Sorry. *(He quickly tries to switch his background back to Ash's)* You don't like roller coasters?

ASH: No. I'm into them. Just like…not Zoom coasters. But I'm hella into roller coasters.

CHARLIE: Maybe one day we can ride one together.

ASH: They're kind of a survival thing, right? Like we practice putting ourselves into dangerous situations.

CHARLIE: Probably why I've been watching lots of horror movies. Lately. Even though I live alone.

ASH: I live alone, too. And yeah, I've been watching horror movies. Big time. Especially if I'm feeling anxious. They somehow make me…

CHARLIE: Less anxious?

ASH: Like, here's a situation way worse than you're in…That's…more than I'd usually admit on a first date.

CHARLIE: Ever seen the movie *Contagion*?

(Ash and Charlie hold up signs that say "Date 2." Both their virtual backgrounds are of a movie theatre audience. The end of a movie plays on their screens. He's screensharing most likely Contagion or a horror flick. She adjusts her hair when she thinks he's watching the movie. He smiles, watching her. She watches him watching. They smile at each other. He turns off screensharing, and his background—revealing his bedroom. Clean—except for a lone sock lying in the background. A moment.)

ASH: I don't usually go home with somebody on a second date.

CHARLIE: Oh, shit. Right. I didn't think—

ASH: No keep it.

CHARLIE: You going to share yours?

ASH: No way. I don't have people over on a second date. Do you?

CHARLIE: No. First date

ASH: For real?

CHARLIE: No. Yeah. Sometimes.

ASH: Thought you said you were awkward.

CHARLIE: Worked for Woody Allen.

ASH: Ugh.

CHARLIE: Kidding. I normally do though—like kiss on a first date. Or have someone over. I usually sleep with girls too soon. You don't think I do?

ASH: I didn't mean it like…Okay, but really?

CHARLIE: I'm a really physical person. Not like in a creepy way. Touch is one of the love languages, right?

ASH: There's a sock on your bed…

(Charlie picks up the sock. He puts it on his hand, revealing it's a sock puppet, hair and all.)

CHARLIE: I was Zoom babysitting for my niece. *(He notices a fly in his space, swats at it with the sock puppet)* Damn fly!

ASH: It's to your left! No. Wait. *(Orienting herself)* To your right. *(A moment, they laugh)* Is this our lobster moment? *Annie Hall.* "It's behind the fridge!" "Talk to it! You speak fly!"

(Charlie laughs with the sock puppet. Ash drops her virtual background, revealing her room. A moment. They both feel naked.)

CHARLIE: Nice.

ASH: Yeah?

CHARLIE: Yeah. Normally this would be where I'd kiss you.

ASH: That'd probably still be too early for me.

CHARLIE: Or hold hands…

(A moment as they both reach towards the camera.)

ASH: Hold on. Close your eyes. Put your fingers close to your face. But like not on your face. I don't encourage that. Actually, open your eyes for a second. Do this. *(She holds her palms together about a centimeter apart)* Eyes shut. *(They both shut their eyes)* Do you feel my heat? I feel yours.

CHARLIE: Uh, what?

ASH: Like we're touching hands.

CHARLIE: *(Jokingly)* This is maybe moving too fast. "Like palm to palm do holy palmers kiss?"

ASH: Wow. Yeah. R&J. That's soooo…

CHARLIE: Sexy?

ASH: Suuurre.

CHARLIE: Yeah. I guess it didn't end well for Romeo and Juliet.

ASH: Shhhhh…God, I haven't even hugged anyone since early March.

CHARLIE: Actually, this is kinda sexy…

ASH: Somehow touching on a second date is easier through Zoom.

(They each hold their palms together. A moment. They each hold up a sign that says "Date 3." Immediately, they jump into it.)

ASH: No recording.

CHARLIE: Promise.

(She removes her shirt revealing her bra (a camisole works, too). He removes his top. They remove their clothes down to their undergar-

ments and stare at each other. They hold up a sign that says "Date 5." They are both out of breath, clearly post-Zoom sex.)

ASH: *(Holding herself)* I'm holding you.
CHARLIE: I'm holding you.

(He holds himself. A moment. He sneaks the sock puppet sock on when her eyes are closed.)

CHARLIE: Hey. Open your eyes. *(She does, then as sock puppet:)* I want to meet. In person.

(Ash throws her shirt on.)

ASH: *(Throwing her shirt on)* No.
CHARLIE: *(As sock puppet)* We're both quarantining
ASH: Exactly.
CHARLIE: *(Throwing his shirt back on)* I could go to your place.
ASH: Washington Heights all the way to Brooklyn?
CHARLIE: I'd do it.
ASH: This whole thing's probably only possible because of Zoom.
CHARLIE: I'd so do it.
ASH: No.

(They stare at one another longingly. They hold up signs that say Date 6. She also has made a sock puppet.)

CHARLIE: *(As sock puppet)* You're sure?
ASH *(As sock puppet)* Abso-fuckin-lutely.
CHARLIE: *(As sock puppet)* What if we just took a socially responsible walk!?
ASH: Is that what they're calling it these days?

(They hold up signs that say "Date 12." Charlie is shirtless.)

ASH: Okay…
CHARLIE: Really?!
ASH: *(Nodding)* Yeah.

(Her video shuts off. He holds up a sign that says "Date 14." For a long beat, Charlie sits alone. He checks his watch. Starts reaching for his phone. She appears with her video turned off.)

CHARLIE: Ash? Seeing you was…wow. Your Internet shaky or something? *(No response)* Okay…*(We hear a cough from her end)* Ash? Alright there? *(We hear another cough)* Oh, haha. Okay. I see you sent a pdf. One sec. Oh, shit? No…you're sure? Sometimes there's false positives! *(She coughs, and he considers…)* We'll…we'll get through this. Ash, can you turn your camera on?
ASH: *(Through coughs)* You don't want to see me right now.
CHARLIE: I kinda do…

(Ash disappears. Charlie sits alone. He holds up another sign. "Date 15." She's still not there. A long moment. He holds up another sign "Date 16." She appears with her camera off again.)

CHARLIE: I know. We shouldn't have…met up. I'm sorry I. I've been thinking. Okay? Sometimes love is sick. Love is a sickness. *(Thinks about it)* I'm not even sure what the hell I'm saying anymore. I'm an idiot. I'm an idiot. *(She coughs)* Also, I'm apparently asymptomatic.
ASH: Seriously?
CHARLIE: Yeah. I got my test back today. Sorry. I'm an idiot. But Ash, when I touched your hand—I know this sounds corny—but I

felt fire. And it wasn't from your eighty-five percent alcohol hand sanitizer—which, by the way, you should be really careful about because some of that shit can kill you. Okay. I'll stop. It's…it must be all the isolation talking. *(He holds his palms together)* I'm…I'm touching your hand. You touching my hand? *(No response)* I'll just… assume you are. You know, Romeo and Juliet—they were killed by the plague. Not like directly. But the dude who was supposed to be delivering the news to Romeo that Juliet's not actually dead never reaches Romeo because he gets stuck somewhere quarantining. I read that online. So, they die. Because some dude stayed inside… Not that that's—I guess that's kind of depressing and like antithetical to my goal here—which is to cheer you up. *(She coughs)* I'm…Look, I'm sorry. Meeting up was irresponsible. Like I should've gotten tested. We should have gotten tested. *(A moment, trying to cheer her up)* Here. I just found a poem. A Shakespearean sonnet. I Googled sonnets that have to do with illness and love. Because the bard sure as shit is going to beat me on that. Ready?

(He screenshares. We see the following text as he reads it.)

CHARLIE: My love is as a fever, longing still
For that which longer nurseth the disease,
Feeding on that which doth preserve the ill,
Th' uncertain sickly appetite to please.
My reason, the physician to my love,
Angry that his prescriptions are not kept,
Hath left me, and I desperate now approve
Desire is death, which physic did except.
Past cure I am, now reason is past care,
And frantic-mad with evermore unrest;
My thoughts and my discourse as madmen's are,

At random from the truth vainly expressed:
For I have sworn thee fair, and thought thee bright,
Who art as black as hell, as dark as night.

(A moment. He quickly ends the screenshare.)

CHARLIE: Wow. That did not go where I expected.
ASH: *(Turning her video on)* Seriously, Sonnet 147?
CHARLIE: Ash. You look…great. *(She holds her middle fingers up)* Okay…I get it. You want me to go?

(A moment.)

ASH: Don't leave.
CHARLIE: Okay.

(They watch each other. Charlie puts the sock puppet on. He gives her a nod with it. She smiles. She coughs. She puts her own sock puppet on. She coughs, jokingly making it look like the puppet is also coughing.)

CHARLIE: *(As puppet)* I'm not leaving.

(He makes kissing sounds with his sock puppet. They move their sock puppets towards the camera to make the sock puppets kiss. A moment as they look at each other.)

TIME IS ELASTIC AND IT'LL SNAP YOU IN THE END
by Paige Zubel

My therapist asks me if I want to die. I say no, not really, not particularly, not today. Today, I like being alive. Today, I like smoking. Eating greasy foods. Sex. Not necessarily in that order. I like the vibration on my phone that tells me, in this moment, someone is thinking about you. I like my cat, how she needs me more than I need her, and that makes me feel powerful. How she curves into the small of my belly at night like she and I are a whittled set.

My neighborhood in ten years' time will be whiter. It will be more expensive. It will be chrome and sleek and shiny and I will hate all of it. The bodega around the corner will probably be gone, and that makes me sad. Richard is so kind. His eyes have the kind of light that feels like a hug. He has children and those children will need money from the bodega that Richard probably won't be able to keep. I met one of his children once—she was young and liked pink and unicorns and I couldn't help but think if she and I were the same age, we definitely would not be friends. She held my hand and asked if I liked dogs. It was the purest question I've been asked in a long time. I don't know if I will be here in ten years, to see the changes, to find out if Richard and his bodega and his children will be all right. Today, I only feel certain about today.

She calls me in the middle of the night to say she has to leave. She has to leave right now. In the middle of the end of the world she has booked an eighteen-hour flight to the other hemisphere of the planet because this country just isn't safe anymore. I tell her, the virus is everywhere. She tells me, it's not the virus I'm running from. She is Asian American. She makes posts about the Chinese Virus. She is scared. And I, wrapped in the skin that is my skin, have been naïve. She tells me, I'm sorry. I tell her, there's no room for that, not when you need to be safe, please be safe. She tells me she'll call when she can, and I tell her to enjoy her time with family when they live so far, and I wonder if this is really what a pandemic is: the splintering of families of choice. Ten years ago, I would have predicted the future and known with the certainty that teenagers hold round in their guts that we would see each other again. Today, I can't predict tomorrow, and I just don't know.

Ten years ago, I was fifteen. I was freshly gay. I had just kissed a girl for the first time and a boy for the first time and was immensely confused. Both of my grandparents were still alive. I didn't smoke or drink. I played baseball with the boys and was good at it. Now my grandparents' wedding rings are around my neck, and I don't remember how to pitch, and I don't kiss boys anymore. And thinking about my neighborhood in ten years means I have to think about myself in ten years and that gives me anxiety, because how many more wedding rings will I have around my neck then?

BREATH
by Philip Zwerling

CHARACTERS

SANDY 25-35, Male
SUE 25-35, Female

SETTING

May 20, 2020; An apartment on the Upper West Side of Manhattan, not far from the American Natural History Museum.

(At Rise, a small apartment is furnished in a contemporary style for a young couple with little money. A large couch center stage faces the audience. Sandy sits on the couch cradling Sue's head in his lap. She lies prone on the couch with her back towards the audience.)

SANDY: *(Bending his head down near to Sue's, then straightening up)* I know. I know these rainy days get me down too. I just want to crawl into bed and pull the covers over my head. Remember when we celebrated National "Stay In Bed Day" years ago? If only we could do that for a month.

(A phone rings in another room.)

SANDY: Don't worry I'll call them back. It's probably just your mother again. Let it ring. I just don't seem to have the energy to get up and do much of anything these days. *(He sighs and then coughs, then coughs again)* I sound like you, don't I. You know, I don't think I would have made it through this without you. *(He squeezes Sue's shoulders)* Who else would I spend three months with in a tiny apartment? *(He kisses her hair)* Really, I never would have made it on my own…and not with anyone else either. I love you. I hope this will all be over soon. *(He coughs)* Remember last year? When we went to Yellowstone in January? We bought snow pants and gloves and hand warmers and insulated underwear. We looked like the Michelin Man wearing all these clothes layered one on top of the other. But it was so beautiful. So quiet after all the noise in the city. You could hear the bison snorting in the silence, stamping their feet in the snow and see their breath like smoke burning in the freezing air.

(He is wracked by a coughing spell. He gasps for air. He claws at his chest desperately trying to breathe. As he writhes, he lets go of Sue and her body falls out of his lap and onto the floor. She is dead. Lights out. Coughing fills the theater.)

Contributor Biographies

Lindsay Adams is an award-winning, internationally-produced playwright. Her plays, *River Like Sin* and *Rattler* have been honored by the O'Neill National Playwrights Conference, and Her Own Devices received the Judith Barlow Prize. Her work has been produced, developed, and commissioned across the US and the UK. She is a resident playwright at the Midwest Dramatists Center and a proud member of the Dramatists Guild. MFA: Catholic University of America. PhD: (in process) Saint Louis University.

Maripat Allen has had one acts, ten-minute plays, and a full-length comedy produced in Michigan, Indiana, Massachusetts, New York, Maryland, England (London), and Australia. She won the first place Community Theatre Association of Michigan award for a full-length drama, *We Gather Together*, in 2014, and in 2021 for her collection *Love Among Mortals*. Maripat's plays can be seen on the New Play Exchange.

Cris Eli Blak wrote and co-produced the short film *The Brother's Survivor*, which won a Bronze Remi Award and is also the recipient of the Christopher Hewitt Award. As a playwright he has had his work produced, performed, and/or published by Urban Stages, Cleveland Public Theatre, The Queen's Theatre (London), Derby City Playwrights, Scribe Stages, Illuminate Theatre, among others.

Mark Borkowski is an award-winning playwright and screenwriter whose work has been produced around the world. Publications include: *Don't Listen To What It Sounds Like and A Gravedigger's Tale* (Smith & Kraus Anthologies), *Shadow Saint, Dead Monkey, Savage Ink, HOLD*

(Collective NY Anthologies), *Tattoo* (Crack the Spine). Sirens in Limbo had a reading at The Actor's Studio in New York, directed by Amanda Moresco. The cast included Greta Seacat, Maggie Wagner, and Julie Janney.

Louisa Burns-Bisogno is an award-winning screenwriter, playwright, director, author, and international media consultant with over 100 on-screen credits. Her movies have been produced on cable TV and on all the major U.S. networks. In Fall 2019, she co-created and produced *Sisters By Choice*, an Italian sitcom. Louisa is a professor of playwriting, screenwriting, and multimedia at Western Connecticut State University and has given seminars at the Universite Roma Tre.

As a teen, **Coleman** fled Oklahoma. He hid out in the Finger Lakes until his arrest. Upon release, he pretended to study in Ann Arbor, then disguised himself as various professionals in the alleys, lofts and high-rises of Chicago. Eventually, he moved to a cabin in Wisconsin, became a lumberjack, and that's okay. He raises chickens, trains dogs and writes plays to amuse and frighten himself. He rides a bike.

Liz Coley is the published author of psychological thriller *Pretty Girl-13* and numerous anthologized SciFi short stories. In 2016, she met playwriting and fell in love. The affair continues. Her work has been read and produced in San Diego and Cincinnati. She manages Next Stage Cincinnati Playwrights, a local critique and support group. Liz can be found virtually as LizColeyBooks on social media and at LizColey.com.

Richard Lyons Conlon is a Resident Playwright Alumnus at Chicago Dramatists and member of the Dramatists Guild, Richard has written 45+ plays, including: *7 Minutes to Live* (Eugene O'Neill Playwrights Conference Semi-Finalist) and *One Time* (record-breaking run at Next Act Theatre). Theatres he's worked with: Chicago Dramatists, Victory Gardens, American

Blues Theater, Ubiquitous Players, Second City, Raven, Naked Angels, Urban Stages, PlayGround Experiment, Equity Library Theatre, Vulcan Theatre, and Rhino Theatre.

Sean Crawford is a Boston-based playwright whose works have appeared in these and other events: MadLab's Theatre Roulette, the InspiraTO Festival, the North Park Playwright Festival, and the Boston Theater Marathon. He is a graduate of Emerson College's MFA in Creative Writing program.

Phil Darg is the author of plays/musicals including: *Sasquatched! The Musica*l (NYMF 2013 Next Link); *The Pound: A Musical for the Dogs* (2017 Theatre Now New York Sound Bites); *The ABC's of LGBT at the Rainbow Valley B 'n B* (winner, 2020 Robert J. Pickering Award for Playwriting Excellence); *Evolution* (winner, 2018 William Faulkner Literary Competition); Thespis (third place, 2020 Tennessee Williams One-Act Play Contest); Hero (Alternative Theater, New York); Facility (2017 William Inge). For more information, visit www.PhilDarg.com.

Jared Eberlein (Playwright) Work includes: *The Facts of Life; The Man in The Iron Mask; Precious Thieves; Jack...*; *The Heir of Pretending* and *Click!* His play, Fall with Me, is the 2019 winner of Dayton Playhouse's FutureFest, and was developed with the Garry Marshall Theater, Silverthorne Theatre Company, and Capital Rep. He's been a finalist in the Samuel French Off-Off-Broadway Play Festival, playwright-in-residence for the Choate Summer Theatre Institute, and a Masterclass Fellow (New World Theatre).

Joel Fishbane's plays have been performed in Canada, the US, and overseas and have been honored in such festivals and competitions as the Samuel French New Canadian Play Contest, the Toronto Fringe New Play Contest,Dayton Playhouse Futurefest, and the NAAA Playreading Festival. For more information, please visit www.joelfishbane.net.

Bonnie Milne Gardner, an award-winning playwright of over 40 plays, is a member of Dramatists Guild and Honor Roll. Productions include Cleveland Play House, San Diego's Human Rights Festival, and New School for Drama, and Publications by Next Stage Press and Scripts for Stage. Her comedy *Wedding Blisters* was a finalist in the AACT 2022 New Play Fest. Gardner is Emerita Professor at Ohio Wesleyan University, currently living in Asheville, North Carolina.

Valerie Gramling's work as a playwright/adapter and director includes *Noah's Flood* and *Everyman*, Renaissance Center Theatre Company, Amherst, MA; Between the Mists, Gilgamesh Theatre Group, NYC, and The Tell-Tale Tale, Magic If Ensemble, Anchorage, AK. Additional directing credits include works at The Metropolitan Playhouse and Oasis Theatre Company in NYC, and at Source Theatre and Washington Stage Guild in Washington, DC. She is currently a Senior Lecturer in English at the University of Miami.

Playwright/Actor/Reality Star **Joe Gulla**'s plays have been performed Off-Broadway, nationally and internationally. He is best known for his award-winning shows, *The Bronx Queen, Garbo, Gay.Porn.Mafia, Sleeping With The Fish* and his sold-out engagements at New York City's Joe's Pub at The Public Theater and *Feinstein's/54 Below*.

Alli Hartley-Kong is a playwright, poet, and museum educator. Her work has appeared in Hyperallergic, Smithsonian, the Endometriosis Foundation Blossom Blog, and numerous other publications. Her short plays and monologues have been produced by Single Carrot Theatre, Central Square Theatre, the Barn Theatre (Montville NJ), and Irvington Theatre, among other online streaming opportunities. By day, she works as a museum educator and digital strategist.

Daniel Ho was born in Wappingers Falls, New York, and currently lives in

Long Island City. He studied theatre at Washington University, the University at Albany, and the Einhorn School for the Performing Arts. His plays have been produced by Capital Repertory Theatre, Second Generation Theatre, the Long Island City Arts Project, and Second Generation Theatre Company.

Charles L. Hughes was born and raised in a small West Texas town. Diagnosed with Asperger's Syndrome at a young age, the careful observation of human behavior and communication in all their contradiction and paradox was a necessity, an experience he likes to think leaves its mark on each of his works in one way or another.

Andra Laine Hunter resides in Dallas, Texas, and her plays have been performed around the United States. She is the founder and artistic director of the Linden Grove Theatre Co. Her play *Star Bright* was a finalist for the 2020 City Theatre National Short Playwriting Award. She is currently pursuing a MFA in Playwriting from Spalding University. When not writing, she hangs out with her family, two dogs, and ten chickens.

Caytha Jentis is an award-winning screenwriter and playwright. Her play *It's All About the Kids* won the NJ Playwrights Competition and was subsequently turned into a film. Caytha is currently working on a new one act stage play. Her body of work can be found at www.foxmeadowfilms.com.

Kathleen Kaan is a native New Yorker and studied at The American Academy of Dramatic Arts. An accomplished singer, Kathleen entertained audiences internationally. Her play *Teddy's Doll House* will be featured in 2022 NY Winter Fest. Kathleen's two short plays *Lost & Found* and *Remember* are introduced in 2022 Virtual Arts Festival.

Leon H. Kalayjian has written several plays including; *Murder with Grace, Where There's no Will,* and *Guess Who's Coming to Seder*, all with Concord Theatricals. His latest work is a musical, Stealing Shakespeare, which was performed by Padua Franciscan High School in June 2021. Leon has many other plays with Brooklyn, Heuer and Off the Wall publishers.

Arden Kass is an award-winning playwright, screenwriter, librettist and independent producer. Current projects include a musical update of the myth of Athena and Arachne, a drama about fallout from Me Too, a TV mini-series based on William Carlos Williams' *The Doctor Stories* and a screenplay about an iconoclastic 20th Century woman photographer. Pre-pandemic she was developing her all-women vaudeville, *Behold Her: 5,000 Years of Jewish Women and Beauty*, for a NY production.

Greg Lam is a playwright, screenwriter, and board game designer who has recently moved to the Bay Area after a lifetime in the Boston area. He is the co-creator of the *Boston Podcast Players* podcast (bostonpodcastplayers.com) Boston's virtual podcast stage for new works by local playwrights. He is the co-founder of the Asian-American Playwright Collective. For more about Greg, visit https://greglam.wixsite.com/home.

Australian-Canadian academic, playwright and dramaturg **Toby Malone** has worked as a theatre artist in Australia, Canada, the United Kingdom, and the United States, and has published work in Shakespeare Survey, Literature/Film Quarterly, Canadian Theatre Review, Borrowers and Lenders, and in published collections with Routledge, Cambridge, Palgrave Macmillan, and Oxford. He is currently Assistant Professor of Dramaturgy, Theatre History, and Criticism at SUNY Oswego.

David Don Miller is the commissioned book writer of new musical *Goodbye New York,* finalist at the New York New Works Theatre Festival. Miller's hard-hitting look at urban education *Why You Beasting?* was a Time Out NY Critics' Pick at the New York International Fringe Festival. Other plays include *Bacon Clickbait* (finalist at both New York New Works Theatre Festival and Theatreworks New Milford), and *A Sad and Merry Madness* (semi-finalist,

American Shakespeare Center).

Robert Paul Moreira teaches fiction and playwriting at the University of Texas Rio Grande Valley. He is the editor of ***¡Arriba** Baseball!: A Collection of Latina/o Baseball Fiction* (2013) and author of the story collection *Scores.* His latest collection, *Dig,* was published by Frayed Edge Press in Fall 2022. Robert's plays include *Roses From Castile, Miriam's Song, Proxima b, Dick Tea,* and a children's play, *Kiki. Malinalli, a musical,* was published by FlowerSong Press in 2022.

Laura Neill's work has been developed or produced by the O'Neill National Playwrights Conference (Winter People), SpeakEasy Stage Company (Just Cause), ScriptWorks (Public Property), OperaHub (Divas), Wilbury Theatre Group (Skin and Bones), and Fresh Ink Theatre (Don't Give Up The Ship). Laura has taught courses on creative writing and theatre at universities across the country. MFA: Boston University. Representation: Katie Gamelli at A3 Artists Agency. For more information, visit https://laurajneill.wixsite.com/plays.

Joyce Newman Scott started college in her fifties after a successful career as an actor. She studied Screenwriting at the University of Miami and Creative Writing at Florida International University. Her short stories have appeared in multiple anthologies. *The Menopausal Freshman* monologue was chosen by the Burning Man Festival in the U.K., soon to be published by Smith and Kraus in The Best Women's Monologues of 2021. She is a proud member of S.A.G./A.F.T.R.A. and D.G.A.

Serena Norr's plays have been performed at the Omaha Fringe Festival, White Plains Performing Arts Center, the New Deal Creative Arts Center, NYC at the Players Theater with the Rogue Theater Festival, the Short Play Festival, and University of Alabama as well as fifteen Zoom productions during COVID. She is a member of the Dramatists Guild, Westchester

Collaborative Theater, Cut Edge Collective, and participant in the 2021 Kennedy Center Playwriting Intensive and Women's Theatre Festival (WTF) Directing Program.

Ayvaunn Penn (Columbia University Playwriting Dean's Fellow) teaches theatre at Texas Christian University (TCU). She is a playwright-director and lyricist-composer passionate about theatre for social change and nurturing future generations of theatre artists. Her piece, *For Bo: A Play Inspired by the Murder of Botham Jean by Officer Amber Guyger* is a Eugene O'Neill National Playwrights Conference 2020 finalist and helped TCU earn the 2020 Higher Education Excellence in Diversity Award.

Joni Ravenna is an award-winning playwright, TV writer and journalist whose articles appear regularly. She was host and head writer of the 13-part series, *Earth Trek* (PBS) and the ACE-nominated 36-part-series, *Great Sports Vacations*—(The Travel Channel, Fox Sports)—while also writing select segments for E! and ESPN. In 2021, several of her plays were produced around the country including the "spellbinding" (Hollywood Examiner) *Beethoven and Misfortune Cookies.*

Robin Rice has written over 70 plays (including 22 full-lengths), produced worldwide from Off-Broadway to London, South Korea to South Africa. Publishers include Samuel French, Original Works, Next Stage Press. Magical realism pushes the sides off boxes so his stories expand visions and blur the edges of reality. He is a lifetime member of the Dramatist Guild. www.RobinRicePlaywright.com.

Rachel Rios has an MFA in Playwriting from The Catholic University of America and a BA in English and Theatre from Loyola Marymount University. Past Credits include: *Floss* (Keegan Theatre's WOMXN on Fire Festival; John Cauble Award National Semi Finalist; Northwestern), *Tilting* (Fountain Theatre Rapid Development Series), *The Bachelors* (Tavern Rakes), *Caution:*

Children at Play (Fresh PRODUCE'd), *Playing with Ringworm* (Kennedy Center's Page to Stage Festival), *Tamales* (Bay Area Playwright Festival Semi Finalist). www.rachelrios.com.

Lavinia Roberts is an award-winning playwright and educator. She is published with Applause Books, Big Dog Plays, Brooklyn Publishers, Eldridge Publishing, Heuer Publishing, Plays: The Drama Magazine for Young People, Pioneer Drama, Redleaf Press, Smith and Kraus, and others. She has received productions in fifty states and internationally in Australia, Bermuda, Canada, Ireland, Singapore, South Africa, South Korea, Taiwan, Turkey, and The United Kingdom.

Rich Rubin's plays have been produced throughout the U.S., as well as in Europe, Asia, Australia, New Zealand, Canada and Mexico. His full-length plays include *Picasso in Paris* (winner, 2020 Julie Harris Playwright Award) and *Kafka's Joke* (finalist, 2020 Woodward International Playwriting Prize). Member: Dramatists Guild, New Play Exchange, and Portland's LineStorm Playwrights and Nameless Playwrights. For more information, visit www.richrubinplaywright.com.

Jack Rushton is the Director of New Play Development-The Greenwich Theatre Company. Forty of his short plays have been produced at more than 150 Festivals and Workshops across the country, including *Movie Reel* which has been performed at The Westcliffe, Colorado Center for the Arts, The Historic Zodiak Theater, The Forge Theater Lab, and The Loud Voices, Silent Streets Project in London, England. For more about Jack's work, please visit www.jack-rushton.com.

Alvaro Saar Rios' plays have been performed in New York City, Hawaii, Chicago, and Texas. His award-winning play *Luchadora!* is published by Dramatic Publishing Inc. He is a veteran of the US Army and co-founder of The Royal Mexican Players, a national touring performance troupe.

Originally from Texas, Alvaro lives in Chicago and teaches playwriting at the University of Wisconsin-Milwaukee. He is a Resident Playwright at Chicago Dramatists and Playwright-In-Residence at Milwaukee's First Stage.

Martin Settle is a writer in Charlotte, North Carolina. Settle has taught English for 32 years, the last 17 of which were at UNC Charlotte. Mr. Settle has published five books (a memoir, an art design book, and three books of poetry). In addition, he has been awarded The Thomas McDill Award (North Carolina Poetry Society), The Poetry of Courage Award (North Carolina Poetry Society), the Nazim Hikmet Poetry Award, and the Griffin-Farlow Haiku Award. For more information, visit www.martinsettleartist.com.

Joseph Sexton's plays have been produced by Love Creek Productions, The Players Theater, From the Couch in NYC, and also workshopped by RisingSun Performance Company as part of their summer Laboratorium series. Joseph has been acting, directing and writing in NYC since 2011. He studied fine art and economics at the University of Washington and then obtained an MFA from Long Island University. He currently resides in Brooklyn, NY.

Leda Siskind's plays have been produced in Los Angeles at the Pierson Playhouse, Theatre 40, The Complex and Lounge Theatres. Her plays *All My Distances Are Far* and *Surveillance* are now available at Stage Rights publishing and on Amazon. She is a proud member of AEA, SAG and the Dramatists Guild.

Kyle A. Smith's plays include *The Part of Me* (Madlab Theatre, Princess Grace Finalist), *Unstuck in Time* (No Frills Theater), *Whiteout* (Shakespeare's New Contemporaries Semi-Finalist), *Blinded* (Goldberg Prize Finalist), *Miss Conduct* (1st place New Thrills Theater Fest), *Miss Direction* (Adelphi

University, Queen's Theater), *Miss Orientation* (Adelphi University), *Frisky* (Emerging Artist's Theatre, Equity Library Theatre), and *Don* (Winner Equity Library Theatre Fall Festival, Finalist Secret Theatre's One Act Festival). For more information, visit www.kyleanthonysmith.com.

Amy Tofte is an award-winning playwright and screenwriter who won the 2015 Nicholl Fellowship in screenwriting from the Academy of Motion Picture Arts and Sciences. She has been in residence at the Autry Museum of the American West, Brush Creek, The Kennedy Center, and Yaddo, with work produced and developed throughout the United States, Australia, the United Kingdom, and twice at the Edinburgh Fringe Festival. She is a proud member of The Dramatists Guild.

Produced on four continents and in 40 states, **Rosemary Frisino Toohey** has had more than 300 productions of her plays around the world. In London she was Audience Favorite in the British Theatre Challenge and in New York she won the Next Generation Playwriting Contest. She tied as Gold Medal Winner in the Italian American Theatre of Chicago's First Playwright Competition, and she's won the Baltimore Playwrights Festival three times. For more information, visit www.frisinotoohey.com.

Molly Wagner is an NYC-based playwright from "Chicago" (St. Charles, IL) whose work has been developed throughout The United States, on Zoom, and in Canada by theatres such as Loft Ensemble, Clamour! Theatre Company, The Bechdel Group, Flush Ink Productions, and Wayward Sister's Theatre Ensemble. Molly earned her BFA from Ball State University.

Robert Walikis is a writer, playwright, poet, and songwriter. His work has appeared in the online journal *Literary North*. Rob graduated from Cornell University and lives in Irvine, California with his wife-partner-writer Diana Mullins. He makes maps and tells stories.

Brian Wallace has had his plays staged around the USA, Canada, and in Australia. He is a regular contributor to the Fireside Mystery Theatre podcast in NYC. He shares all performance royalties with the original casts, and rights may be obtained by contacting wallaceplayrights@gmail.com.

Deborah Yarchun's honors include two Jerome Fellowships at The Playwrights' Center, a Dramatists Guild Foundation Fellowship, Dartmouth's 2020 Neukom Literary Arts Award for Playwriting, an EST/Sloan Commission, and The Kennedy Center's Jean Kennedy Smith Playwriting Award. She earned her MFA from the University of Iowa where she was an Iowa Arts Fellow. You can learn more about her work at www.DeborahYarchun.com.

Paige Zubel (she/they) is a Philadelphia-based playwright, dramaturg, and producer. Their plays have been developed and produced by 50+ theatre companies, including Berridge Conservatory (*Amos and the Stars*, France), Normal Ave (*Dead Meat*, NYC), and What If? Productions (*A String Between Man and the World*, NC). They are the Associate Artistic Director of Shakespeare in Clark Park, Resident Dramaturg of Paper Doll Ensemble, and were the recipient of a National New Play Network Producer in Residence Grant.

Philip Zwerling, Ph.D., served as Director of the Creative Writing Program at the University of Texas Rio Grande Valley, until his retirement in 2018. He is the author, co-author, or editor of six books, including *After School Theater Programs for At Risk Teenagers*, *The Theater of Lee Blessing*, and, most recently, a full-length play, *Locked*.

Printed in the USA
CPSIA information can be obtained
at www.ICGtesting.com
LVHW040046201024
794167LV00005B/444